Agenda 1970:
proposals for a creative politics

Edited by
TREVOR LLOYD / JACK McLEOD

UNIVERSITY OF TORONTO PRESS

© University of Toronto Press 1968
Printed in Canada

SBN 8020 1571 9 (cloth) / 8020 6092 7 (paper)

Foreword

F. R. SCOTT

THESE ESSAYS ON public policy and Canada's future are presented by a group of professors who believe that academics can and should emerge from the ivory tower into the public forum. The thrust of their work is toward reform. A university need not blindly copy the society about it, but can play its part in the reshaping of that society.

Is this not an idea very much in the air today? Are not students complaining that universities too often provide an education adapted to the immediate needs of the outside world and do not sufficiently assert their own intellectual independence? Are universities not being challenged again to help build a new social order and not just to supply manpower for the old? In the physical sciences, the university that discovers a revolutionary principle or technique is rightly hailed as having contributed to progress; but in the professions and the social sciences, proposals for radical change are less easily accepted. Dean Manning of Stanford University Law School stated recently that the one hundred and thirty accredited law schools in the United States were almost carbon copies of one another in curricula and teaching methods, adhering to a model crystallized at the turn of the century. The root causes of this condition would be many, but undoubtedly our traditional system of university government is one reason for the slowness of adaptation and experiment. The similarity between the governing elites outside the university and those within is obvious. Fortunately university government in Canada is now undergoing an agonizing reappraisal. For this the students must be given some credit, though there has been a steadily increasing influence coming from the organized teaching profession itself.

There is something about the present university and world situation which makes me cast my mind back to the 1930s. My memory ranges back now over five decades, all spent in and around universities. These 1960s have been revolutionary by comparison with the fifties, which seemed to me to be a grey period when most students were interested in highly paid jobs and we seemed content to help them find them. North America was elaborating that civilization which has led to the war in Viet Nam and race riots in the cities. Is this a comment on its educational system? The 1940s were of course the period of the Second World War and of post-war reconstruction. By skilful wartime economic planning and controls Canada pulled herself rapidly out of economic depression and soon had an industrial machine that doubled its previous output. There was a lesson in economics that I am not sure has yet been learned. We used to say to ourselves after the war began and suddenly there was no shortage of money, "Never again shall we say we can't do something because there is no money." Yet what are we saying about medicare today?

But it was the 1930s which were in my experience the most revolutionary of these five decades. I had come out of the twenties primarily interested in literature. I had found T. S. Eliot's "The Waste Land" more revolutionary than the Communist Manifesto, but the crash of 1929 and ten years of economic depression were a traumatic shock that politicized my generation much as, I think, current disturbances are politicizing the present generation. Already the withdrawn hippies are becoming the involved activists. Students in the thirties were moved to rebel in many ways, but not directly against their university administration. The capitalist system, having virtually collapsed, became the enemy against which criticism was most directed. Government was seen as an agency in society too feeble to cope with the disaster unless its powers were greatly enlarged. In Canada this meant principally a turning toward the federal government for assistance, since the provinces were bankrupt. There was a great involvement in politics, for it was through political action that it was hoped to move governments to restore prosperity.

Hence in that decade we saw the emergence of no less than five political parties in Canada, namely the Communist party, the CCF party, the Reconstruction party, the Social Credit party, and in Quebec the Union Nationale. Even poets and artists were pushed in the direction of social consciousness and toward involvement in political movements. What is essential to remember from this whole disturbed yet creative period, is that the vision of a new and better social order was very much in the minds of young and old alike, and the universities were all to some extent awakened by the ferment. But authority itself was not in question; anarchy was only too evident.

Today there is a rising protest against authority in general. Or, as one McGill student put it to me, "It is not authority we object to, it is the idea of it." This feeling is world-wide and transcends ideological frontiers. I notice more similarity in techniques of demonstration and violence than in the formulation of the aims being sought. West German students demonstrate against emergency laws, while Flemish students close the University of Louvain because it continues to teach in French. We are too close to the nazi and fascist movements not to realize that violence in itself is blind. When the McGill students are exhorted in the *McGill Daily*, which all students are obliged to pay for whether they read it or not, to continue the fight so that "we can bring the administration to its knees," one wonders whether this is really inspired by new insights into the problems of education and government. (Anyway, I suspect all the university administrations are already on their knees – praying!)

Nevertheless in all this turmoil I believe that there is moving a new spirit of individual responsibility and individual freedom and that we are challenged to redefine our attitude to all forms of government and all systems of education. Underneath the noise and shouting one can hear that profound cry: "Be yourself, do your thing."

It was the gross injustice, inefficiency, and waste suddenly exposed in the 1930s which jolted every one into some kind of action. Poverty amidst plenty, mass unemployment, the inhibiting dominance of ancient myths such as "sound money," "balanced budget," and "private enterprise" – these were painfully obvious. Suppose I were to ask a graduating class today to put itself thirty years ahead and then to look back on the society it is about to enter. Would you not see plenty of absurdities and wastages? Wars actual and threatening? The widening gap between rich and poor nations? Some millions of Canadians living in abject poverty? Slums in our big cities tolerated while high-rise apartments drain off investment? The desecration of the air waves and the degradation of a great means of human communication by commercialized advertising? The frustration of town planning and of the beautification of our cities through the private ownership of land? The timidity of governments in promoting the public interest against those over-mighty subjects, the private corporations? Our taxation system which, as the Carter Commission proved, makes low-income individuals and families pay a higher proportion of their incomes in all kinds of taxes than do the rich? Our failure to see language and minority rights as human rights needing protection all across Canada? Our slowness in freeing education from the pressure of external private interests and the frustration of mass student production? This list is partial; everyone can add more items.

Norman Bethune is said to have made his great impression on the Chinese people through his faith that every obstacle was an opportunity. What a wealth of opportunities we have! The excitement of living is in making something new, something our own. The poet is merely a maker; that is what the root of the word means. He creates with words, but that which makes him create is the spirit of man within him. This same creative spirit works through all people in different ways, and it may emerge as a work by a Henry Moore or in opening new avenues for human rights.

In this light, the state too can be a work of art, as the Swiss historian Burkhardt pointed out long ago; it can be the outcome of calculation, reflection, and, above all, imagination. The French students who took over the Odeon Theatre in May 1968 cried out "l'imagination prend le pouvoir." Under the circumstances this may have been a little naive, for they had to leave the theatre and go back to a more normal life. But again we see the profound desire to release man the creator through the making of better social institutions.

I have always felt that politics was an art not only in the sense of being the art of the possible, but being the art of removing the obstacles surrounding each individual which prevent him being himself and doing his thing. It is the art of making artists more possible. This is why we must experiment with new forms of university environment, new kinds of learning. If some young people feel they must opt out of the struggle and start their full enjoyment of life now, I cannot say they are wrong. I would even include them in the guaranteed annual income which is long overdue. But we have not yet reached that happy state when we can leave the preservation of peace and the creation of a just society to the computer. Wherever we look there is great work to be done. No creative mind wants to be left out of it.

Contents

1

Introduction:
Our Ideological Tradition

TREVOR LLOYD

SO FAR AS THERE is a unifying force to these essays, it comes
from the fact that all the writers are, in a very general sense, part
of a single tradition of thought. What emerges is an attempt to
trace the interactions between the growth of government and the
changing attitude to government taken by the liberal intellectuals.
The contributors to this book fit into this category: they are all
descendants of Locke rather than Rousseau or de Maistre. But
although they have this common background, they do not end up
in the same place.

Two closely connected changes have affected the way people
think about governments and their role. Governments have grown
bigger, not just in absolute terms, but in comparison with every
other institution in the country. A century ago education was still
primarily a religious question – the churches were often in charge
of it, and even when they were squeezed out they showed a great
willingness to get back in again. Social security was still primarily
a matter for the family: families stayed together, with several
generations under one roof, and it was taken for granted that
children would be brought up and old people looked after without any help from the government. If the family broke down, some

mean and meagre assistance was available, but only as a last resort.

Defence expenditure in time of peace was very low; even when war came it was usually ended swiftly by a decisive battle, so that it did not cost much. The reason why nobody thought of Keynes' economic system earlier is that until 1914 the proportion of the national income spent by government was very low. Even a dramatic increase would have had very little effect on the economy as a whole; the psychological harm to confidence caused by an unbalanced budget would probably have outweighed the stimulus to the economy provided by any budget deficit that could have been run up by any pre-1914 government. A hundred years ago the government of a normal prosperous country in the North Atlantic area spent a tenth or a twentieth of the national income; today the governments in this region spend, with slight variations from country to country, about a third of the national income. A hundred years ago it was much easier to think of a government as one institution among many, competing to reduce the others to its will, than would now be the case; conversely, it is easier to think of government as a superior authority arbitrating impartially among inferior authorities, such as business and labour, than would have been the case a century ago.

At the same time as this very large change in the amount of power has taken place, there has been a great alteration in the attitude taken to the power of government: in the nineteenth century "liberals" or "the left" or "the party of progress" were devoted to reducing the powers of the state, but in the twentieth century the left tends to be in favour of expanding state power. The change has been so large that some people deny that there is any logical connection between the "liberals" of a hundred years ago and those of the present day. The pro-government "liberals" of the present day, it is sometimes suggested, have seen a good name under which to masquerade, and have gone ahead without paying any attention to the principles for which the name used to stand. At the level of party politics, what could an easily recognizable nineteenth-century Liberal like George Brown have in common with Eric Keirans? At the level of political philosophy, what right have these men to claim any sort of descent from Bentham and Adam Smith? Surely – and this is the moment to put the knife in – these pro-government liberals have all been infected by Marxism.

Governments a hundred and fifty or two hundred years ago were called hard names like "Old Corruption" (Bentham, referring to the British government) or "the Family Compact," and they deserved it. The net effect of government was to take money from the great majority of the population and give it to a small minority at the top. Revenue was raised mainly by indirect taxation which included a great many customs duties levied on necessities consumed by the poor; the Corn Laws in England were a textbook example of taxes that made the poor poorer and the rich richer. Once the revenue had been raised, a very large proportion of it was spent on paying the salaries of men from the upper classes who held government jobs, and these people further enriched themselves by accepting bribes. Historians have tried to justify this arrangement by saying that (*a*) holders of government offices did do some work in return for their salaries and (*b*) bribes were regarded by everybody as a perfectly normal thing. To the first point one can only reply "and so they should"; to the second, that nobody except recipients and potential recipients of bribes seems to have expressed satisfaction with the system.

When Adam Smith and his successors asked for limitations on the activity of government, they were attacking a system which redistributed money toward the rich. This is not to say that they would have approved of a system that redistributed money toward the poor, but only that they never had to consider the question. There were very few ways in which it was possible to redistribute money toward the poor; the most that could be done for them was to stop taking their money from them by way of taxes, and this was what the classical economists had in mind when they said that revenue should be raised as far as possible by direct taxes or by indirect taxes on luxuries. By 1848 radical thinkers were asking (in the Communist Manifesto) for a high and graduated income-tax, but although they knew how to transfer the burden of taxation to the rich, they had relatively few proposals for spending this money on the poor. Social welfare was a very unimportant part of the business of government, as the BNA Act shows.

Apart from the religious and cultural reasons for leaving welfare in the hands of the provinces, one important consideration was that welfare did not take up much government time and revenue, for it had always been considered a matter of merely local concern.

The churches still had a very large responsibility for such education and welfare services as did exist. Governments had no desire to challenge their position and very little desire to extend the role of government in this direction. But by 1867 the first part of the program of the left, as put forward by Adam Smith and Bentham, had been carried out: government had become reasonably efficient, relatively uncorrupt, and much less concerned to benefit the rich. What was next on the agenda (to use the word Bentham invented to cover just this problem)? That the government should do things for people that they could not do for themselves.

The emergence of the state as an institution for helping people was first introduced to the English-speaking world by the disciples of Hegel. He had been the first modern political theorist to have an entirely favourable view of an active government. Marx was torn between his Hegelian upbringing and his later acquaintance with ninetenth-century liberalism, but, so far as the role of the state was concerned, nineteenth-century liberalism triumphed. He believed, just as Bentham had done, that government was the executive committee of the ruling class. He thought that when the ruling class had been deposed and the traces of it eradicated, the state would wither away. In the next generation, the blend of Hegel and Bentham formed a slightly different mixture: English Hegelians like T. H. Green were able to think of government as something morally neutral rather than the instrument of upper-class domination that it had been in the past.

In the last hundred years people have found three things that the government can do better than individuals could do for themselves: it can help the economy develop, it can make war, and it can look after the poor and helpless. In Canada the role of government as a development agency was well established: the Canadian liberals who fought the Family Compact were much more ready than Adam Smith to think of the state as an instrument to help build canals and railways. The economic philosophy behind the National Policy of tariffs and a transcontinental railway was, of course, quite different from that of the Corn Laws in England, but its fiscal effects were very similar. Certainly in the short run, and possibly in the long run as well, the tariff took money from the poor and placed it in the pockets of the rich, though this was disguised to some extent by the fact that it also redistributed money among the poor.

It was quite understandable, both in the terms of Adam Smith and in the terms of the present day, that liberals in the 1880s and 1890s thought free trade was the great issue. The government was undertaking a new task, that of promoting national unity by economic development, but was doing so in the old spirit of helping the rich to grow richer at the expense of the general public. The liberal view had always been that, if there was an extra dollar to spare, it should go to the poor man rather than the rich, because the poor man needed it more, and the National Policy appeared to offend against this principle. Liberals still believed that a government which did anything more than the bare minimum of providing a police force and defending the country would be inefficient and would redistribute money toward the rich.

Early in this century the Liberal government in Canada found itself drawn, by processes that no biographer of Laurier has really dared to face, into the business of helping businessmen. Adam Smith would pretty certainly have seen the Canadian Northern railway as a device for putting the people's money into the pockets of Mackenzie and Mann. At the same time liberals in most English-speaking countries were slowly coming to realize that the state, whether it helped the rich or not, could help the poor by schemes of social welfare and social insurance. A number of these schemes were inspired by the example of Germany. Under Bismarck the ruling class had no desire to part with its political power, but on the other hand it had no inhibitions about using the power of the state in a way that helped the community as a whole. Whether Bismarck did this out of a desire for healthy and efficient cannon-fodder, or because he thought it would check the progress of the Socialist party, or because he had a Hegelian idea of the state is not easy to find out. On the whole the people in English-speaking countries who imitated his social policy were sorry for the poor and wanted to do something to help.

Naturally this impulse was felt primarily by liberals. In the years before 1914, Lloyd George, Woodrow Wilson, and the youthful Mackenzie King were beginning to adjust themselves to the idea of using the state to help the poor rather than limiting it so that it should not be used to help the rich. Their policies were suddenly cut across by the First World War. Between 1914 and 1918 all the old ideas about limiting the powers of the state were set aside: the success of the state became the supreme objective, and the power of the state to direct its subjects expanded in all directions. Canada was fortunate enough not to be involved in war as totally and completely as Britain, France, and Germany were involved in the First War or as Britain, Germany, and Russia were involved in the Second. Internal tensions and quarrels showed that Canada was not committed to either war as a single undivided unit which commanded the total loyalty of all citizens, but the two wars did increase the overall power of government in Canada. Constitutional lawyers may find it more interesting to look at the way the federal government increased its power at the expense of the provincial governments in wartime, but so far as citizens were concerned the overall increase of government power was more important than the redistribution of power between different authorities.

Not that citizens minded the increase in the power of government. The first result of it, and one that gave universal satisfaction, was that Canada emerged from the two wars on the winning and not on the losing side. At the same time the ability of the government to stimulate the economy and to provide the benefits of social welfare had been demonstrated. The lessons of the First War were not absorbed, and it was not really until the Second War that the government became accepted by everybody as the instrument to solve most problems. There are still disputes about whether the federal or the provincial government should do the work, and people have differing estimates of the amount that the government can afford to do, but not many people think they would be better off if the government stopped trying to help them.

Political parties in Europe and in the United States were affected decisively by the First World War. From Land's End to Vladivostock, effective power on the left passed into the hands of socialist or communist parties. These parties disagreed about the importance of democratic institutions, but they agreed that the state should be active and interventionist and that it should use its power in a way that would redistribute money toward the poor. Whether this is what actually happened in communist countries is another and a very complicated question; all that matters at present is that according to their theory communist governments should, like the social democrats of western Europe, use the power of the state to help the poor people who need it most. Social democrats are likely to stick to this policy, if only for electoral reasons, but communists have at times used the power of the state in a way that benefits the party bureaucracy more than anyone else.

In the United States it was clear, in the aftermath of the First World War, that no American socialist party was going to emerge as an organization that could win elections. But by the thirties the economic situation had pulled the Democratic party into a position where it had to help the poor and the unemployed first and think of reasons afterwards. It is possible that the Democratic party would have found its intellectual position a little clearer if it had taken up socialism, but it would probably not have won many elections and on the whole – given the American constitution, which makes it very hard to pass social welfare legislation – the absence of an effective socialist party has not retarded the movement of the United States in a direction welcomed by socialists. The rhetoric of the Democratic party is a curious blend of Hamiltonian praise of governmental activity and Jeffersonian egalitarianism, but this does not make its policies any less coherent.

It is quite possible that, if a socialist party had survived and had become the major party of the left, American politics might have possessed more moral and intellectual clarity. The existence of a strong socialist minor party could have had an obscuring rather than a clarifying effect, a situation like that of Canada since the First World War. Canada has had a socialist party (the Ginger Group, the CCF, the NDP) for almost all of that time, and the socialist party has usually been the point at which new ideas have entered the Canadian political scene. This intellectual fecundity has not been caused simply by the merits of its members. Since 1918, most of the new thinking about the old-established liberal ideas of liberty, equality, and fraternity has been conducted by asking whether socialism will help them or not. The successive socialist parties in Canada have been in touch with the world of ideas outside Canada and have introduced ideas from abroad and ideas of its own into Canadian political life.

Canada has also had a Liberal party, and for most of the time since the First World War has had a Liberal government. Original thinking within the Liberal party has not been encouraged. This has led to the curious situation that, if a man has new ideas in the liberal tradition that he wants carried out, he is best advised to join the socialist party and introduce them there, with some degree of assurance that they will be taken up by the Liberals. Of course, a man who wants political power for himself may be well advised to enter Parliament as a Liberal, though he should remember that the Liberals regard service as a back-bencher as a disqualification for being prime minister.

The absence of political thinking within the party of government has not prevented political development from taking place. Canada has not been able to stay outside the general current of change and the power of government has increased. Wars have had a considerable effect, assistance for economic development has continued (sometimes helping rich men from the public purse, as in the case of the Trans-Canada Pipeline), and institutions like the churches and the family have given up some of their former tasks and passed them on to the government. It has taken up the task, as in other countries, but with less understanding and control. In Europe the situation can be discussed in terms of socialism and resistance to socialism; in the United States there is a Democratic policy to be argued about; but in Canada political discussion has to begin by finding whether the Liberal party is the "true church" or the hippopotamus wallowing in the mud.

The power of government has increased without anyone who held power explaining what it was increasing for, and intellectual opinion has offered no surer guide. The theory has been advanced that the Liberal party is just a collection of brokers of power, selling everybody out to the highest bidder. The Liberal party has attracted a good many people who expect to do well out of holding power without any fuss about principles. Because Conservatism stood for a hierarchical society with WASPs at the top and socialism was identified with anti-clericalism and centralization, the Liberal party has gained the solid support of Quebec, though the Quebec Liberals represented as wide a range of thought as all of English-speaking Canada put together.

But even if Quebec and the liberal Catholic approach were left out, the Canadian Liberal party would suffer because the political thought of the nineteenth-century liberals now flows in so many different channels. The contributors to this book provide examples. It is possible to take an approach based on a literal reading of Adam Smith and approve of equality but want to keep the role of the state as small as possible. A fairly extreme example of this at the present day is the suggestion that the government should redistribute income by means of a negative income-tax but scrap all other welfare services. None of the contributors is as extreme as this, and in fact most of them are less distrustful of the state or are not convinced that people's needs can be quantified by the revenue department. As a result a number of the contributors prefer a second approach, and want an active state which tries to bring about greater equality.

A third approach, which has some points of similarity with the second, is in favour of government action but is less concerned about equality. There may, for instance, be good nationalist reasons for buying out American investors in Canada and there may be good educational reasons for spending money on grants or stipends for students, but in both cases the net effect might be to spend the taxpayer's money on schemes that would benefit the investing and university-attending (i.e., affluent) section of the community. Adam Smith would probably have denounced such schemes as a way to give the money of the poor to the rich, but there are undoubtedly people in the liberal tradition who would like to spend money in this sort of way and some of their views are represented in this book.

For logical completeness a fourth group descended from Adam Smith should be mentioned, although it is not to be found in these essays. Some people with no interest in his views of equality take up his attacks on government activity. The supporters of this approach tend to be an unappetizing collection of people who want lower taxes and see no plausible way of diverting government revenue to the support of their own enterprises. Their lack of fidelity to Adam Smith is demonstrated by their hostility to the income tax and their preference for the sales tax.

Adam Smith may not have believed that the power of the state could be used in a way that would help the poor, but in the nineteenth century Bentham clearly believed that if it could be done, it ought to be done, and later on John Stuart Mill thought that it could and should be done. "Liberalism," Matthew Arnold said in 1880, "is about equality," and the liberal political economists would always have liked greater equality of wealth, if it were possible. It is always reasonable to ask a liberal, when he proposes some extension of state power, why he thinks his particular proposal will promote equality. And, very often, a perfectly reasonable answer can be given: medicare is a good example of the sort of step that increases the role of the government and does something to help the great bulk of the community. In fact, it is so good an example that it is in danger of going sour. If it had come in the forties it would have been a measure so striking and novel that it would have been a good example of the way governments can act to help the people; by now medicare is coming so slowly and so grudgingly that it is bound to look like a vote-catcher's bargain or an attempt to "bribe the people with their own money."

In examples like medicare, the two principles of Adam Smith – that governments should be weakened and that life should be made easier for the poor – have worked like badly set blades on a pair of scissors, destroying each other instead of cutting properly. And the principles look like being harder than ever to apply in the future. The classical economists wrote almost exclusively about the position of adult men who were able to look after themselves, and a good deal of the time they were really writing about skilled craftsmen and businessmen impeded by the aristocracy. The economists were ready to admit that women and children were in a different position. If they had looked at the really poor men of their own day, they might have admitted that the poor were also in a different position. Undoubtedly the poor at the present day have great difficulty understanding the society in which they find themselves. Very few people who have been enrolled in trade unions could any longer be classified as poor; one of the great services that trade unions render to the community is to provide their members with a way of fitting into society. But most of the poor are very confused by the world and it is not clear what liberalism has to offer. A simple application of Adam Smith's principles will do very little good. It is a question of helping people who are not able to deal with the whole mass of institutions that already exist, and cutting down on government will not make the other institutions less confusing or less menacing.

While government in Canada has grown so much, nobody has really understood why it has grown and looks like going on growing. One practical result has been that the growth of government activity has been exploited by certain groups for the purpose of self-enrichment. Another has been that increased government power has not always had the humanitarian results which alone could justify it in the minds of liberals. There seem to be five possible lines of development in party politics, three of them rather unlikely: Canadians may decide that change ought, as far as possible, to be avoided and society should be stabilized under a conservative government which could reconcile people to immobility; or a new efflorescence of life may adapt the liberal principles of the late eighteenth century to the present day; or people may become reconciled to the present way of doing things. It seems more likely that either the Canadian political scene will rearrange itself in a way that will establish a socialist party as the normal instrument for carrying out political change (with either the Liberal or the Conservative party as the upholder of stability), or the existing Liberal party will take up socialism, using the word in the sense that the Liberals on the left wing of the party would say that they are socialists.

Is there any real distinction that can be made between liberals and socialists, using both words in the broad sense employed in this essay, rather than in terms of party divisions? The difference which means most today is concerned with the distribution of money and of power. Very roughly, a liberal would feel that as long as everybody got a reasonable amount of money or power there would be no danger that some people were getting too much. A socialist would feel that limiting the amount of money or power given to people at the top of society was well worth doing for its own sake. The liberal attitude is that men's freedom is limited only by the rule that they must not interfere with other people. Of course, this rule can be interpreted with varying degrees of strictness, and this can lead to sharp restrictions on anybody's right to acquire very large quantities of power or money. Obviously a liberal is not going to allow anybody to make a fortune by selling adulterated food or faulty machinery. A more rigorous liberal would not allow anybody to make a fortune by accumulating untaxed capital gains when other incomes are taxed fairly heavily. An almost fanatically conscientious liberal would say that nobody had a right to have a fortune at all when there were still poor people in the country.

The more determined of these liberals would no doubt find themselves proposing the same policies as people who called themselves socialists. Even so, the socialist reason for advocating these policies would be slightly different. The socialist attitude is that a community is driven out of control and destroyed by excess. Too much wealth, too much poverty, too much power in the hands of any one group will destroy the community. Under a capitalist system there is always the possibility that management and share-holders will have too much power, and it can be added that under a syndicalist system, in which wage-earners owned the industries in which they worked, trade unions might have too much power. The community has to protect itself against the danger of excess. On the whole it looks as if this can be done only by mobilizing the legal force of the community, which is to be found in the government.

By now liberals and socialists have a fair amount of common ground. They see the government as an instrument for doing good, rather than a dangerous weapon to be locked away as much as possible. And they agree that an egalitarian policy is a good policy – neither a liberal nor a socialist could accept an ordered and hierarchical society. "No man is good enough to be another's master" was in fact said by an early socialist, but it is a good liberal sentiment as well. Equality is one of the three master-words of the French Revolution; what about the other two? On the whole liberals are, as the name suggests, attracted by the idea of liberty; socialists are attracted by the idea of fraternity. Liberty looks easy enough to define, at least in broad outline, though there are difficulties about drawing the line between one man's liberty and another's. Fraternity, on the other hand, sounds rather a sloppy word. People are not going to live together as brothers, so a policy of fraternity will not work.

This may be true. Perhaps all that can be said is: so much the worse for the human race. The failure to bring Quebec into a Canadian community, the failure to bring negroes into a United States community, the failure to bring coloured immigrants into a British community are visible signs that people are not living together as brothers. The results of these failures are destructive enough to show that the preservation of the community is a worthwhile objective. This is not a simple question of law and order: if people are discontented enough to riot, sending policemen out to hit them on the head will not cure their discontent. At best it will give the government a breathing space in which to work out policies for rebuilding the community, and at worst it will accelerate the collapse of the community.

Liberalism does not really have very much to say about the preservation of the community; socialism is concerned with communities at all levels of complexity, from union locals to internationalism. A determined emphasis on freedom says very little about what a community under strain should do. Clearly anyone on the left would agree that people are entitled to demonstrate against harsh laws and discrimination. And to commit acts of civil disobedience? Yes. And to riot? Presumably. And to loot and burn? If the community is disintegrating, the government has either to give people freedom to loot and burn, or to send in soldiers to shoot them down. Neither choice is pleasant. Extreme situations of this sort can probably be avoided in Canada; the community here is not under really intense strain.

Fraternity may be a sloppy word, but the underlying principle of preserving the community is obviously important. This is a political matter, not a question of personal satisfaction. Too many people expect politics to provide relief for their psychological problems. The most easily apparent example of this is the readiness of the public to snatch at some reasonably intelligent and attractive political leader and imagine that he is going to solve all their difficulties. Political leaders find it hard enough to solve political problems, without becoming psychiatrists-at-large at the same time. The community, at least in the first instance, is a matter of political arrangement, not of private life. Beatrice Webb had very high hopes for the socialist commonwealth, but she admitted that people were still going to be unhappy; she offered the example that, when two men were in love with the same woman, one of the men was going to be unhappy, socialism or no socialism. The people who took part in the French Revolution may have felt that fraternity held out some possibility of reducing restrictions and inhibitions which produce needless unhappiness, but they were primarily concerned with the arrangement of public life.

"Holding the community together" is rather a defensive objective for a government to undertake, and yet it is the necessary preliminary to everything else. We have reached a point at which institutions are put under more strain than for many years past – strain which results from the pressure of change untempered by a program for change. The rate of change is unlikely to slow down in the near future, and so people have to find a way of adjusting themselves to what is happening. It is the contention of the essays in this book that the government will have to do more and more to make adjustment to change possible.

2

The Emotional Revolution

JOHN RICH

THE WAY THINGS are going, we may all fall off the edge of our present world within the next thirty-five years. The future can be predicted with some accuracy by extrapolation as long as there is no "quantum jump"; but these sudden jumps seem to occur just as trend curves flatten out. For example, if we plot the speed by which man could travel, first by ship, then by train, plane, and ballistic missile, we find that as each device reaches its maximum efficiency a new technique is discovered. Now the speed does not increase in a straight line, but in an upward-bending curve. The same curve is seen when we plot world population, life expectancy, and many other human statistics.[1] The intriguing thing is that these curves all approach infinity around the year 2000, thirty years from now. A rough parallel is seen if we imagine driving a car over a sphere; the gradient becomes steeper and steeper until we start falling vertically – and that is what the trend curves are telling us. For example, unless some new situation intervenes to change the increase in life expectancy, it has been said that anybody born after the year 2000 will live for ever. Other predictions are less extreme; Gordon Taylor[2] says that fifty years will have been added

1 / S. Neiger, unpublished paper given at the Toronto Psychiatric Hospital, 1965.
2 / *The Biological Time Bomb* (London, 1968), p. 206.

to our life expectancy by 2012 AD and that there will have been a definite prolongation by the end of this century.

Before this is dismissed as science fiction, it is worth noting that the scientists predicted in 1930 that we would not have a controlled nuclear reaction in less than seventy years; it came within ten. Using the curve I have been describing, however, scientists of the US Air Force predicted the date by which orbital velocity would be achieved – they were only two years out.

Taylor also predicted that physical pain will be abolished (or abolishable) by the end of the century, and that hybridization (the grafting of, say, human arms onto lower animals) and cloning (the reproduction of an indefinite number of exact copies of an individual) are within sight. He writes that cloning holds out "the possibility *right away* of producing exact copies of prize bulls . . . [and] exceptional human beings." It has already been done in plants. When these possibilities are combined with our present ability to keep frozen sperm alive so that a woman can have her husband's children long after his death, and the ovum-implanting techniques that will soon make it possible for a woman to bear a child who is neither hers nor her husband's, we can see that once again science is presenting us with ethical choices that we have not even begun to discuss. The current controversies on the morality of contraception, abortion, and the use of a nuclear bomb are taking their place with discussions on the ethics of usury and whether God objects to man travelling faster than a horse can gallop.

Pity the political commentator. A newspaper or magazine read a month after publication has the air of an archaeological specimen. If the commentator was wrong, his assessment seems ludicrous (for example, the spate of reassuring accounts coming out of Vietnam in December 1967 to the effect that 70 per cent of the South was "secure"). If he is right, his remarks, read a month later, seem trite and self-evident. I myself was interviewed for a TV series toward the end of 1967 on the hippies. As I was working quite closely with them and their peers I felt that my points were reasonably up-to-date, yet by the time the program went on the air the whole "movement" had changed or perhaps disappeared; my remarks had a quaintly old-fashioned air.[3]

The Flower Children faded away with the end of the summer in 1967 and were replaced by a mass of other adolescents – who, in spite of their long hair and beads, were not hip at all. The hippies had been above average in socio-economic background, intelligence, and sophistication. The replacements came from that usually submerged mass of emotionally disturbed, hung-up, delinquent kids who have always been with us.

Even the Diggers were taken by surprise, and the Diggers were virtually hippies themselves. In Toronto, in the fall of 1967, they wanted to set up a Hippie Haven, but bureaucratic and other difficulties prevented the implementation of their plan until early 1968. Instead of a house given over to poetry, guitar-playing, and idealistic discussion they found that they were running a cross between a Salvation Army hostel and a mental hospital. (The Diggers pulled out after a few weeks of this; apparently loving one's fellow humans is too hard if they really need it.)

This did not happen only in Yorkville. The scene in New York's Village and San Francisco's Haight-Ashbury districts also changed fundamentally in the same few short months. Does this mean that the hippie "movement" is dead, was a fad for a summer, and that the kids who comprised it are all getting their hair cut and applying to Dow Chemicals for jobs? I think not. Even if events do occur so fast that they take people by surprise, there is, I suggest, an underlying trend that is consistent even if it expresses itself in different ways and with different slogans. Nobody expected the strikes and riots in France in May, 1968 – the trade unions and Communist party were evidently as surprised as anybody and for several days were clearly trying to catch up with events. Within a week, however, the commentators were saying that the French people had become tired of the centralized paternalism that had endured for nearly two centuries and was now personified by De Gaulle. But this was no *French* revolt, it was a *human* revolt.

3 / It will probably be the same with this chapter by the time it appears in print.

Although the students who began it had different slogans from their colleagues in Berkeley in 1964, the London School of Economics in 1967, and Columbia in 1968, they had much in common. As the *Observer* put it editorially, "There is no doubt that many students feel that their rejection of 'bourgeois' values goes far beyond their own circumstances and those of their particular country. What they are really rejecting is the technological age itself, its bureaucracies, its self-love, its requirement that students be trained to become loyal servants of some monster organisation of statistical efficiency."[4]

In a wider field, banning the Bomb became less important than civil rights, partly because we have learned to live with the Bomb now that the first horror has worn off (most of today's young people have never known a world without it) and partly because the danger of nuclear war seems to have faded. But both the anti-Bomb and the civil rights campaigns have something in common: a desperate plea for the rights of individual human beings to live, a refusal to sacrifice them, or to be sacrificed, for the "system." The "system" that the university students were fighting was not authority as such (as some Establishment spokesmen have so glibly said) but the authority which has become dehumanized and infra-human, a "system" that has forgotten what it is supposed to be achieving, a way of life that has nothing to do with life.

Can we make any sort of guess at the sort of world we shall see? I think we can, if we have the courage to study what is happening around us now, and do not write it off because the implications are too disturbing. We are witnessing a fundamental change in human attitudes, shown essentially by young men and women under twenty-five. This change is happening because, without it, western man is in a blind alley. John Wilkinson writes, "... What has happened is that today's version of the quantitative society, 'cybernation', confronts us with a possibility of the imminent destruction of *all* human values. ... The inability of even the highest levels of management, financial, political or military, to control the apparatuses of which they are nominally in charge has become apparent, except to the limited extent that these pretended makers of policy can discover and render themselves subservient

4 / *Observer* (London), May 19, 1968.

to technical imperatives."[5] In this he follows Ellul who tells us bluntly that there is no way out: "Enclosed within his artificial creation, man finds that there is 'no exit'; that he cannot pierce the shell of technology to find again the ancient milieu to which he was adapted for hundreds of thousands of years. ... In our cities there is no more day or night or heat or cold. But there is over-population, thraldom to press and television, total absence of purpose. ..."[6]

More recently, Malcolm Muggeridge wrote: "There is so much power and so little strength, so much wealth and so little ease, so much information and so little knowledge. A great and widening abyss, as it seems to me, yawns between the happening and the recounting; between the event and the image, the achievement and the dream. In the vast and intricate processing of news, the news gets lost; within seconds of the bullet entering Martin Luther King there is no bullet, no King, only a story."[7]

It is no new thing for living organisms to get themselves into this sort of blind alley. When the first reptiles crawled out of the swamps, a few of them adapted their fore-limbs into wings, be-coming the birds. For a long time they were the most advanced of living creatures, but although wings are useful, they are less useful than a prehensile hand. Less differentiated animals were able to put their fore-limbs to better use. If previous evolutionary pro-gress is any guide, there seem to be two possibilities; one is that the human race has effectively destroyed itself, although we may be around for a few thousands of years yet. The dinosaurs lived on this earth for much longer than humans have so far managed; they died out because their environment changed and they did not have the brains or bodies to adapt to the new situation. We humans have enough intelligence to modify our physical environ-ment within the limits that our highly vulnerable bodies require; on the other hand our emotional instability makes it not at all unlikely that we shall be unable to meet the demands of our social

5 / *The Quantitative Society or What Are You to Do with Noodle?* (Santa Barbara, Calif.: Center for the Study of Democratic Institutions, n.d.).

6 / Jacques Ellul, *The Technological Society* (New York, 1965), pp. 428–9.

7 / "Adrift in America," *Observer* (London), May 19, 1968.

environment. For example, if we are unable to solve the problem of nuclear war, we shall presumably wipe ourselves out by high explosives or by poisoning the environment with radio-activity. In other words, we shall go the way of the dinosaurs and many other extinct animals, because we cannot adapt to a new environment, although in this case it is our own stupidity that will have made the environment intolerable.

Ardrey has pointed out that evolution occurs because those animals whose behaviour is most appropriate are the ones who survive – and that morphological change, or "selection," follows this.[8] As human behaviour is so highly modifiable compared with that of lower animals we will presumably see a change within a few generations, instead of one extending over thousands. An alternative (or additional) possibility is that of "mutation." This is an apparently chance change in the genetic structure of the species. Most mutations are deleterious, and the mutant has a physical or mental deformity, or cannot live at all. There are, however, a few mutations which allow the new individual to adapt more effectively to his environment. Leslie Fiedler argues that we are currently witnessing an analogous change in the social attitudes of young people.[9] It is true that many, or perhaps all, the values espoused by those now under thirty have been held by various groups in the past. The idea that loving your enemy is better than going to war with him is not new. Freer sexual behaviour (with different moral rules or none at all) has been advocated often enough. Many men in many centuries have tried to get back to a mythical world based on other values than those of work and success. What is new, in my own opinion, is that this attitude is no longer confined to a small group of intellectuals and idealists. Very few of the young people who show this most clearly seem to have arrived at their conclusions by any clear logical thought, but rather they are being swept along by largely unconscious processes. It is their very inability to formulate and explain their point of view (unlike the highly articulate "Bloomsbury Group" and others)

8 / Robert Ardrey, *The Territorial Imperative* (New York, 1966), chap. 1.
9 / Leslie A. Fiedler, "The New Mutants," *Partisan Review*, vol. 32, no. 4 (1965), p. 505.

that leads to so much misunderstanding of what they are trying to say. There is no reason to suppose that this is a mutation in the genetic sense, but the analogy is very close.

Some people, of course, will argue that we do not need any mutations; that our present environment represents "progress." It is already obvious that I do not accept this point of view, and see our world much as Galbraith does – we produce more and more cars and have nowhere to park them; we produce labour-saving devices, but have nowhere to go for a walk; we buy TV sets for our children, but cannot afford cultural programs which don't have a high enough mass appeal; we produce surpluses of food and then have to produce millions of appetite-controlling drugs; we spend billions on making people dissatisfied, driving them into the rat-race, and cannot afford hospitals and clinics to keep them going; we go for a picnic in our two-tone car with power steering, eat food which is perfectly packaged, from a portable icebox, and have to sit beside a polluted river looking at billboards.[10] Is disagreement on whether technological advance is synonymous with "progress" merely a matter of opinion, a matter of difference in values? Or is it possible to look back and detect a general direction of change, so that we can have some objective measurement of which change is forward, which is back, which is leading us into a blind alley?

Teilhard de Chardin addressed himself to this question[11] when he was unable to reconcile his religious belief that Man is pretty important with his scientific recognition that we are minute and vulnerable animals, living brief lives on a speck of dust in the immeasurable distances of the known universe. He suggested that one can in fact see a steady (although not regular) progression from simplicity to complexity. The earliest nebulae consisted of very simple atoms, which became condensed into heavier atoms, thence into simple molecules. Eventually after billions of years, these molecules became sufficiently complex for life to be possible. The simplest life consisted of unicellular animals, which then became more complex in their turn, to become multi-cellular. As the

10 / John Kenneth Galbraith, *The Affluent Society* (Boston, 1958), chap. 18.
11 / In *The Phenomenon of Man* (London, 1959).

complexity increased, the cells forming the organism became more and more specialized, so that the adequate functioning of the organism became possible only when each type of cell was playing its part, and conversely the differentiated cells were unable to live without the help of the others. The human race has already become a multi-cellular organism in this sense; few of us could live without the smooth functioning of other members of the human family, unlike the caveman, who was almost entirely self-sufficient.

It would follow from this hypothesis that the most "advanced" human being is the one who is most integrated into the human family. No doubt an amoeba would argue that he was far superior to any of the highly specialized cells found in the human central nervous system, because he can get along by himself in the water, can absorb and excrete food, and can take primitive defensive measures against threats to his integrity. What is more, he can, when the time is ripe, divide himself into two and maintain the species. Those of us who are not amoebae would grant him these points, but would insist that the specialized brain cell which can do none of these things by itself is still a more advanced form of life. Our remote descendants, looking back on the self-contained entrepreneur of the twentieth century, and comparing him with the highly specialized and differentiated human who has become part of a larger and more complex organism, will (I am sure) regard the entrepreneur, the individualist, as a primitive form of life. Loss of individuality can be often seen as a higher level of existence – "It is not that the raindrop has entered the ocean, but the ocean has entered the raindrop."

It is probably no coincidence that Maslow's "self-actualizing person" has several of the characteristics I have been describing; this person has "increased identification with the human species." He writes: "Examples of this kind of transcendence are Walt Whitman or William James who were profoundly American, most *purely* American, and yet were also very purely supra-cultural, internationalist members of the whole human species. They were universal men not *in spite* of their being Americans, but just *because* they were such good Americans. So, too, Martin Buber, a Jewish philosopher, was *also* more than Jewish. Hokusai, profoundly Japanese, was a universal artist. Probably *any* universal art cannot be rootless. *Merely* regional art is different from the regionally rooted art that becomes broadly general – human. We may remind ourselves here also of Piaget's children who could not conceive of being simultaneously Genevan and Swiss until they matured to the point of being able to include one within the other and both simultaneously in a hierarchically-integrated way."[12]

The technological marvels of our present society have arisen largely because of our emphasis on two aspects of human experience. One is competition, the other is the use of intellect and reason. Of course, we have never been all that reasonable; our behaviour has always been emotional in origin, but we justify it by rationalization. The Age of Enlightenment with its glorification of science was itself an over-reaction against the Christian Church, which had anathematized reason as the handmaid of the devil, and had successfully stopped nearly all scientific experimentation for a thousand years. At the same time, although it was formally committed to love as the basic law, the Church soon perverted this into some of the most vicious and widespread cruelty of recorded history. Our rejection of this is still one-sided; the price we have been paying since the seventeenth century is a large one; our emphasis on competition has largely prevented us from learning the techniques of co-operation, and the emphasis on reason has largely blinded us to the validities of emotional experience. Emotional experience has been expressed in "art," which is separate from "real life," and for several centuries has been largely despised as being some sort of frill that can be indulged in when work is over. Emotional expression is then confined to those primitive and irrational impulses which manage to escape our rational control. It is precisely because we have neglected awareness of our emotional selves that our emotions are likely to overwhelm us and bring the whole intellectual pyramid, balanced delicately on its apex, falling to the ground. Scientific study of emotion is not, of course, any substitute.

The essence of Fiedler's paper[13] is that the new mutants among us are less preoccupied with the old exclusive emphasis on reason

12 / Abraham H. Maslow, *Toward a Psychology of Being* (New York, 1962).
13 / "The New Mutants"; see footnote 9.

and competition. He begins by pointing out that every period of literature has shown particular sensitivities and corresponding obtuseness; the present emphasis is on novels about the future (not about utopias, which have always been written, but which have not been described as realizable possibilities so much as a frame of reference for measuring or satirizing the present world). He suggests that science fiction "reflects a growing sense of the irrelevance of the past and even of the present." Fiedler's use of the word "irrelevance" is no accident – that is the basic challenge put to our present concepts and values by the members of the coming generation.

When I began to collect material for this paper, I tried to find a word that would express the philosophy of the "New Youth." Until I realized the significance of my difficulty, I was constantly frustrated by having each possible word – such as "movement," "New Left" – derided as completely missing the point. Eventually I got the message: all the words or phrases I could think of had connotations in a frame of reference that was simply not applicable to what I was trying to describe. In short, the words and names themselves were irrelevant. This is one reason why communication between the generations has broken down so sadly and the younger generation write us off and say, "Nobody over 30 can understand." They are not rebelling against us, as young people have always rebelled against older ones, they are not trying to measure up to us or surpass us, they are not competing with us; they are playing a different game with different rules.

As Lennie Bruce said in his autobiography,[14] "We push our kids to set up charge accounts to buy more and more consumer junk – so who's the junkie?" Looking at their elders and betters having a couple of stiff drinks *before* the party, able to enjoy sex only when high, indulging in wife-swapping, polluting our air and water, saying that the only way to save a Vietnamese town was to destroy it, turning our ravines into expressways and calling all this the "Great Society," they turn to us and say with more amusement than indignation, "Are *you* telling *us* how to live?"

14 / How to Talk Dirty and Influence People (Chicago, 1963).

However, even when we have recognized that their rules are different, it is far from easy to find out what they are. This is partly because the young people are themselves not clear about what the rules are, and partly because we have been so conditioned by two thousand years of rational thinking that we keep slipping back into it and using a scientific, cognitive frame of reference. Collingwood has argued that we can approach a concept as art, religion, history, science, or philosophy.[15] We can discuss Shakespeare's *Julius Caesar* as poor history or as good art; each approach, historical or artistic, has its own validity, but validity in one frame of reference is no guide to validity in another. For example, the churches have traditionally got themselves into difficulties by trying to describe transcendental religious experience in scientific terms; it may be religiously true that the sun goes around the earth; it is certainly scientifically false.

A youth may wear his hair long because he is trying to prove his independence, but he may not be trying to "prove" anything. To ask him what it "means" is as pointless a question as asking what abstract art "means." Representational art can be judged both in artistic terms and in terms of the accuracy of its reproduction. Abstract art can be discussed only in artistic terms. Similarly, it seems to me that many of the statements made by young people today are statements of emotional truth, and not necessarily of rational or cognitive truth. This was illustrated by a patient of mine who had been wondering if her boyfriend was going to marry her. She told me that he said, "I love you," and when she asked, "Do you mean that?" he replied, "Now you've spoilt it." When he made his remark he was expressing a sudden, spontaneous feeling of love for her. Her question had the implication of asking if he was prepared to marry her; in his reply he meant that this was an entirely different question. In a purely emotional frame of reference, it is irrelevant to talk of marriage in the circumstances, but it is also true that love does carry implications for action and commitment that extend beyond the spontaneous and possibly transitory feeling. It seems to me that the young person who emphasizes the validity of love without

15 / R. G. Collingwood, *Speculum Mentis* (Oxford, 1924).

formal or social commitment is reacting against a world and a civilization in which all the emphasis has been on formal and social commitment without the underlying spontaneity and emotional reality.

This view has also been expressed by Irving Howe.[16] He said that the "movement" springs from a genuine moral feeling – a sense of outrage. With this he detects a corresponding weakness, a lack of clear ideas, "a feeling that it's wrong – or middle-class – to think systematically." He is inclined to forgive this lack of systematic thinking because our present society is so deficient in attractive or even firm values; it is "so ready to substitute success for significance," that the reaction against it must be undifferentiated. Nevertheless, he suggests, they do seek for a distinction of style because they share with the middle class the idea that fundamental values are embodied in externals of dress, appearance, furnishing, and speech. Howe also said that the third characteristic of the "movement" is that it shares with totalitarianism a contempt for history. "What attracts them is the surface of vitality, the appearance of freshness, the drama of gesture." It is this fascination with charisma that attracts them to such figures as Mao or Castro. Howe's last point seems to me to be plausible; on the other hand my own impression is that the young people who are such fervent admirers of either leader tend to be the ones who are showing the classical adolescent rebellion; not the ones who are active in the civil rights movement or who personify the "sense of outrage" that Howe is describing earlier.

It is hard to say what connection there is between the "movement" and communism. For that matter it is hard at the time of writing to know what is the connection between Cuban communism, Mao communism and Russian communism. The current heroes of the more militant young people are certainly communists or Marxists of a sort: Ché Guevara, Régis Debray, and Herbert Marcuse. Nevertheless Marcuse's main complaint is against technocracy rather than capitalism. He says that, both in the East and the West, the people are kept quiet by being told what they want,

16 / "The New Radicalism: Round Two," *Partisan Review*, vol. 32, no. 3 (1965), p. 341.

"they enjoy a comfortable, smooth, reasonable, democratic un-freedom." He feels that only the intellectuals can form the small enlightened core that can change this situation, and there is no question that his ideas have inspired many students in both West Germany and France. Commenting on these "New Heroes" of today's youth, Neal Ascherson summarizes their attitude as fol-lows: "Parliaments are moribund; liberalism is a dangerous sham concealing the most efficient repression ever known. Moscow and Washington are power bureaucracies brainwashing their masses by a manipulated press into believing they are content."[17] They believe that capitalism leads to technocratic fascism and that it must go to make way for a new human being who will be unex-ploited, creative in a leisure granted by automation, spontaneous, uninhibited, social.

Nat Hentoff writes that in the "movement" there is "no cohesive design for a new society, but the beginning of a consensus about the irrelevancy of most traditional American radical styles and the corrolary recognition – often more visceral than ideological – of ... the root failures of the present society and the prospects of a far worse society of technological necessity."[18] To prevent this there must be a fundamental change in values as well as in institutions.

To return to Fiedler's article: he remarks on the repetitive theme in current literature of the end of Man, not by the Bomb but by mutation, and illustrates this by A. C. Clarke's *Childhood's End*. This novel ends when the children, who are mutants, "take off" into outer space. Fiedler suggests that this is (whether Clarke knows it or not) a metaphor, an allegory – it is *inner* space that they are moving to. Fiedler says that these new mutants are already among us, we see them as beatniks, hipsters, rounders, or drop-outs. They are trying to disengage from the twin assumptions of our society – humanism (both bourgeois and Marxist) and reason (from Socrates through the Renaissance and the Age of Enlightenment). Fiedler remarks that he discovered he was already living in the past when he heard one of the students say,

17 / "The New Heroes," *Observer* (London), June 2, 1968.
18 / "Is There a New Radicalism?" *Partisan Review*, vol. 32, no. 2 (1965), p. 183.

"Freud is a fink." (It is worth noting that Freud's teaching was largely misunderstood by the people who reacted so hysterically to his insights and discussions of sex. Freud believed in and advocated the greater understanding of impulses and drives, only so they might be more effectively controlled by the ego, the mediator of rational control.)

Much has been written about the Berkeley riot of 1964. It has been generally recognized that this revolt was the prototype for much unrest in universities elsewhere, both in North America and in Europe. Because of this, there has been much thought given to various interpretations. These have been summed up by J. R. Seeley,[19] who lists many of the standard "explanations." These include the suggestion that the students were spoilt children who already had too much, that it was an accidental spill-over from civil rights activities, that it was an irrational plot to destroy a great university for the sheer joy of doing so, that it was a communist conspiracy. Seeley points out that all these explanations have the hidden motivation of exculpating the administration and of trivializing and patronizing the students. He suggests that we should begin by asking what the students in fact did say. They were indicting the administration (i.e., the government) of the university – it was more an attack on the monarchy than on the monarch. Few of them wanted Clark Kerr to go, at least at the time; and it is interesting to note that the somewhat similar revolt at the London School of Economics in 1967 had many of the earmarks that Seeley had earlier described for the Berkeley situation. The students at LSE chose as their target a recently appointed member of the Establishment, whom they accused of having been a supporter of the Smith regime in Rhodesia. It is not altogether clear whether or not this was a fair accusation. His supporters claim that he had in fact done his best to maintain the integrity of his university there in spite of the difficulties imposed by the Smith government. However, the important point is that this issue was merely a precipitating factor; the essential protest, in both Berkeley and London, was against certain assumptions on the part of the university government. The students at Columbia were pro-

19 / In *Quo warranto: The Berkeley Issue* (Santa Barbara, Calif.: Center for the Study of Democratic Institutions, n.d.).

testing, among other things, the building of a gymnasium on open ground that had been previously available to their neighbours in Harlem.

Seeley argues that the detailed content of the students' complaints is unimportant. Basically they are questioning the legitimacy of the government. They ask by what right they are being governed, a fundamental question that must be put by all free men who are asked to conform to any law. The variety of answers they were given illustrates the shaky basis on which the university government was, in fact, established: they were told that their attendance at the university was a privilege, not a right, that the Board of Regents had power whether the students liked it or not, that the university was a private institution, that it was a public institution; they were told that somebody must govern. Seeley points out that any government that lacks legitimacy in the eyes of its subjects is doomed sooner or later. All government depends on tradition, reason, or charisma, or a mixture of these. Few North American universities can claim the first; few are lucky enough to have a dean or president with charismatic authority; this means that they must depend on reason – that is, *moral* reason. Seeley asks what is, in fact, the moral basis for the laws issued by a university government. He remarks that board members are not elected publicly or by any proof of professional or academic competence; neither are they there by the consent of the governed. In his encyclical *Pacem in terris*, Pope John XXIII wrote: "Human society can be neither well ordered nor prosperous unless it has some people invested with a legitimate authority to preserve its institutions. ... Authority must derive its obligatory force from the moral order. ..."

We have already seen that young people are also disinclined to accept the moral order of the society in which the university is placed. This is partly because the society itself seems to have very few firm values, partly because there is rejection even of the values to which society pays lip service. Our educational system generally, both high schools and universities, pretends to value learning for its own sake, but in fact subordinates this to "success." It is increasingly obvious that the best way to succeed in this sort of institution is to repeat what you are told and not to ask questions, to become a junior "organization man" as soon as possible and not rock the boat. But even if we except many university teachers and other educators from this cynical philosophy, the fact still remains that they are dedicated to intellectual excellence, to the pursuit of knowledge for its own sake, and we have seen that this assumption of intellect and reason as the *only* valid criteria has been rejected by many young people. In short, many of them are dropping out of university or school, or are rebelling against it, because they simply do not accept the moral right of the establishment to promulgate the laws to which the students are expected to conform.

In this context a couple of other pithy remarks by Seeley are worth quoting. "The educators speak of 'educating the whole child', but unless he checks pretty nearly everything that makes him a child and a human being at the door, they panic." He says that we program the children in our schools like computers, and all we have left at the end is marginal differentiation among them. He also remarks, "It is a post-Renaissance heresy that somehow knowledge exists apart from the life into which it enters, and that life exists in a medium other than the knowing of it."

Fiedler makes much the same point about the Berkeley revolt. He says that the students were protesting against the assumption of the bourgeois protestant humanist viewpoint, with man justified by rationality, work, duty, vocation, and success; childhood and youth being a period of preparation (under the guidance of successful older people). He tells the story of a lady in California who was applying to have a local café closed, and in her evidence described her distress in looking in the window and seeing a young man "just standing there, looking – nonchalant." Fiedler points out that the origin of nonchalant means "without heat" or "cool." I would like to digress here to suggest that there is not too great a distinction between nonchalance and "the end of desire" that is held by Buddhists to be a prerequisite for Enlightenment. The acceptance of ourselves and of each other, the insistence that attempts to change the world by striving are based on illusion, are attitudes common to both Eastern philosophies and the Beat point of view. The rejection of cognitive classification, on which all Western science is based, is emphasized throughout Buddhist teaching. Many others have pointed out the dangers of classification; de Chardin talks of the way in which concepts become "unravelled at the edges" as soon as one tries to state them. Lao Tzu said, many centuries ago, "Inasmuch as names are given, one should also know where to stop."

It is interesting that this rejection of overdrawn distinctions is one of the characteristics of the New Youth listed by Seeley in another paper, delivered in Toronto in 1966.[20] A glance through this list shows how close his views are to those already quoted by Hentoff and Fiedler. He says that there is rejection of the combative virtues and competition in favour of love in all its forms. There is rejection of work as *inherently* valuable and of generalized rules in favour of assessment of a unique situation. There is rejection of segmental responses and overdrawn distinctions (e.g., male–female, right–wrong, inner–outer world) in favour of global or integrated responses. Rejection of the idolatry of self and extended self for "something more than tolerance." A refusal to be obsessed with scarcity and consequent hoarding of material goods, in favour of things that are "good only in the giving," such as the making of music.

There is ample and obvious evidence to support his view that the New Youth rejects the concept of right and wrong based on rigid and unalterable rules, and also on the traditional concepts of masculinity and femininity. "Moral relativism" is the name given to the former; in the sexual field it is exemplified by the humanistic liberalism espoused by Isadore Rubin and Lester Kirkendall. Many theologians are also advocating a morality based on a total assessment of a given situation in all its aspects rather than on legalisms; this is one of the basic points made by Ernest Harrison in *A Church without God*[21] and by H. A. Williams[22] who writes: "A great deal of what Christians often call virtue, on closer inspection turns out to be cowardice of this

20 / "Time's Future in Our Time," unpublished paper presented at the (Ontario Education) Minister's Conference on Recreation.
21 / Toronto, 1966.
22 / "Theology and Self-Awareness," in A. R. Vidler, ed., *Soundings: Essays concerning Christian Understanding* (Cambridge, 1962).

kind – a refusal to give myself away because I am too frightened to do it. This is most obviously true in the sphere of sexual ethics, because here more than anywhere there seems to be an enormous amount of double-think. If I am to give myself away to another person, I cannot, in any circumstances, exploit her or him. To exploit is to withhold. It is totally incompatible with giving. But this is not at all the same thing as saying that in certain specifiable circumstances I must always be exploiting and never giving. Yet this is what the Church says about sexual intercourse outside marriage. Such intercourse may be often, perhaps almost always, an exploitation, unilateral or mutual. But there are cases where it need not be and isn't."

It is ironic that some of the hippie habits that arouse the most public antagonism are those that were not merely socially approved but considered to be the mark of a true Christian in previous centuries. St. Anthony is said never to have washed his feet in his whole life. St. Simeon Stylites lived with a rope knotted round and embedded in his flesh, thus producing "a horrible stench, intolerable to the bystanders. ... worms dropped from him wherever he moved and they filled his bed." And "throughout the monastic period cleanliness of either the clothes or the body was regarded as pollution of the soul, a sign of sinful pride."[23] Harvey Cox has made a similar point in a recent article.[24] He points out that St. Francis of Assisi was the son of a well-to-do merchant but lived in poverty and refused to make any provisions for the next day. He describes the hippies as, "A secular version of the historic American quest for faith that rules the heart, a religion that one can experience deeply and feel intensely. The love-ins are our twentieth century equivalent of the nineteenth century Methodist Camp meetings." Cox felt that the Easter Sunday love-in in Central Park in 1967 seemed much closer to the Easter spirit than did the parade in front of St. Patrick's. He quotes one hippie as saying, "Jesus was here this morning, so was Buddha." Cox goes on to ask why this movement began at this period of history. He suggests that this is because society

23 / Homer W. Smith, *Man and His Gods* (Boston, 1952), p. 382.
24 / "God and the Hippies," *Playboy*, Jan. 1968.

can now afford it; the traditional Christian virtue of charity is now a function of the state. He also asks why the hippies have become so interested in oriental faiths rather than Christianity, and readers of his previous work will not be surprised to hear that he blames the Church for being too bland, too wealthy, and as having sold out for the *status quo*. It has been activist and competitive, it has neglected an important part of its heritage – the mystical element – which would have appealed to the hippies. He is particularly critical of the Church's behaviour in turning its back on man's age-old search for the ecstatic and the mystical. He writes, "Christianity is challenged to exhibit a sensitivity to the religious needs of post-industrial man it has not yet displayed."

In addition to their disapproval of washing, the early Christians were notorious for their lack of interest in work. Cox remarks, "Much to the embarrassment of generations of preachers, Jesus commended Mary, who was simply sitting and talking with him, rather than Martha, who was busily preparing supper. It is hard to make Jesus an exemplar of the Protestant work ethic."

Another reason for the hippies' refusal to go along with the established churches is the latter's hypocritical attitude to sex. The hippies hardly provide an adequate ethic for our time, "but it does challenge the Church to devise a sexual ethic that will transcend present prudery and hypocrisy."

Cox is not starry-eyed about the hippies, however. He remarks that perhaps the greatest danger that the "movement" must confront is that its present theology, however confused and eclectic, still contains very little corrective to just plain self-indulgence. "This ... can lead to a terrible arrogance and to a kind of self-righteousness." Not only is their theology confused but they are politically naive. "Pot and barefoot frolicking isn't much use to hungry people in India. But most of the people who voice this criticism of the Hippies aren't doing much about it either." This echoes the remarks of Pierre de Lattre, a clergyman writing of the Beats in San Francisco a decade ago; he felt that this group was grossly misunderstood by the public and afforded a genuine example of Christianity in action. He felt that they had withdrawn from their society because none of the political parties at the time offered a valid alternative to acceptance of the Bomb and Madison Avenue. In this context it is worth noting that Senator Eugene McCarthy's entry into the presidential nominations early in 1968 did offer a genuine alternative, and, in the words of his wife, "What happened is that Gene's step forward released a spiritual log-jam in America." Paul Johnson, writing in the *New Statesman*, said, "For too long, those of us who care about politics have been imprisoned in the stale triangle formed by communism, fascism and bourgeois democracy. Appalled by the choice between the two authoritarianisms, most of us have struggled wearily to humanise the third, cobbling together every ramshackle variety of 'democratic socialism' in a vain attempt to combine material progress, on a mass basis, with a raised quality of life. Often enough we have got neither."[25] An editorial writer in the *Montreal Star* in May 1968 – in the middle of the French strikes – suggested that the workers' rejection of wage concessions might mean that they hoped to receive even more money, but it was equally likely that they "are groping for new meaning and answers, the pursuit of which has been ignored."

The blurring between the masculine and feminine images is seen most obviously in the long hair worn by young men and the male costume favoured by so many young women. It must, however, be recognized that there are other reasons for this reduction in differentiation. From Man's earliest history, the male's peculiar contribution has been a greater physical strength than the female's, and a greater delight and skill in physical combat. Within living memory physical strength has become of little value; most of the hard work has been taken over by machines. What is more, the male has little opportunity for displaying skill in physical combat; even in war, only a very small proportion of the armed services is involved in actual combat, and even those men who are, seldom require the traditional combative skills. A woman can navigate an aircraft as well as a man, or can program a radar tracking computer. It is an inescapable fact that women have redefined their role during the last fifty years, but men have not

25 / Vol. 75 (May 24, 1968), p. 675.

made a corresponding adjustment. In some ways, the new status of women offers them considerable advantages; in others they are at a disadvantage. Although they now have the vote, and almost all jobs and professions are open to them equally with men (a residual difficulty in obtaining the very top positions is rapidly disappearing), this new freedom really gives them an opportunity to be like men, rather than to continue as women. If a woman enters the industrial or business world, she does so as an individual human being and not as part of the family. Until fifty years ago, the woman played an essential part in the economy, but as a wife and mother. Any farm depended as much on the smooth and efficient functioning of the mother as on the competence of the farmer himself. Her new freedom has faced her with a choice of neglecting her family because she is out at work or of walking off the job whenever the children are sick. However, although women have not solved this problem, generally speaking, they do seem to have solved a large part of the emotional concomitant; when the suffragettes were active, many of the women who were trying to break into the masculine world dressed like men – with flat heels, tweedy clothes, and an Eton crop. Nowadays the only women who dress like this are those with psychosexual problems; when women wear slacks or men's shirts nowadays they do so with an undeniably feminine style. Again, on the side of advantage, it is a fact that women are now freed from the threat or fear of repeated pregnancies, especially as contraception is now under their own control and not that of their husbands. The other side of this coin is the possibility that the majority of women do in fact need the fulfilment of being wives and mothers; the corresponding masculine need is probably achievement in a wider world. The unfortunate thing for women is that a man can achieve what success he needs in part of the day, and then come home and be a father and husband, whereas the woman cannot be a part-time mother to anything like the same extent. This would not be a problem if men were to accept a much greater responsibility for parenthood. If husband and wife each have important and responsible jobs, it is taken for granted that it is the wife who stays at home when the children are sick, that it is she who will leave her job when her husband's career demands it. There is no reason at all why the husband should not stay home to look after the children because his wife's career is important; nor is there any reason why the family's location and living arrangements should not be determined at least as much by the woman's career requirements as those of the man.

Nelson N. Foote points out that it requires strength to be a lover, but a greater strength to be a husband, and greater strength still to be a father.[26] He suggests that the sort of acceptance of responsibility that I have just described is in fact a sign of strength and not of weakness. It seems to me that the blurring of sexual roles and external appearance, seen in long hair in boys or male attire on girls, is not so much an abandonment of their sexuality as much as a more solid awareness and acceptance of themselves as individuals, with a correspondingly diminished need to demonstrate their masculinity by conforming to orthodox masculine appearance. If one were to put the question, "What are you?" to a hundred men at random, almost all of them would reply by stating his occupation. It is only the few individualists, like Zorba the Greek, who would answer, "I am a man." Our present society demands so many roles of each of us – insurance salesman, husband, father, member of Kiwanis, suburban home-owner, etc., etc. – that there often seems to be no real human being left underneath. This is shown dramatically and commonly when many men retire; having become nothing more than workers, they fall to pieces when this role is no longer required of them. This is a problem that will become increasingly important as automation proceeds. If jobs disappear, or even if they only become less dominant in our lives, we shall be forced back more and more into ourselves as individuals. There are no signs that the educational system in general is preparing the coming generation for this; the whole system is geared essentially to externally imposed criteria, not to self-discovery.

LSD and other hallucinogens are very valuable drugs when used with adequate precautions, but indiscriminate use is highly dan-

26 / "Masculinity and Femininity," unpublished speech at Conference on Sex Education, Washington DC, 1966.

gerous. Nevertheless, although this is well known, they are increasingly popular, and this reflects a search for other forms of reality than the ones offered by the outer world. Mark Harris saw the hippies as Puritan Americans, "gorged with moral purpose, and loath to confess that their captivation was basically the pursuit of pleasure. They therefore attached to the mystique of LSD the conviction that by opening their minds to chemical visions they were gaining insights from which society should soon profit ...". However, this was not as effective as they had hoped. "Visions of community seen under LSD have not been imparted to anyone, remain visible only to Hippies, or entering the visual scene only in the form of commentary upon LSD itself, jokes and claims for its efficacy growing shriller with the increase of dependence. Yet the argument had been that LSD inspired transcendance, that it was, as one Hippie phrased it, 'a stepping-stone to get out of your environment and look at it'."[27]

Of course, the outer world is not entirely commercialized; the visual and plastic arts in particular have, for some decades, paid relatively little attention to the representation of physical reality. It is worth remembering that representational art covers only a small part of human history or geography; the "primitive" art of Africa, the stylised and symbolic art of China, are closely related in many ways to so-called "modern painting." Pop art may or may not be aesthetically pleasing, but the artist is trying to force us to look at and pay attention to the world around us, even if that is the traditional Campbell's soup can. He is saying, like the Buddhist, "Don't ask what it *means*, don't ask what it's *for*, look at it as it *is*." In a way, the current popularity of "camp" derives from the same insights. The essential quality of camp is hard to pin down, but it seems to me that it lies in its essential artificiality. It is not only meaningless and purposeless, but is ostentatiously and satirically so. It is not merely decoration for its own sake; it insists that the words, the mannerisms, the concepts, the values that we thought were solid and important are in fact superficial and affected.

27 / Mark Harris, "The Flowering of the Hippies," *Atlantic Monthly*, Sept. 1967, pp. 63–72.

The James Bond movies are great favourites of camp connoisseurs. The blue-eyed upstanding hero of the nineteenth-century novels and melodramas was seen as a poseur as soon as society asked about his unconscious motivations. We sighed with relief when we did not have to emulate these paragons, and instead we projected ourselves into novels as the non-hero; but there was still enough of the Walter Mitty left in us to be dissatisfied with this colourless creature. Accordingly we set up the super-hero, like James Bond. At the same time we could not really take him seriously and, recognizing this, the film-makers turned him into a satire. It is clear that we need new heroes, and the paper by Foote already quoted points the way. The hero always has been, and always must be, strong; but the traditional form of strength – physical and combative – is no longer acceptable. (When Hollywood caught on to this idea, it thought it was breaking new ground by casting a priest or some other man of peace in the role of hero, but over and over again, when the chips were down, and he had the eyeball-to-eyeball confrontation with the villain, he used his fists – showing thereby that he was a man after all, and also completely missing the point.) The "movement" does have its heroes, but these are not the heroes of Kipling and Henty. The new mutants recognize that it takes at least as much courage to be a Gandhi as to be a Gordon. It is relatively easy to find physical strength and bravery in the middle of a battle; it is far harder to find the moral strength *not* to hit back when attacked. This, then, is the strength of the coming heroes, the true sign of manhood and maturity. A man who is strong in this sense does not have to reject skills that have no basis in physical strength, such as delight in poetry, music, and all the "feminine" arts. The old hero solved his problems by relying on his physical strength and bravery – by hitting somebody. The new hero solves the problem by showing the moral strength of love and tolerance. As our economic structure is based on competition rather than co-operation, it seems inevitable that it will be fundamentally changed if this other philosophy becomes dominant.

Although members of the "movement" commonly reject the term "New Left," and although there are major differences between this movement and the traditional political radicalism, they would surely reject even more vehemently the label of "New Right." When they do become involved in political action, it is always on the side of the Left. Thelma McCormack wrote in 1950, "Nothing divides the generation over thirty from the generation under thirty so decisively as the preoccupation with self, which runs through the New Left thought."[28] She goes on to say that the earlier Leftists developed the ability to subordinate themselves in collective action in order to achieve these goals. I think she is right up to a point, but has missed the essential nature of their preoccupation. They are interested in themselves, and in discovering who they are, but not in the self-centred, essentially hostile way exemplified by Ayn Rand's heroes. To subordinate oneself in collective experience is one thing; to subordinate oneself in collective action is quite another. This latter type of subordination is an enlargement of one's ego, a way of increasing one's personal strength, but not necessarily one's personal understanding.

In 1965 a series of writers in the *Partisan Review* contributed to a discussion of "The New Radicalism." Two opposing views became apparent; some writers felt that the present civil rights movement and its supporters among today's youth derive from traditional radical attitudes, through David Lillienthal, TVA, work camps, etc. It would follow from this assumption that the "New Left" must ally itself with the workers, must find where the present power really lies, and must know how to counter it. It must develop techniques for helping the poor and under-privileged find and sustain their own leadership. This view, held by Max Hentoff and others, was opposed by Michael Harrington who claimed that the issue is not an economic one. "The Negroes have probably done more for the whites than for themselves, for while they have won some modest, token, integration, they have given our entire nation a gift of conscience." Harrington goes on to point out that Lenin saw a labour aristocracy thriving on the super profits of imperialism, but now some leftists regard *all*

28 / "The Motivation of Radicals," *American Journal of Sociology*, vol. 56, no. 1 (1950).

labour as a labour aristocracy, the only proletariat being the poor. "The centre for social change is not the factory but the slum," and the root problems are rates and welfare rather than wages and working conditions. Hentoff was also opposed by Stephen Rousseas, who argued that Hentoff's view was a naive restatement of Marxism and pointed out that "Scarcity no longer exists." The problem is one of misallocation because of political rigidities. In fact, real wages have followed technological advance fairly closely, which has led to a phenomenal stability in labour's relative share of the total output. The intellectuals have failed to keep up with the new problems because they have "turned their eyes inwards and are steadfastly gazing into their psyches when not losing their selves in their specialties." They have, as a result, become politically ineffectual and, by default, defenders of the *status quo*. In a counter-attack, Hentoff wrote that "the young are not so much disrespectful of radical tradition as they are disrespectful of those aging Radicals who try to conceal and influence them in terms of the thirties." The enemy now, he says, is basically different, and young people are not following the old-line parties because they are still fighting the old battles – he excepts the Trotskyites who are "rigidly irrelevant." It is not so much that the "movement" has ignored the workers, but it is the other way around.

It is certainly true that many young idealists feel today that everybody over thirty must have sold out; they see such union leaders as Walter Reuther as firm supporters of the establishment and the *status quo*. Far less has been written about conditions in Canada, but we see a similar disenchantment. The New Democratic party is often accused of still fighting the battles of the 1930s, with slogans about thirty years out of date, and giving answers to problems that have been largely solved. Most Liberals and Conservatives are not even asking the questions. Be this as it may, I still feel that it is not entirely wrong to apply the term "left" to the "movement." There is, I think, an underlying emotional attitude, common to both the traditional radical and the new radical. The difference lies in the fact that the old-line radical tried to achieve social justice by rational planning and political coalition. The new radical is more concerned with immediate, spontaneous personal action. They are both concerned with the "have-nots," but what the dispossessed did not have in the 1930s was different from what the dispossessed do not have today. Thirty years ago they did not have money, and they were essentially workers; now they do not have human dignity and they are a much less clearly defined group of Negroes, slum dwellers, and problem families.

Several attempts have been made by psychologists and others to align political and emotional attitudes. Himmelstrand[29] has studied this in Sweden, and Eysenck[30] did so in Britain. By means of questionnaires and statistical analysis, Eysenck was able to extract two axes, one of radical-conservatism, the other of tough- and tender-mindedness. He found that tough-minded radicals tended to approve of companionate marriage and to be in favour of liberalization of divorce and abortion laws. Tender-minded radicals were pacifist, opposed to the death penalty, felt that patriotism worked against peace, and were concerned with curing rather than punishing criminals. Tough-minded conservatives, on the other hand, believed in the flogging of criminals, were in favour of capital punishment, nationalism, and were racially prejudiced. The tender-minded conservatives advocated a "return to religion," Sunday observance, etc. A much more comprehensive study by Adorno et al. in 1950[31] describes "a basically hierarchical, authoritarian, ... power-oriented exploitively dependent attitude to one's sex partner and one's god, and may well culminate in a political philosophy and social outlook which has no room for anything but a desperate clinging to what appears to be strong and a disdainful rejection of whatever is relegated to the bottom. ... On the other hand, there is a pattern character-

29 / U. Himmelstrand, *Social Pressures, Attitudes, and Democratic Processes* (Stockholm, 1960).

30 / H. J. Eysenck, "General Social Attitudes," *Journal of Social Psychology*, vol. 19 (1944), pp. 207–27; and "Primary Social Attitudes," *International Journal of Opinion and Attitude Research*, vol. 1 (1947), pp. 49–84.

31 / T. W. Adorno et al., *The Authoritarian Personality* (New York, 1950), p. 971.

ized chiefly by affectionate, basically equalitarian and permissive interpersonal relationships." Even though there have been a few studies which tend to support Eysenck's findings in this field (such as Warburton's study of the 1931 German general election,[32] one of the confusing factors has been that authoritarian personalities can and do reach prominence in left-wing parties. Emotionally, they differ very little from their counterparts in right-wing parties; they merely hit different people.

Nevertheless it does seem to me that the left-wing political philosophy is related more to the "affectionate, equalitarian, and permissive" personality, whereas the right-wing political attitude is essentially authoritarian and exploitative. In short, if we are thinking in terms of attitudes and personality we can properly call the "movement" left-wing, but if we are thinking in terms of specific goals and, more particularly, of techniques to achieve them, it is not in the left-wing tradition.

Members of the "movement" want *participatory* democracy, which is the opposite of authoritarianism; for this reason many writers have felt that they are immune to the dangers of being taken over by authoritarian parties, however hysterical are the warnings given by middle-aged democratic socialists. (This does not apply to that small band of devout Trotskyites, who are rigid, fanatical, authoritarian, and essentially rebellious, but they do not have any marked effect on the "movement" as a whole.) Paul Goodman is one of those who sees the "movement" as a descendant of earlier radicalism. "Poignantly, in their ignorance of American history, they do not recognize that they are Congregationalists, town-meeting Democrats, Jeffersonians, Populists." He, like many other writers, points out that this generation is the first really post-Freudian one. The sort of upbringing they have had is "fatal to suburban squeamishness, race and moral prejudices, and keeping up appearances. ... As a style they go in for direct confrontation and sometimes brutal frankness." It is this preference for direct confrontation that makes them particularly

32 / F. W. Warburton, "Social Attitudes as Measured by Factorial Analysis of Voting Behaviour," *Bulletin of the British Psychological Society*, vol. 41 (1960), pp. 5–8.

irritated by the impersonal and distant relationships they find with their teachers. They are also intolerant of the double-talk used all around them by administrators, politicians, advertisers, and the mass media. "These official people are not even lying; rather, there is an unbridgeable chasm between the statements made 'on the record' for systemic reasons, or the image of the corporation, and what is intended and actually performed. I have seen mature graduate students crack up in giggles of anxiety listening to the Secretary of State expound our foreign policy; when I questioned them afterwards, some said that he was like a mechanical man, others that he was demented. And most campus blow-ups have been finally caused by administrators' animal inability to speak plain. The students have faithfully observed due process and manfully stated their case, but the administrators simply cannot talk like human beings."[33]

This, then, is the crux of the whole matter. As a society we are in danger of losing (or perhaps already have lost) those human qualities that make life worth living. Because of it, I am suggesting that there is a spontaneous revolution of the coming generation.

At this point the "practical" man will – if he accepts the contention that an emotional revolution is underway – ask what should be done about it. The only answer is: "Get with it." Psychiatrists rarely tell their patients what to do, because carrying out instructions blindly never works. We cannot make decisions for our patients; all we can do is to offer them new interpretations of their situations, so that they themselves will know what has to be done. I was talking to a school teacher recently who complained that her students had asked for responsibility but had refused to accept it when offered; it turned out that they had refused to take over "lunch duty" from the staff. She was quite unable to see that this was not the sort of responsibility they were talking about – it was merely carrying out somebody else's rules. "Surely you aren't suggesting that students should write the school rules?" she asked in horror. Then, having been quite unable to accept what the students were in fact saying, she asked again what responsibilities they should be given.

33 / *Playboy*, Feb. 1967, p. 110.

I have little hope that the various establishments – political, financial, military, educational – will be able to accept the implications of the revolution. I think that they will try to set up some phony concessions and will be swept aside by sheer force of numbers. The "movement" will not be satisfied with face-saving de-escalation; they refuse to take part in war at all. They will not settle for improved welfare payments for negroes; they want them to be fully accepted. They do not want to patch up the slums; they want to destroy the society that makes slums inevitable. They do not want a society that is "free" only in that the slave can become a slave owner; they want to abolish slavery.

They did not decide to do all this; they do not know how they are going to achieve it. The early mammals did not decide to develop prehensile fore-limbs – it happened to them. The coming generation is following a similar evolutionary imperative. We cannot predict how they will evolve, and it is possible that the reaction against reason, science, and technology will go too far. If everybody contemplates the infinite instead of fixing the drains many of us will die of cholera. At some point in the future Man will have to integrate all these truths, and in the meantime there will be conflict, confusion, and compromise. But – unless the military men destroy the human race to save it from communism/ capitalism – the revolution is the first step toward saving us from the nightmare world into which we have been drifting.

3

Post-Capitalist Society*

JACK McLEOD

> The historian who does not grasp the fact that man-
> kind, whatever else it is doing, is making an agon-
> ized transition from societies based on private
> property to societies which are not, is in my view
> out of touch with what is happening in the second
> half of the twentieth century. I hasten to add that
> the new societies may not be more humane than
> those they replace. Still, the interesting question of
> our time will appear to future historians as that one
> – namely, Is a humane socialism possible? – rather
> than that which presently pre-occupies the Ameri-
> can psyche, Will capitalism or socialism prevail?
> And from where I stand, this is ground for hope.
> STAUGHTON LYND

READERS OF THE Schulz comic strip "Peanuts" may recall the
cartoon in which Lucy is reading a book to Linus. "It says here
that people used to believe that the world was flat," says Lucy. A

---

*This essay is highly eclectic. It is an attempt to synopsize and popu-
larize certain ideas which are "in the air" in academic circles, as well as to
give this book a sharper focus. In borrowing ideas from various authors, I
am most heavily indebted to Daniel Bell, Charles A. Reich, and Karl
Polanyi.

The leading quotation from Staughton Lynd is from his "Historical Past
and Existentialist Present," in Theodore Roszak, ed., *The Dissenting
Academy* (New York, 1966), p. 109.

long silence follows until little Linus finally inquiries with innocent bewilderment, "And what do we believe nowadays?"

Linus is Everyman. The old beliefs and ideologies are hollow and inadequate. Whether Daniel Bell is correct in pointing to an end of ideology, or whether we are simply suffering from confusion over ideologies, I do not know. My own suspicion is that we may be entering an era in which there will be a renaissance of political theory and ideology. But at least it is clear that our former market mentality is obsolete.

The capitalist mentality, with its emphasis on private property and self-regulating markets, reduced both land and labour to "commodities," which could be bought and sold for profit. The grotesque and immoral enormity of this fundamental feature of capitalism can be seen if we remind ourselves that "land" is simply another name for nature, and that "labour" is only another name for man. Here is the basis for the late Karl Polanyi's thesis that market destroys community.[1] From Polanyi and others we learned, or should have learned, that markets can organize material interests only, and not all of these, and that an agglomeration of material interests is not enough to constitute a true community.

In effect liberal capitalism was man's initial response to the benefits and agonies of the Industrial Revolution. In order to provide scope for the use of machine technology, we transformed the organic and hierarchical medieval economy into a self-adjusting system of markets, and cast our thoughts and values in the mould of the market. Liberal capitalism was utopian in the sense that it assumed away all of the most fundamental questions of society. It assumed that private and public economic interests would always conveniently coincide. They did not. We discovered that the unregulated market did not produce full employment, economic stability, or adequate social capital such as hospitals and schools. The market did not produce economic justice or any real sense of community. Instead of utopia, the market created an impersonal and bloody battleground upon which affluent but alienated economic atoms called "individuals" could struggle for

1 / Karl Polanyi, *The Great Transformation* (Boston, 1957).

gain, while the sullen poor looked on helplessly. In short, the market proved splendidly productive but essentially amoral.

Today it is no longer possible to accept unquestioningly the validity of the orthodox capitalist values of possessive individualism, private property, and the unregulated market. The market is now regulated almost everywhere by the state in the defence of more humanistic values and, except in the minds of the most unreconstructed conservatives, capitalism is either dead or completely transformed. As Polanyi wrote in 1947: "Outside the United States, liberal capitalism can hardly be said to exist any more. How to organize human life in a machine society is a question that confronts us anew. Behind the fading fabric of competitive capitalism there looms the portent of an industrial civilization, with its paralyzing division of labour, standardization of life, supremacy of mechanism over organism, and organization over spontaneity. Science itself is haunted by insanity. ... The search for industrial democracy is not merely the search for a solution to the problems of capitalism, as most people imagine. It is a search for an answer to industry itself."[2]

Just as we learned in the past to regulate and control markets, it is now imperative that we learn to control technology. Technological change can no longer we taken for granted. Shallow critics of contemporary society tend either to worship or to deplore modern technology, but neither response is intelligent, and neither response will suffice. How to control technology is *the* new political problem. It is a problem to which this book provides some guidance but no adequate answers. That statement should neither shame the authors nor surprise the reader, because no one has yet succeeded in finding the "right" answers. It has become fashionable to observe that we live in a "technological society," and increasing numbers of intellectuals, led by McLuhan[3] and Ellul,[4] are trying to solve the mystery of technological change, but the

2 / "Our Obsolete Market Mentality", *Commentary*, vol. 3, no. 2 (Feb. 1947), p. 109.
3 / Marshall McLuhan, *Understanding Media* (New York, 1964).
4 / J. Ellul, *The Technological Society* (New York, 1965).

mystery remains. We can scarcely blame the politicians for bumbling and fumbling this crucial issue of our age, because they have received little or no guidance from the intellectuals whose job it is to study and interpret contemporary problems. But we can at least recognize the terrifying magnitude of the task.

There is an analogy between the rise of liberal capitalism and the rise of the new technology, an analogy which may place the problem of technological control in its proper perspective. Technological development today is in the enshrined position that was accorded to the market in nineteenth-century capitalism. Unguided and self-directed technology is the free market all over again. Those scientists who exhort us to let technology have its head and solve all problems for us strikingly resemble the advocates of the unregulated market a century ago. The arguments justifying *laissez faire* were little different from those justifying unrestrained technology, and the arguments are as blindly utopian today as they were then. Failure to control technology will result in the same social disruption and chaos that resulted from our failures to control the market.[5] Once again the name of the game is control, the ability to control gigantic forces which are imperfectly understood. Our future depends upon contemporary success in developing new social theories as the basis for political action.

In this essay I will outline some of the reasons for the rise of "big government" and the decline of private property in the twentieth century. The role of the newly emergent technocratic elite will be indicated, followed by a speculative sketch of the general shape of the future. The concluding section will suggest several means of coping with what I call the "medieval future."

I

Seeing the future is relatively easy, since "mere facts" don't impede our view; seeing the present is much more difficult. McLuhan is right when he says that the immediate environment tends to be "invisible"; we can imagine the future and we can get some perspective on the past, but it is much less easy to perceive and

5 / W. H. Ferry, "Must We rewrite the Constitution to Control Technology?" *Saturday Review*, March 2, 1968, p. 50.

comprehend the present. Although it is obvious that we live in an age of big government and the welfare state, most of us are confused as to how and why the size of government has grown so enormous. The introductory essay by Trevor Lloyd provides us with insights into the changing nature of political ideology which has accelerated the rise of the positive state. However, there are other important reasons why the size of government has increased so rapidly. Most of these reasons are obvious, yet so familiar that they tend to be neglected or even "invisible."

The twentieth century has displayed three leading characteristics: it has been an age of "total war," the age of the emergence of the welfare state, and an age of rapid technological innovation. These three characteristics of our age are tightly interwoven. The recent spread of mass democracy has enabled more people and more groups to make greater demands on government; ordinary people as well as special interest groups learned to use the vote as a stick with which to beat government, demanding that the state should do more, expand its functions, and grow larger. The state also became a more positive instrument of social control during periods of wartime emergency in which politicians and civil servants learned to regulate and direct all aspects of economic life for wartime purposes.

Techniques developed for regulation of the economy in war could also be applied during peace time. The social dislocation and economic chaos of the Great Depression in the 1930s quickened demands for still further experiments with government intervention in the market. By the 1930s the end of free farm land and the closing of the agricultural frontier shut off an important social safety valve; no longer could the unemployed or the economically disadvantaged go west to take up free homesteads. Increasingly our social concerns shifted from rural to urban problems, and the family farm or the church and similar informal charitable institutions could no longer cope with problems of welfare. Concentration of much economic enterprise into giant corporations and monopolies meant that only the institution of the state was sufficiently powerful to offset the abuses of commercial power. As new problems of economic insecurity emerged, people began to assume that the state should "do something," and the role of government further expanded.

Even if important shifts in public opinion had not occurred, modern technology would have made an expansion of government inevitable. In the nineteenth century, government had a limited and relatively static technology to deal with,[6] and it is not surprising that there was a long period in which the negative or "nightwatchman" state was accepted as the norm. But in the twentieth century our norm has been rapid scientific innovation. Science has provided one of the strongest pushes toward the rise of the positive state. For better or for worse, new inventions such as automobiles, planes, and television required new governmental regulation and increased functions for the state.

Not only new machines but also innovations in intellectual technology have caused important alterations in society. The nature of technology itself has changed. There is at least a sense in which most nineteenth century know-how was mainly "curative." Medical technology, for example, was devoted to attempts to cure, and machine technology was devoted mainly to curing or relieving man of the worst excesses of physical toil. In the twentieth century, however, a more important part of our technology became "preventive." The rise of preventive medicine threw new burdens on the state, and the know-how produced by the more sophisticated discipline of Keynesian economics enabled society (again through the agency of government) to offset the wild oscillations of the business cycle and prevent the worse aspects of economic dislocation. It might also be argued that recent innovations in political technology, employing such things as royal commissions and social science research, advisory boards, public opinion polls, and the well-organized mass political party, are "preventive" in that they have given governments an opportunity – not always

6 / Obviously I am using "technology" in the broadest sense to include knowledge and educational skills as well as applied inventions. No one needs to be reminded that there was an Industrial Revolution prior to the twentieth century, or that the inventions of the steam engine and summer fallow techniques, for example, were important. I am suggesting only that the rate of general technological change was slower in the nineteenth century, and that the possession and application of knowledge was much less widespread.

taken – to anticipate and take steps to correct the most overt political dissatisfactions within society.

All of these tangled and complicated factors, together with shifts in political ideology, have combined in the twentieth century to bring about the rise of the positive state or big government. The ascendancy of the modern state over other social institutions has created a mixed public and private economy, a system which is most often labelled as "collectivist." Modern collectivism resulted from the decline of previous forms of capitalism. Under nineteenth-century liberal capitalism it was assumed that the role of government should be limited and that private property was the essential basis of individual liberty. As A. A. Berle summarized this doctrine, "If a man was to be free, able to speak his own mind, depict his own thought and develop his own personality, he would have to have a base apart from one that was politically or ecclesiastically organized and controlled." Under capitalism that base was private property.

In the collectivist society, private property is no longer the primary institution of economic life. The old forms of property have been eroded, and if we are to protect that most important achievement of liberal capitalism – individual freedom – new bulwarks for liberty must be found. Most of the evidence suggests that property is not very private any more.

What is property? In law school professors often indulge in whimsical sport with their students trying to arrive at a definition of property. First the traditional image – land and physical possessions – is pooh-poohed. Then the search is pursued through contract rights and other intangibles until the class thinks it has the answer: property is "rights." But what is a right? A right is a claim which can be substantiated in law and which a court will enforce. It follows that property is a right of use or disposition which will be enforced by a court. On that day, says David Bazelon, "the legal elite is prepared to go out, tautology in hand, and grow rich defending and creating such rights."[7]

Still, a twinge of doubt remains. We poor mortals who are not

7 / "Facts and Fictions of US Capitalism," in H. C. Harlan, ed., *Readings in Economics and Politics* (New York, 1961), pp. 267–8. See also Bazelon's *The Paper Economy* (New York, 1963).

lawyers are uncertain about our rights. Insecure, aggressive, and acquisitive beings that we are, we want a more concrete sense of ownership, particularly ownership of something tangible. Surely if the ordinary man can aspire to possess anything he can hope to own his own dwelling, a house. Surely a house is private property? Legalistic definitions apart, can't ownership of a house be simple? It cannot.

Consider: You will probably need to borrow some part of the down-payment. You may be deterred by the high interest rates which are set, for the most part, by the state. Your ability to borrow will be determined by your social status which is in turn based upon your income. Your status and income are determined largely by your possession of technology, that is to say, your education, which was provided by the state. Many buyers discover that they can afford the purchase price of the house, yet cannot afford the extra fixed costs involved, the high real estate taxes which are imposed by the state. The realization begins to creep over you that the role of the state is crucial even in the purchase of a home.

Nor is that the end of the story. The re-sale value of your house is in large measure determined by government regulation of the economy which may produce either general inflation or deflation of prices. You may also become aware that the value of your house has been largely determined by its location in relation to zoning by-laws and government-created facilities such as schools, parks, and public transport. Even the use and enjoyment of your home are influenced by the state. In addition to the provision of essential services such as water, sewers, and police and fire protection, you will find that what you can and cannot do with the house will be determined by the state. If you want to renovate or build an extra room, you must first apply to some municipal government agency for a permit.

In what sense, then, can you be said to "own" the house as private property? Your ownership is private in a very limited sense at best. Although some of the above factors were present in the nineteenth century, the shift in the extent and degree of social control over property now amounts to a change in "kind" of property.

Some legal theorists attempt to get around these difficulties by extending the definition of property until it comes to mean "the legitimate power to initiate decisions on the use of economic assets." This definition leaps over the awkward question of whether property can be regarded as private any longer. It implies no less than the truth, that the state now directly or indirectly determines the use of most property. The state has undermined the traditional bulwark of individual liberty.

Students of political economy have long been familiar with the notion that private property is declining as the principal basis of economic activity. The writings of James Burnham, Berle and Means, and more recently J. K. Galbraith's *The New Industrial State*, have emphasized the fragmentation of ownership which occurs through shareholding when the scale of economic enterprise becomes vast, and the widening gap between ownership and managerial control of giant corporations. Those who "own" do not control, and those who control do not "own." It is almost risible to ask who "owns" the CPR or International Nickel. It is equally risible to suggest that any government could permit the CPR or the Argus Corporation to go bankrupt. Witness how quickly government moved when the financial difficulties of Dosco threatened to withdraw an important source of employment from a community. "The mature corporation, as it develops," says Galbraith, "becomes part of the larger administrative complex associated with the state. In time the line between the two will disappear. Man will look back in amusement at the pretense that once caused people to refer to General Dynamics ... and AT & T as *private* business."[8]

The source of economic power has shifted. As private property has declined in importance, possession of know-how or technology has become the chief economic asset and the most dynamic factor of production. Economic power always lies with that factor of production hardest to obtain or replace. In the medieval period power lay in land. Under liberal capitalism power lay with investment capital. Now technology has become the most scarce and the most productive factor.

The significance of this shift of economic power is not yet gener-

8 / *The New Industrial State* (Boston, 1967), p. 393.

ally appreciated, although we have at least taken the first step toward greater understanding of the new industrial system. Giant corporations tend to act in a similar manner whether they are owned publicly or privately, and the line between public and private ownership is no longer distinct. Andrew Shonfield, in his notable book *Modern Capitalism*, suggests that the important discovery of the 1950s was that the leftist emphasis on nationalization of industry was mistaken, and that the question of who owns the corporation no longer matters very much.[9]

On empirical grounds there is still a strong case to be made for nationalization of certain key industries. A compelling case can be argued that the insurance industry, for example, is a "natural monopoly" and should be publicly owned. But even socialists have begun to concede that nationalization should no longer be regarded as essential. This revisionist thinking was reflected in the CCF's Winnipeg Manifesto in 1956, and Anthony Crosland has stated: "The basic fact is the large corporation, facing fundamental similar problems, acting in fundamentally the same way, whether publicly or privately owned."[10]

But most people have not yet made the second necessary intellectual leap. While we have perceived that the lines between public and private property have become blurred, we have failed to appreciate the full significance of the newly emergent technological elite. Writers like Bazelon[11] and Galbraith have only recently pointed to the appearance of a "new class" or "technostructure" as the most dynamic and powerful group within the industrial system. Galbraith calls the new elite "the association of men of diverse technical knowledge, experience or other talent which modern industrial technology and planning require."[12]

9 / *Modern Capitalism: The Changing Balance of Public and Private Power* (London, 1965), pp. 378–9. The sub-title indicates the basic theme of this important book, but on the first page Shonfield begs the whole question of whether or not the new system can still be called "capitalism."

10 / C. A. R. Crosland, *The Future of Socialism* (London, 1957), p. 480.

11 / David T. Bazelon, *Power in America: The Politics of the New Class* (New York, 1967).

12 / *The New Industrial State*, p. 59.

II

Both business and government increasingly depend on sophisticated technical expertise. The function of decision-making and the exercise of power is being transferred from capitalists and politicians to the most skilled and educated experts, salaried professional technocrats such as engineers, economists, and scientists who advise and formulate policy for business and government. These experts are important not because of what they own but because of what they know. Their possession of technology gives them special status, and their status gives them power.

Nor is this phenomenon limited to the western world. Milovan Djilas' book, *The New Class*, emphasized fifteen years ago that, although most private property had been abolished in the communist world, membership in the political party or managerial rank in industry or possession of technical skill conferred upon a new class special status and power almost tantamount to a new form of property. The two rival economic systems are thus more and more similar; the nature of power and property is changing in all parts of the industrial world on both sides of the Iron Curtain.

Less and less is wealth or privilege a function of ownership. It is not simply because they lack private property that the poor are poor. Rather, it is because they do not possess the technology which would enable them to be productive. No guaranteed annual income scheme will do anything to increase their productivity (i.e., their possession of technology) or release them from the bondage of ignorance. Similarly the new technological elite do not own appreciable quantities of private property in any traditional sense. They acquire wealth and privilege because they possess the technology which makes them the most productive and valued factor in the new economy. Talent is always the most scarce resource. The technocrats receive lavish rewards in the form of income and status. They enjoy a high degree of job security, large salaries and fringe benefits, a high degree of social mobility, and rejoice in those prestigious symbols of having "arrived," the credit card and the expense account.

The nineteenth-century legal scholar Sir Henry Maine remarked that the transition from the medieval economy to capitalism was marked by a transition from *status* to *contractus* as the basis of property. Modern collectivism has now reversed the process until *contractus* is being replaced by *status* as the source of wealth. Instead of private property, the exalted status of the new elite is based upon their control of technology, and their possession of valuable techniques is the result of the education which they have acquired from institutions in the public sector.

Therefore, we are forced to re-examine the relationship of the state to the new forms of property. We have come to accept without question the fact that the state can regulate and even expropriate so-called private property. We must also recognize that an increasingly important function of the state is to *create* property. It does so mainly through expenditures on research and development.

In order to maintain high levels of employment and income, the contemporary state has become obsessed with economic growth. Economic growth is in large measure dependent upon technological innovation. Schumpeter and others have stressed that the enormous productivity of liberal capitalism was found in the entrepreneur as "creative innovator"; the entrepreneur took the risk, applied or created the technology, and provided the driving force to the economy. Individual capitalist entrepreneurs still exist, but they are more likely in the future to be scientists who become businessmen than businessmen who become scientists.

We have invented new patterns of invention. An expanding economy must place heavy emphasis upon research and development so that new technology can be created and applied. Research in both universities and businesses is subsidized by the state, and the economy depends upon the state-financed academic institutions to provide the personnel for research and technological advance. Even the bastion of capitalism, the United States, has come to rely upon vast flows of government funds to support research and development work in the giant corporations and in the universities. Research funds are no longer allocated by competitive bids for fixed price contracts. Instead the government finances technological innovation by research teams through the mechanism of the cost-plus-fixed-fee arrangement.

Dupré and Lakoff have stressed the way in which this radical arrangement has transformed the us economy: "The negotiated cost-plus-fixed-fee contract by-passes the market mechanism. Competition is restricted to those firms with whom negotiation takes place. This competition is based on technical and managerial capabilities rather than on price. Because the government stands ready to reimburse all reasonable costs and to provide necessary capital equipment, the firm assumes no financial risk. Indeed government, rather than business, assumes the role of the entrepreneur."[13] Schumpeter's creative innovator has been replaced by the state.

Contracts for research are only one means by which government creates new forms of wealth or property. It need hardly be said that in Canada government has woefully neglected expenditures on education and research, and that this has been a major factor in the siphoning-off of our creative talent to the United States, and our reliance upon imported technology through American subsidiaries. That much has long been apparent to everyone except our politicians. But even the unimaginative Canadian government has become an important source of wealth. This wealth pours forth in many forms: money, benefits, services, franchises, and licences. Government has become a fount of largess on a grand scale.

The valuables dispensed by the state take many forms, but they all share one characteristic. They are steadily replacing the traditional forms of wealth and property. "Social insurance substitutes for savings; a government contract replaces a businessman's customers and good will. The wealth of more and more [citizens] depends upon a relationship to government."[14]

The state creates jobs, either directly through government agencies or indirectly through monetary and fiscal policies. The government provides income and monetary benefits to most citizens through an elaborate scheme of welfare payments, including

13 / J. S. Dupré and S. A. Lakoff, *Science and the Nation* (Englewood Cliffs, NJ, 1962), p. 30.
14 / Charles A. Reich, "The New Property," *The Public Interest*, no. 3 (spring 1966), p. 57. I have leaned heavily on Professor Reich's work.

pensions, unemployment compensation, family allowances, veterans' benefits, and a whole host of welfare arrangements at the national, provincial, and local levels. Many industries, including transportation, mining, agriculture, and manufacturing, receive public benefits either through direct subsidies or indirect tariff protection. The government dispenses commercial franchises and occupational licences to innumerable professional and commercial groups. The government provides countless contracts to businessmen for the supply of goods and services, and permits commercial utilization of the public domain by dispensing rights to exploit public resources in oil, minerals, timber, and water. We have come to look upon government as a cornucopia.

Government is, in fact, the prime mover of a dynamic economy. Even the Americans have discovered that the principal creator of new jobs is the public rather than the private sector of the economy. In the decade of the 1950s, nine out of every ten *new* jobs added to the US economy were generated by the remarkable growth of the not-for-profit sector, by the enormously enlarged role of the government at all levels, particularly in the fields of education, research, health, and welfare.[15] As the 45th annual report of the National Bureau of Economic Research put it, "The US is now a service economy – i.e. we are the first nation in the history of the world in which more than half of the employed population is *not* involved in the production of food, clothing, houses, automobiles and other tangible goods." Automation tends to limit or diminish the number of jobs in the manufacturing sector of the economy, and that, coupled with continued prosperity, tends to shift employment from the industrial to the "service" sector of the economy. In the future, more and more people will work in the service trades and in the not-for-profit or governmental areas.

As these trends become more pronounced and better known in both the American and Canadian settings, we may see an end to the Berle-Galbraith myth of the dominance of the large corpora-

15 / Ginsberg, Hiestand, and Reubens, *The Pluralistic Economy* (New York, 1965). Compare also Robert Heilbroner, *The Limits of American Capitalism* (New York, 1966).

tion in our society. The political power of the giant commercial corporations may continue for some time, but the corporation is likely to decline in economic and social importance relative to the power of government during the next decade. Large sections of the service sector of the economy, including restaurants, barber shops, dry-cleaning plants, health and educational facilities, tend to be controlled by small business firms or by government, not by giant corporations. "Big business" may decline in significance; at least it need not be the bogeyman of the new society. "In actual fact, large corporations are not and have never been the dominant form of American enterprise. Most people do not work, and never have worked, for large corporations; most production does not take place and never has taken place in large corporations. This assumption was primarily based on extrapolation of trends from the 19th century, but the trend is now reversed and this assumption is no longer tenable. In the future, the large corporation is likely to be overshadowed by the hospitals, universities, research institutes, government agencies, and professional organizations that are the hallmarks of a service economy. One ironic aspect of Galbraith's thesis is that he personally is employed by an organization (Harvard University) that is tiny compared with General Motors or us Steel, but he and his colleagues have more power and influence in the United States than any ten large corporations."[16]

In a technological and service economy such as Canada is now developing, the emphasis shifts from the private to the public sector. The difficulty is that we have not yet made the appropriate intellectual shift enabling us to grapple with reality. The rigidity of our mentality is such that we still tend to think of the government-financed parts of the economy, including education, health, transportation, and public housing, as a burden on our lives and our tax dollars. The economic realities have changed, but our attitudes and public ideologies have not yet caught up. We continue to mouth clichés about the private sector being an area of freedom in the economy, and the public sector being an

16 / Victor Fuchs, "The First Service Economy," *The Public Interest*, no. 2 (winter 1966), p. 10.

area of burden, bureaucracy, and non-freedom. In part, we are the victims of advertising which accustoms us to think of public enterprise as bad and private enterprise as good. Private enterprise spends far more on advertising and opinion-manipulation than does government enterprise, which may account for how we have been brainwashed. However, the truth is that the public sector contains the most important necessities and essential services of modern living. Without the public economic sector, we would be poorer, stupider, and less free.

Freedom is no longer based primarily upon private property. If we define freedom as degree of choice for an individual within society, it is clear that the factors which give the individual the greatest degree of choice, opportunity, or freedom are to be found within the public sector. People may be "free" to fly to the Riviera, or buy a newspaper plant or a TV broadcasting station to publish their opinions, but most of them lack the financial means to do so.

At the elementary level of day-to-day living most people's freedom is enhanced and expanded by government activity and the public sector. Our physical mobility is increased by state-built roads and public transit. Our incomes are increased by the education which the state provides. We are given a wider degree of choice through our state-created opportunities to use parks, museums, hospitals, art galleries, and the theatres and concert halls which are community-owned. Our opportunities for day-to-day choices and our degree of practical freedom depend less and less on private property, and more and more upon services provided by the state. Far more than we realize, our liberty is state-created, and collectivism enhances freedom.

But will we be more free, or less free, in the future? Can new bulwarks be found for the preservation of individual liberty? The task of defending liberty will be very difficult, for already changes in technology present new threats to freedom.

Individual technicians are declining in importance and groups of inter-related technicians are becoming more important. Like the economy itself, the "technostructure" is becoming collectivised; like property, technology can no longer be regarded as private.

In years gone by, says Daniel Bell, "one's achievement was an individual fact – as a doctor, lawyer, professor, businessman; in the reality of today, one's achievement, status, and prestige are rooted in particular *collectivities* (the corporation, being attached to a "name" hospital, teaching in a prestigious university, membership in a law firm), and the individual's role is necessarily submerged in the achievement of the collectivity. Within each collectivity and profession, the proliferation of tasks calls for narrower and narrower specialization and this proliferation requires larger collectivities, and the consequent growth of hierarchies and bureaucracies."[17]

Large-scale organization generates many social perils, as every reader of W. H. Whyte's *The Organization Man* knows. Authoritarianism, the tendency to timid conformity and mediocrity, the discouragement of individual eccentricity, excellence, or distinction, and the substitution of "group think" for individual creativity: all of these are potential threats that lurk in the shadows of the "organization" or collectivity, be it an industrial corporation, a labour union, a multi-versity, or a government department.

There is at least one more major threat to individual liberty implied by the emergence of the technological elite. I have argued above that a difference between late-nineteenth- and early twentieth-century technology was the shift from a "curative" to a "preventive" emphasis. The applied science of tomorrow will again be different. Principally it will be a "manipulative" technology enabling us to control society and shape its ends. We will have the ability to select and create our own environment instead of having our physical milieu imposed on us by the ugly vicissitudes of the market.

The natural and social sciences have provided us with a vast new "industry of discovery." The computer technology associated with linear programming, econometric and simulation models, cybernetics, information theory, and cost-effectiveness systems analysis, now permits us to construct models of the future and to assess in advance the possible consequences of altering the variables. This new manipulative technology facilitates the

17 / Daniel Bell, "The Dispossessed," in D. Bell, ed., *The Radical Right* (Garden City, NY, 1964), p. 21.

identification and speedy solution of social problems. We will be able to choose and create "total environments."

The question must be asked: What if you and I do not like the results? Montreal's Expo, for example, demonstrated the exhilarating possibilities of a "total environment" which was functionally and esthetically a triumph. But the people did not choose it democratically. The overall plan of Expo was created and imposed on its physical space by experts. A form of benign authoritarianism was required to ensure that every element harmonized with every other element, right down to the design of the street signs and the garbage cans.

When a total environment "works," it is grand. But what if it doesn't work? What if the social plans of the technicians do not square with the values and wishes of the people? Consumers will rebel. They will demand a voice in the planning process and in the setting of social objectives. In self-defence and in the name of democracy and freedom, citizens will insist upon exercising some degree of control over the technocrats. Ways must be found to enable total planning to proceed in accordance with the expressed desires of the people, to encourage participatory democracy in the planning process, to enable citizens at least to engage in a dialogue with the experts.

If there is any single resounding lesson to be learned from the experience of the Company of Young Canadians and the American War on Poverty, it is that participatory democracy is essential before social planning can succeed. Already university students (and even high school students), as the vanguard of the future, have made it clear that they will demand a voice in the decision-making processes of education, that they will no longer be contented and passive consumers of whatever the educational technicians deign to provide.

As one student leader was quoted during the 1967 strike at McGill University, "It is not authority we object to, it's the *idea* of authority." In other words, authority is "them," but "we" as consumers of technology will not accept manipulation by "them" from above. The hip way of putting this – "never trust anyone over thirty" – reflects a hard truth: never trust promises or programs imposed by establishments and experts. Young people perceive that liberty is increasingly threatened by the techno-structure; technocratic authority must be resisted by protest marches, sit-ins, civil disobedience, and strikes; in the long run, liberty must be defended through the development of direct participatory democracy. Our whole concept of freedom, no longer based on property but on status and public rights, will require extensive adjustment and redefinition in the future.

III

The rate of social change is now so rapid that tomorrow is almost upon us. Fortunately, contemporary social science has become future-oriented. This is a new and hopeful phenomenon. For a time, the designing of utopias went out of intellectual fashion in the twentieth century, partly because most utopian visions and ideologies tended to be either apocalyptic or totalitarian or both, and partly because thinkers in the 1940s and 1950s were pre-occupied with more immediate practical concerns. But in the 1960s, the future has again become an "in" subject to study. Recently there has been a burst of books published which deal with the world of tomorrow: notable among these are *The Future* by Theodore Gordon, *Inventing the Future* by Dennis Gabor, *The Image of the Future* by F. L. Polak, *Profiles of the Future* by Arthur C. Clarke, and *The Next Hundred Years* by Brown, Bonner, and Weir. Of these, much the best and most neglected is the two-volume study by Professor Polak.

The theme of Polak's remarkable work[18] is that the key to the dynamics of any culture is its dominant image of the future. The quality, though not necessarily the content, of this image tends to be self-fulfilling. The important thing about the image of the future, Polak argues, is that it should be glorious so that it will breed in men's minds faith or optimism upon which they can act, and thus provide a sense of purpose and cohesion to a society.

Only a moment's reflection is required to discover reasons why the future has suddenly become such an acceptable if not obses-sive topic. Ours is an intensely hedonistic and utilitarian culture. The welfare state in which we find ourselves is dedicated to the implicit assumption that every individual is entitled to happiness,

18 / *The Image of the Future*, trans. Elise Boulding (New York, 1961).

and that one of the functions of government is to try and assure him at least the preconditions of happiness. There are dangers in encouraging politicians to dictate how we should "build a new Jerusalem in this green and pleasant land"; happiness is a highly subjective state which cannot be defined, let alone measured and imposed. However, there may be even greater dangers threatening a society in which politicians and the people have *no* concept of a better future.

The plain fact is that the *conditions* of happiness – economic security, equality of opportunity, education, medical care, decent housing, and clean air and water – necessarily involve a high degree of collective action through the agency of government. Since we demand security today as a means toward happiness tomorrow, a society which expects the state to create the social preconditions of happiness must become future-oriented. Our concern with the future is thus linked to the emergence of the welfare state.[19]

Many other factors have also combined to quicken our tendency to look ahead into time. The relative stability of the economy in the 1960s has enabled corporate business to anticipate long-run changes in demand and supply and to plan ahead. Increasing sophistication in post-Keynesian economics has made economic forecasting a much more precise and useful tool than was dreamed of even thirty years ago. Government, like business, now looks ahead and economic planning has become a standard and respectable technique of economic management by the state.

Science has provided us with new tools with which to create the new society. Computer technology has given us better handles with which to grasp the future. The heightened role of science, including social science, and the increasing emphasis on research have brought with them a new optimistic temper. A. N. Whitehead observed that science has brought about a "change in the rate of change." Knowledge is growing at an "exponential rate," doubling much faster than ever before. "Whatever caveats one may have about the genuine accretions of knowledge that might be reflected simply in the doubling of publications, the idea of the

19 / Daniel Bell, "The Study of the Future," *The Public Interest*, no. 1 (fall 1965), p. 120.

information explosion has reinforced the sense many people have – although it cannot be measured – that technology is increasing at an accelerating rate, and that new inventions, new modes of communication, new knowledge will demand new social forms necessary to cope with these changes."[20]

There is at least one more major reason for our growing preoccupation with the future. Young people, who are now proportionately more numerous and influential than in the past hundred years, are impatient with the old order and tend to be forward-looking. Whether in politics, in dress, or in way of life, young people worship style and innovation since they have very little else left to worship. No one needs to tell them that "the medium is the message" because they have grown up in a medium-full and message-less culture. Young people are more aware than the rest of us that the western society is undergoing an acute crisis of values. They recognize that the old value-creating and value-sustaining institutions have been eroded. The family, the church, and the school no longer exercise clear moral authority in matters of economic and political life, sexual conduct, or ethical conduct. Young people are searching for new values and a new sense of "community." They demand a different and better future.

If the hydrogen bomb permits us any future at all, its shape is to some degree predictable. Populations will grow larger and more of us will live in big cities. Urban concentration will wedge most of us into less space. Overcrowding will cause either more tension and mental illness, or more mental escapism through increased use of psychedelic chemicals, or both. Stresses which have driven people to drink will continue, but we will probably turn to the less harmful use of marijuana. Pot will be legalized, and the state may have to take direct control of the manufacturing and distribution of all drugs.

More aspects of our lives will be automated. Technological unemployment may well cause great social upheavals. Since the computer is simply automated information-processing, and since information must be fundamentally public, the computer industry will come to be regarded as a public utility and will be publicly owned or regulated, just as population concentration will require

20 / *Ibid.*, p. 122.

that urban land be publicly owned and simply leased to individuals. Computerized data banks will facilitate social planning, augment the power of the planners, and necessitate the legal protection of individual privacy.

The public sector will grow still larger in relation to the private sector of the economy, but the lines between them will be less distinct. Research will be recognized as a major industry with high social priority. Research will be rushed to meet urgent public needs such as electric cars and reform of educational methods. Levels of education and income generally will rise, but the growing income gap between the highly educated groups that control technology, and those who do not, will cause social tension between the two groups and necessitate the raising of basic income floors for all. The "class struggle" will centre on the control of technology.

Diverting as such speculation may be, it does not answer our questions about the shape of the future and the possible degree of individual liberty. From the preceding discussion of collectivism and technology, do suggestive patterns emerge which may hint at the most likely configuration of the new society? Surely the answer is yes.

Our hyper-collectivist world of tomorrow will not resemble liberal capitalism so much as the pre-capitalist medieval society. Such historical parallels are, of course, not exact, but the comparisons between the feudal past and the collectivist future are provocative and striking. Only an extreme romanticist would pretend that individuals in the feudal order were as happy or free as we are today, and the comparison between the two eras is by no means precise, but the parallel between past medievalism and future collectivism is too important to be ignored.[21]

21 / I first caught a glimpse of this parallel in 1954 when Professor K. A. H. Buckley introduced me to Karl Polanyi's *The Great Transformation* and J. M. Clark's *Alternative to Serfdom,* both seminal works. After preparing an earlier draft of this paper in 1966, I discovered that C. A. Reich had already formulated the concept in great detail in "The New Property," *Yale Law Journal,* vol. 73, no. 5 (April, 1964), pp. 733 ff., and in the article of the same title cited in n. 14. See also A. M. Ross, "A New Industrial Feudalism," *American Economic Review,* vol. 48 (Dec. 1958), pp. 903 ff.

Whereas in medieval society power was shared by the secular princes and the pervasive institution of the Church, future collectivism will be marked by a sharing of power between the secular technologists and the dominant institution of the state.

Our "medieval future" will be characterized by these factors:

1 / It will be assumed that the community (then represented by the Church, now by the state) can intervene into and regulate and control almost all aspects of life.

2 / The free market will decline further, and the setting or administering of a "just price" will be done either by the state or by state-regulated corporations.

3 / Private property will be replaced by the concept of "stewardship" or limited control over property, and lines between public and private property will be blurred.

4 / As in the medieval period, "rights" and the "common" will be more important than private property, and more and more property will be publicly created.

5 / Political conflict will be less over the possession of private property and more concerned with the possession of technology and the establishment of individual and community "rights."

6 / An individual's rights, income, and liberty will be dependent largely upon his status, which will be dependent upon his usefulness to the community or the state, and his usefulness will be dependent in turn upon his education.

7 / Just as the medieval priests preserved culture, in the future technology will be possessed and expanded by the professions and the universities, which will be organized into powerful and largely autonomous associations or guilds, and which may resist popular control.

8 / Those who possess know-how will control the levers of power. The priests of the new society will be the highly educated mandarins who possess the new technological theology, the manipulators of scientific social theories, the Galbraiths, the McLuhans, the Watkinses.

9 / The consumers will rebel against the technocratic elite and demand participatory democracy in the defence of community rights.

In fact we have already arrived at the threshold of the medieval future. The objectives of the pre-capitalist and post-capitalist societies are strikingly similar. Whereas the medieval world sought to defend society against the infidels, we attempt to defend against the communists. Whereas the medieval world tried to defend the sense of community in an age of chaos, we attempt to defend "the public interest" and a sense of community in an age of frightening technological flux. For the objective of glorifying God, we have substituted the glorification of man, but prayer will not suffice to achieve our objectives. We are in desperate need of new social and political theories to interpret and give cohesion to the new society.

The essential contrast of our society with the medieval order is the absence of any one integrating philosophy or ideology. Christian faith gave to the Middle Ages a set of beliefs which the community shared and which gave that society a reassuring sense of purpose and stability. The communist world in our own day has its dogmatic faith. It is not a faith acceptable to us, but it does give cohesion to their world. Marxist dogma provides its adherents with a sense of the inevitability of their triumph and a clear concept of a glorious future.

By contrast, the western world is weakened not by our inability to compete morally or materially, but by the absence of a social philosophy which might give us faith in ourselves and in our society. Our world lacks ideological cohesion and a sense of purpose. We do not have clear concepts of a glorious future. We live not in the Middle Ages, but in the "muddle" ages.[22]

"No one really seems to believe in anything," says Michael Harrington. "For now, there is a crisis of belief and disbelief. The simultaneous undermining of confidence in the ... Western ideals of man was parallel to, and related to, the decline of both the capitalist and socialist ideologies. So there is a massive intersection of uncertainties, a time of interregnum, of indeterminacy."[23]

A society without an informing theory, philosophy, or ideology

22 / This phrase appears in Irving Babbitt, *Democracy and Leadership* (Boston, 1924, re-issued 1952), p. 200.
23 / *The Accidental Century* (Baltimore, 1966), pp. 146 and 172.

has no coherence and no goals. The previous capitalist society had no goals except those set automatically by the market. Those goals were mainly selfish and grubby, oriented to the possessive individual rather than to the community, and as our standard of living rose we began to appreciate that the acquisitive life is existentially unsatisfying. A society without clear objectives is a drifting society, an aimless non-community. Its future cannot be glorious until it can consciously invent a concept of a better tomorrow. Our lack of social theory and our consequent paralysis of values in a world of technological flux means that we are being dragged unwillingly into the future by events rather than by our own rational choice. As A. J. Liebling observed, "A man is not really free if he can't see where he's going."

At least it is apparent that theories of possessive individualism and our orthodox capitalist mentality are obsolete. Although the socialism of the 1930s has been outmoded, the values and the ideals of democratic socialism will be the basis of the new collectivist society.

The future is a function of technology and of human choice. With the new manipulative technology, we can now invent the future. But technology is concerned with means rather than with ends, and technicians should not impose their values on a free society. A great society can be defined as a community which consciously chooses its own goals and which provides opportunities for individuals to participate in the achievement of those goals. As technology sweeps us forward, we are running out of time in which to make conscious choices. Our choices are not between capitalism *or* socialism, but between a more, *or* a less, humane and democratic form of socialism.

In the past the most crucial relationship in society was between the politicians as brokers of power and the businessmen who controlled the capitalist market. In the future the most crucial relationships will be between the people and the politicians on the one hand and the new professional elite which controls technology on the other. The chief issue which we must confront, says the British economist E. J. Mishan, is that of "seeking to adjust the environment to gratify man's nature *or* of adjusting man's nature to an environment determined predominantly by 'efficiency considerations,' that is, by technological advance."[24] Are we to control technology, or is technology to control us? Prime Minister Pierre Trudeau has stated, "We must not be the victims but the masters of change,"[25] but neither he nor anyone else has yet been able to tell us how we are to avoid becoming victims. There are no easy answers.

IV

Such limited salvation as we are likely to achieve will probably come from two sources: from new concepts of rights, and from that medieval invention, the university.

The nerve centre of the post-capitalist society is knowledge. Every human society has always been based upon knowledge, but in the post-capitalist society, what is crucial is not just a shift from private property to knowledge as the new base of power, but a fundamental change in the nature and character of knowledge itself. "What has now become decisive for society is the new centrality of *theoretical* knowledge, the primacy of theory over empiricism, and the codification of knowledge into abstract systems of symbols that can be translated into many different and varied circumstances. Every society now lives by innovation and growth; and it is theoretical knowledge that has become the matrix of innovation."[26] If we do not have a revival of ideology, we can at least anticipate a renaissance of political and social theorizing.

The place where theoretical knowledge is sought, tested, and codified in a disinterested way is the university. The university is becoming the main source of ideas, of social and economic dynamism, and the primary institution of the new society. Just as the business firm was the key institution of liberal capitalism in the past, because of its role in organizing production, the univer-

24 / Ezra J. Mishan, *The Costs of Economic Growth* (New York, 1967), p. xix.
25 / Quoted in the *Toronto Daily Star*, March 30, 1968.
26 / Daniel Bell, "Notes on the Post-Industrial Society", *The Public Interest*, no. 6 (Winter 1967), pp. 28–9. (People who don't read *The Public Interest*, published by Freedom House, 20 West 40 Street, New York, are missing the biggest middle-brow bang for a buck on the market.)

sity is becoming the central institution of the new society because of its role as the principal source of innovation and knowledge.[27]

If it ever was true that those who can, do, and those who cannot, teach, it is true no longer. Academics have ceased to be a leisured class, but have become both knowers and doers whose skills are in great demand. Governments and even businessmen have come to rely upon the universities for research and innovation. From the ranks of university faculties have come the royal commissioners, the experts, the advisers and consultants which have caused some politicians to worry about the "dictatorship of the professoriat."

The increasing importance of the universities makes three things imperative. First, to enable universities to obtain independent sources of the money necessary to conduct education and research autonomously, without fear of direct government control. In order to guarantee academic and technological freedom, it is desirable that both the federal and provincial levels of government participate in the financing of universities, and that an independent commission, similar to the Canada Council, have the power to distribute the vast sums of money required for higher education and research without the possibility of political strings being attached. A measure of popular control will come from within the universities, from the principal consumers, i.e., from students. Second, a new national policy, as urged by the Watkins Report, must stress heavy public investment in brains and technology, or research and development. Third, it will be necessary to encourage a two-way flow of skilled personnel between governments and businesses on the one hand and universities on the other. Professors must gain more direct experience in business and in government; civil servants, business managers, and politicians must obtain experience in universities. The university practice of granting of sabbatical leaves should be extended to business and government personnel so that no one institution within society has a monopoly on technology, and so that technologists can take refresher courses and be continuously educated to expand their skills and productivity.

Since knowledge has replaced private property as the basis of

27 / *Ibid.*, p. 30.

status and power, we require new concepts of rights and new guarantees of status rights in order to protect individual liberty. A constitutional Bill of Rights for Canada, guaranteeing linguistic rights as well as traditional civil liberties, will not by any means be enough to preserve freedom in the technological society. There must be a clear right to an education for every citizen. The state should guarantee the right of every individual to be educated up to the limits of his industry and ability. A sane and just society must guarantee to every citizen the right to a decent income and a right to decent housing. The state must guarantee and protect community rights as well as individual liberties. The community must be acknowledged to have a right to clear air and clean water. E. J. Mishan prefers the concept of "amenity rights" which should be vested in every person. "Men should be invested by law with property rights in privacy, quiet, and clear air – simple things, but for many indispensable to the enjoyment of life."[28]

The American legal theorist Charles A. Reich stresses the need to expand the concept of rights to include the various forms of wealth and income which are generated by the public sector in the collectivist economy. "Eventually those forms of largess which are closely linked to status must be deemed to be held as of right. Like property, such largess could be governed by a system of regulation plus civil or criminal sanctions, rather than a system based upon denial, suspension and revocation. ... The concept of right is most urgently needed with respect to benefits like unemployment compensation, public assistance, and old age insurance. These benefits are based upon a recognition that misfortune and deprivation are often caused by forces far beyond the control of the individual, such as technological change, variations in demands for goods, depressions, or wars. The aim of these benefits is to preserve the self-sufficiency of the individual, to rehabilitate him where necessary, and to allow him to be a valuable member of a family and of a community; in theory they represent part of the individual's rightful share in the commonwealth. Only by making such benefits into rights can the welfare state achieve its goal of providing a secure minimum basis for

28 / *The Costs of Economic Growth*, p. 71.

individual well-being and dignity in a society where each man cannot be wholly the master of his own destiny."[29]

Technology and the rise of big government have given enormous power to the state. Such a concentration of power is always dangerous, particularly to individual liberty. We should not forget that the medieval concept of rights was based upon reciprocal obligations between the individual and the community. The modern state remains the one supreme representative of the community as a whole, and in its welfare capacity of rendering services it seems to be in danger of developing from the negative state, in which people were told merely what they must not do, into the Santa Claus state to which people look for handouts with no thought of reciprocal obligations. A rational and just state, says J. M. Clark, should "start with the duty of self-support. On this one could safely predicate an obligation of the community to see that the members do not lack the means to make their contribution. We are visibly growing toward that two-sided conception. When we have grown fully up to it, we shall have a right to consider that we have become once more an organically constituted society, after a lapse of several centuries."[30]

In our medieval future, technology will continue to create new forms of property and new forms of status which cannot be protected adequately by narrow and obsolete concepts of civil liberties. New forms of power demand new concepts of community rights if men are to remain free.

29 / "The New Property," *Public Interest*, p. 88.
30 / *Alternative to Serfdom* (New York, 1960 reprint), p. 28.

4

Public and Private Space

JOHN O'NEILL

POLITICAL IMAGINATION is shackled by the corporate organization of modern society. The traditional antitheses of individual and state, state and society, public and private rights, conflict and order, no longer serve to orient men's private lives toward their political contexts. Modern society is increasingly consensual and apolitical; it generates a comfortable reality which tempts us to identify the rationality of its industrial metabolism with the whole of rationality and thus to disengage ourselves from the critical tasks of reason. The tendency to identify technological rationality with social rationality is the major threat to the survival of the political imagination.[1] It underlies the liberal abdication of politics in favour of the market economy. By contrast, the subordination of technological rationality to social rationality is the program of a genuine Marxian political economy.

Political economy remains nerveless so long as it rests upon a concept of government which does not question the social distribution of resources between the public and private sectors of the

1 / Herbert Marcuse, *One-Dimensional Man*, Studies in the Ideology of Advanced Industrial Society (Boston, 1964). For the distinction between technical or "functional" rationality and "substantial" rationality see Karl Mannheim, *Man and Society in an Age of Reconstruction* (London, 1940), pp. 51–60.

economy. No modern government can retain power which fails to control industrial technology and the power of large corporations to shape the national ecology and psychic economy of individuals. The corporate economy stands between the state and the individual. Its power to determine the life-style of modern society must be recognized as the principal subject of political economy. The critique of the forces working to produce what Herbert Marcuse has called one-dimensional society must avoid the elitist fiction that mass society is the cause of our political troubles as well as the liberal illusion that pluralistic countervailing power is the only viable formula for political conduct.[2] At the same time, the basic organizational form of modern industrial society is so closely tied to such a small number of corporate and bureaucratic structures that the ideas of pluralism can hardly be said to exercise a qualitative effect upon the system.

"In a specific sense advanced industrial culture is *more* ideological than its predecessor, inasmuch as today the ideology is in the process of production itself. In a provocative form, this proposition reveals the political aspects of the prevailing technological rationality. The productive apparatus and the goods and services which it produces 'sell' or impose the social system as a whole. ... The products indoctrinate and manipulate; they promote a false consciousness which is immune against its falsehood. And as these beneficial products become available to more and more individuals in more social classes, the indoctrination they carry ceases to be publicity; it becomes a way of life. It is a good way of life – much better than before – and as a good way of life, it militates against qualitative change. Thus emerges a pattern of *one-dimensional thought and behavior* in which ideas, aspirations, and objectives that, by their content, transcend the established

2 / "*To be socially integrated in America is to accept propaganda, advertising and speedy obsolescence in consumption.* The fact is that those who fit the image of pluralist man in pluralist society also fit the image of mass man in mass society. Any accurate picture of the shape of modern society must accommodate these ambiguities." Harold L. Wilensky, "Mass Society and Mass Culture: Interdependence of Dependence?" *American Sociological Review*, vol. 29, no. 2 (April 1964), p. 196.

universe of discourse and action are either repelled or reduced to terms of this universe. They are redefined by the rationality of the given system and of its quantitative extension."[3]

One-dimensional society is characterized by a systematic linkage between the subordination of public space to private space through the agency of the corporate economy and an ideological privatization of individual sensibilities which reinforces corporate control over the allocation of social resources and energies. One-dimensional society has its roots in the liberal concept of society as a field in which the private pursuit of economic interests produces public benefits without political intervention. The emergence of a "social universe," which is, strictly speaking, neither public nor private, is a modern phenomenon that arises from the public significance accorded to the business of making a living and that has no counterpart in the ancient world. It is a phenomenon which has forced upon us the hybrid term "political economy" and with it the challenge to rethink the relation between the public and private domains in modern industrial society.

Public and Private Space
In the Graeco-Roman world the boundary between the public and private realms was clear and men were conscious of the threshold between public and private life. Although the ancient city-state grew at the expense of the family household and kinship group, the boundary between the public and private realms was never erased. Indeed, the definition of the public realm as an area of freedom and equality presupposed the recognition of "necessity" in the household economy.[4] The needs of maintenance and reproduction defined the social nature of man and the family, and the sexual and social division of labour between man and woman, master and slave.

In the modern period this ancient boundary between public

3 / Herbert Marcuse, *One-Dimensional Man*, pp. 10–11. For an empirical confirmation of the ideological content of the consumer orientation, see Sanford M. Dornbusch and Lauren C. Hickman, "Other-Directedness in Consumer-Goods Advertising: A Test of Riesman's Historical Typology," *Social Forces*, vol. 38, no. 2, pp. 99–102.
4 / Aristotle, *Politics*, 1252 a.2.

and private realms was dissolved with the emergence of "society" and the liberal concept of mini-government. A whole new world – the social universe – emerged between public and private life. The public significance of the social universe has its roots in the subjectivization of private property and the subordination of government to a minimal agenda in the social equilibration of individual and public interests. The seventeenth century reduced the political domain to the narrow limits of "government" in order to exploit the boundless domain of possessive individualism, which Professor C. B. Macpherson has described as the central impediment of modern liberal-democratic ideology. "Its possessive quality is found in its conception of the individual as essentially the proprietor of his own person or capacities, owing nothing to society for them. The individual was seen neither as a moral whole, nor as part of a larger social whole, but as an owner of himself. The relation of ownership, having become for more and more men the critically important relation determining their actual freedom and actual prospect of realizing full potentialities, was read back into the nature of the individual. ... Society becomes a lot of free individuals related to each other as proprietors of their own capacities and of what they have acquired by their exercise. Society consists of relations of exchange between proprietors. Political society becomes a calculated device for the protection of this property and for the maintenance of an orderly relation of exchange."[5]

The liberal practicality shied away from any utopian conception of the public domain and was content with an order that seemed to emerge through non-intervention in the natural processes, or rather in the metabolism, of society. As Hannah Arendt has argued, this extraordinary identification of society with its economy may be traced in part to the liberal devaluation of politics. "What concerns us in this context is the extraordinary

5 / C. B. Macpherson, *The Political Theory of Possessive Individualism: Hobbes to Locke* (Oxford, 1962), p. 3. The liberal concept of "society" provoked the counterconcept of "organic society" in Conservative and Marxian thought which have more in common than either has with liberalism. Karl Mannheim, *Essays on Sociology and Social Psychology* (New York, 1953), chap. II, "Conservative Thought."

difficulty with which we, because of this development, understand the decisive division between the public and private realms, between the sphere of the polis and the sphere of household and family, and, finally, between activities related to a common world and those related to the maintenance of life, a division upon which all ancient political thought rested as self-evident and axiomatic."[6]

All the spaces of the modern world are absorbed into a single economy whose rhythms are linear and mechanical. The architecture of public and commercial institutions, the furnishings of the home, and even the styles in which we clothe our bodies threaten to destroy the dialectic between the things that are to be shown and the things that are to be hidden. The results vary from the inhuman naked space of the typing-pool to the democratic open spaces of Toronto's new City Hall where the shocking exposure of secretarial knees produced demands for privacy in the design of working areas. Even more desperate is the loss of the values of privacy in the very sanctuary of the home. Le Corbusier has called the modern house "a machine to live in," a machine that mechanizes living in a mechanical world. In a strange, disordered repetition of ancient symbolism, the modern household is hooked into the centre of the universe through its television navel and suspended by an aerial (*universalis columna quasi sustinens omnia*) between heaven and hell. "The Kwakiutl believe that a copper pole passes through the three cosmic levels (underworld, earth, sky); the point at which it enters the sky is the 'door to the world above.' The visible image of this cosmic pillar in the sky is the Milky Way."[7] Through the picture-frame windows of the modern house the metabolism of family life is projected into the public realm and from there it completes its circuit back into the home through a magical aether populated by waxes, deodorants, soap-suds, and tissues.

In one-dimensional society desire born of necessity is no longer domesticated. Now the whole of society is organized to satisfy domestic passions. And this is an arrangement eminently suited

6 / *The Human Condition* (Chicago, 1958), p. 28.
7 / Mircea Eliade, *The Sacred and the Profane* (New York, 1959), p. 35.

to the ethic of individualistic-familism and the socialization of the members of society into their "calling" as consumers whose needs are the self-imposed agency of social control. It is this continuity of psychic and socio-economic space which grounds the coherent fantasy of consumer sovereignty at the same time that it fills the air with the noise and filth that are the by-products of the commercial narcosis.[8]

Metabolism and Political Economy
In the period between the decline of the feudal family order and the rise of modern nation-states geared to a fully industrialized economy there emerged a microcosmic version, in the Court circle and the salon of high society, of the tragic alienation of the individual in a universe hidden from God and abandoned to the play of social forces.[9] Whether it is through the identification of the individual with his title at Court in the *ancien régime* or with his occupational status in the modern corporation, the modern individual encounters a bureaucratization of private sensibilities, a wasteland between the boundaries of the heart and the public presentation of the self.[10] The rise of modern society is the history of the decline of feudal community, the growth of the nation state, industrial technology, and political democracy. But it is also the paradox of the affinity of individualism for conformism through

8 / "To behold, use or perceive any extension of ourselves in technological form is necessarily to embrace it. To listen to radio or to read the printed page is to accept these extensions of ourselves into our personal system and to undergo the 'closure' or displacement of perception that follows automatically. It is this continuous embrace of our own technology in daily use that puts us in the Narcissus role of subliminal awareness and numbness in relation to these images of ourselves. By continuously embracing technologies, we relate ourselves to them as servomechanisms. That is why we must, to use them at all, serve these objects, these extensions of ourselves, as gods or minor religions. An Indian is the servo-mechanism of his canoe, as the cowboy of his horse, or the executive of his clock." Marshall McLuhan, *Understanding Media: The Extensions of Man* (New York, 1965), p. 46.
9 / Lucien Goldmann, *Le dieu caché: Etude sur la vision tragique dans les pensées et dans le théâtre de Racine* (Paris, 1955).
10 / Locke shows no awareness of the alienation of man in society, unlike Hobbes, who, nevertheless, has no solution for it. It is Rousseau who first attempts to link the experience of alienation with social criticism.

the erosion of the communal bases of the family, the guild, the village, and the Church.[11] The emergence of the "total community" has its origins in the growth of rationalism in economics, politics, and religion. In each of these areas modern individualism receives its impulse from the subjectivization of the bases of the feudal community and a simultaneous assimilation of the individual into the abstract community of market society. "Thus, from the viewpoint of this enlightened political economy which has discovered the *subjective* essence of wealth within the framework of private property, the partisans of the monetary system and the mercantilist system, who consider private property as a *purely objective* being for man, are *fetishists* and *Catholics*. Engels is right, therefore, in calling Adam Smith the *Luther of political economy*. Just as Luther recognized religion and *faith* as the essence of the real *world* and for that reason took up a position against Catholic paganism; just as he annulled *external* religiosity while making religiosity the *inner* essence of man; just as he negated the distinction between priest and layman because he transferred the priest into the heart of the layman; so wealth external to man and independent of him (and thus only to be acquired and conserved from outside) is annulled. That is to say, its *external* and *mindless objectivity* is annulled by the fact that private property is incorporated in man himself, and man himself is recognized as its essence. But as a result, man himself is brought into the sphere of private property, just as, with Luther, he is brought into the sphere of religion. Under the guise of recognizing man, political economy, whose principle is labour, carries to its logical conclusion the denial of man. Man himself is no longer in a condition of external tension with the external substance of private property; he has himself become the tension-ridden being of private property. What was previously a phenomenon of *being external to oneself*, a real external manifestation of man, has now become the act of objectification, of alienation. This political economy seems at first, therefore, to recognize man with his

11 / Robert A. Nisbet, *Community and Power* (New York, 1962). Cf. Karl Marx, *Communist Manifesto* (New York, Gateway Editions, 1954), p. 12. Marx's sketch of the breakdown of feudalism is brilliantly developed in Karl Polanyi, *The Great Transformation* (Boston, 1957).

independence, his personal activity, etc. It incorporates private property in the very essence of man, and it is no longer, therefore, conditioned by the local or national *characteristics of private property* regarded as existing outside itself. It manifests a cosmopolitan, universal activity which is destructive of every limit and every bond, and substitutes itself as the *only* policy, the *only* universality, the *only* limit and the *only* bond."[12]

The identification of the metabolism of the household with the national economy, which results in the hybrid concern of "political economy" is the outcome of the alienation of private property and labour from their anchorages in use-values. In their endlessly reproducible forms, as the exchange-values of capital and labour power, private property and labour enter the public realm and subordinate the public realm to the needs of market society. The emancipation of labour is the precondition of the substitution of exchange-values for use-values which leads to the subordination of all fixed forms of life and property to the accumulation and expansion of wealth. In the remarkable passage from the *Economic and Philosophical Manuscripts* quoted above, Marx explains how private property becomes the subjective impulse of industrial activity through its definition as *labour-power*. The Physiocrats identified all wealth with land and cultivation, leaving feudal property intact but shifting the essential definition of land to its economic function and thereby exposing feudal property to the later attacks on ground rent. The objective nature of wealth was also in part shifted to its subjective basis in labour, inasmuch as agriculture was regarded as the source of the productivity of land. Finally, industrial labour emerged as the most general principle of productivity, the factors of production, land, labour, and capital, being nothing else than moments in the dialectic of labour's self-alienation.

Private Opulence and Public Squalor
Marx's expectation remains unfulfilled that capitalism would collapse because of the conflict between the technological rationalization of its economy and the irrationality of its social

12 / *Karl Marx: Early Writings*, T. B. Bottomore, trans. and ed. (London, 1963), pp. 147–8.

and political structure. The question is whether the Marxian diagnosis is as irrelevant as the phenomena of welfare and affluent capitalism[13] are taken to suggest. Certainly, the metabolism of the corporate economy absorbs more than ever the public and private energies of modern society. Under the banner of a neo-feudal ideology of corporate responsibility,[14] a new psychic serfdom to brand-loyalties and occupational status immunizes monopoly capitalism from the processes of social and political criticism. It is increasingly difficult to discuss the nature of the good society where everyone is mesmerized by the *goods* society.

In the North American context, there are historical and environmental factors which contribute to the equation of politics and abundance. "The politics of our democracy was a politics of abundance rather than a politics of individualism, a politics of increasing our wealth quickly rather than dividing it precisely, a politics which smiled both on those who valued abundance as a means to safeguard freedom and on those who valued freedom as an aid in securing abundance."[15] The ideological roots of the affluent society have been traced by John Kenneth Galbraith to the hold upon the liberal mind of certain imperatives which flow from the "conventional wisdom." Adam Smith, Ricardo, and Malthus were clear enough that the mass of men were powerless against the class of property owners. But in view of the factors of scarcity, against which any proposal for social redistribution

13 / For a careful appraisal of the relations between welfare capitalism and the affluent society, see T. H. Marshall, *Sociology at the Crossroads*, (London, 1963), Part Three, "Social Welfare," and Richard M. Titmuss, *Essays on the "Welfare State"*, with a new chapter on "The Irresponsible Society" (London, 1963).

14 / It has been argued that the corporate exercise of political power is in principle continuous with the natural-law tradition of the separation of sacred and profane power and its institutionalization in the countervailing powers of feudal nobility. St. Augustine's "City of God," understood as the theory that in every age there is a moral and philosophical framework which constrains power, has been claimed as the model of corporate politics. Adolf A. Berle, *The Twentieth Century Capitalist Revolution* (London, 1955).

15 / David M. Potter, *People of Plenty: Economic Abundance and the American Character* (Chicago, 1954), p. 126.

could only mean a relapse into barbarism, it seemed that the mutual interests of the rich and the poor lay in the expansion of industrial activity. However, in the conventional wisdom the imperative of production remains just as imperious as it ever was, despite intervening changes in the modern economic environment which have made abundance a technological possibility, if not a sociological certainty. "These – productivity, inequality and insecurity – were the ancient preoccupations of economies. They were never more its preoccupations than in the nineteen thirties as the subject stood in a great valley facing, all unknowingly, a mountainous rise in well-being. We have now had that mountainous rise. In a very large measure the older preoccupations remain."[16] The paradox of the affluent society is that it has exhausted the liberal imagination in a "solution" of the problems of inequality and insecurity through a mindless expansion of production.

The instrument of this paradoxical situation is the corporate organization of the economy whose success in controlling its economic environment[17] has won for it political acceptance from its employees and the stabilizing support of state-administered anti-depressants for those moments in which the soulfulness of the corporation threatens to reach a low-point. The power of the corporation to control its environment assumes a variety of forms, ranging from its ability to control price-cost relationships, levels and composition of investment, the nature of research and innovation, the location of industry with its effects upon local communities and, of course, its power to influence governmental intervention, and, last but not least, the power to shape the physi-

16 / J. K. Galbraith, *The Affluent Society* (Boston, 1958), p. 77.
17 / "By and large, corporations have been able to exert sufficient pressure on governments, and on social institutions generally, to stabilize the field in their favour. *This stabilizing of the environment is the politics of industry.*" John Porter, *The Vertical Mosaic: An Analysis of Social Class and Power in Canada* (Toronto, 1965), p. 269 (my italics). The weakness of government planning in America has been attributed to the competitive nature of its political institutions which weaken it relative to the more monolithic structure of business. Andrew Shonfield, *Modern Capitalism: The Changing Balance of Public and Private Power* (New York, 1965), p. 353.

cal and socio-psychological environment of the consumer public. In each case, these powers of the corporation are of enormous social and political consequence.[18]

In the face of the reality of corporate power, Galbraith's theory of countervailing power is hardly more than a figleaf for corporate respectability and liberal prudishness. It is in any case a desperate gesture in view of Galbraith's own understanding of the corporate practice of integrating its production and sales efforts through the generation of wants. By engineering consumer response, the corporation is able to get an *ex post facto* ratification of its commitment of social resources as determined by corporate agenda. While paying lip-service to consumer sovereignty in the final allocation of social resources, the corporation can in fact assume the conventional distribution of social resources between the public and private sectors of the economy. This presumption is a political reality inasmuch as the demand for public services presently arises out of the needs of low-income groups who are powerless to compete away social resources from the private uses of higher-income groups. It is only in the context of the unequal distribution of income, which remains as much as ever a defining characteristic of affluent capitalism, that one can properly understand the imperative of production or, rather, of *relative overproduction for the private sector*, which in turn promotes the secondary imperatives of consumption and other-direction. Despite the heralds of the age of high mass consumption, the fact is that monopoly capitalism is a production system continually faced with the problem of deficient consumption structurally related to the class distribution of income.[19] Because of this conventional restraint upon the economic space of the capitalist system, it is necessary to invade the psychic space of workers and consumers through raising levels of expectation or through deepening levels of credit.

18 / Carl Kaysen, "The Corporation: How Much Power? What Scope?," and Norton Long, "The Corporation, Its Satellites and the Local Community," in Edward S. Mason, ed., *The Corporation in Modern Society* (Cambridge, Mass., 1961), pp. 85–105, 202–17.

19 / Gabriel Kolko, "The American 'Income Revolution'," in Philip Olson, ed., *America as a Mass Society* (New York, 1963), pp. 103–16; Porter, *The Vertical Mosaic*, pp. 125–32 for an evaluation of the validity of the middle-class and middle-majority image in Canada.

There are, of course, attempts to expand the economic space of the capitalist system through extensions of the public sector, overseas operations, and the conquest of outer space. But in no case do these extensions result in a significant alteration of the flow of social resources between the public and private sectors. The commanding position of the corporation in the face of governmental efforts to redistribute social income is evident from the relative stability of corporate profits after taxes as a share of national income during the last forty years.[20] In effect, the government merely uses the corporation to collect its taxes and is therefore dependent upon the corporate economy's agenda having been substantially realized before it can undertake its own program. Indeed, it must be recognized that the determination of the balance between the public and the private sectors of capitalist society depends increasingly on the identification of welfare and warfare. The American war psychosis is an obvious manifestation of the increasingly militarized production imperatives of the corporate economy. The significance of the social unbalance created by military spending is lost when considered simply as a proportion of total gross national product. From this perspective, the one-tenth of GNP absorbed in military expenditure seems negligible and easily enough absorbed in alternative expenditures. However, once it is realized that military expenditures represent half of total federal government expenditures,[21] it is clear that the issue is neither negligible nor easily corrigible. It is not negligible because it represents the impoverished conception of the public

20 / Irving B. Kravis, "Relative Shares in Fact and Theory," *American Economic Review*, Dec. 1959, p. 931, quoted in Paul A. Baran and Paul M. Sweezy, *Monopoly Capital: An Essay on the American Economic and Social Order* (New York, 1966), p. 148. There is consistent empirical evidence of long-run tax-shifting by corporations. Two recent studies emphasize the long-run maintenance of a stable after-tax rate of return on investment despite substantial increases in corporation income tax, E. M. Lerner and E. S. Hendrikson, "Federal Taxes on Corporate Income and the Rate of Return in Manufacturing 1927–1952," *National Tax Journal*, vol. IX (Sept. 1965), pp. 193–202; R. E. Slitor, "The Enigma of Corporate Tax Incidence," *Public Finance*, vol. XVIII (1963), pp. 328–52.

21 / In a record US budget of $135 billion for the fiscal year 1967 $72.3 billion were allocated to military expenditures, a sum exceeded only by the figure of $81.3 billion spent in 1945. *Globe and Mail*, Toronto, Jan. 25, 1967, p. 1.

domain in capitalist society. Nor is it easily corrigible, since to find alternative paths of governmental spending involves a reconsideration of the balance between the public and private sectors which would expose the poverty of the liberal ideology.

The institution of advertising can now be understood as the essential means of expanding the economic space of capitalism in a manner compatible with the liberal ideology. What Galbraith calls the "dependence effect" is in reality a political option which, if unrelated to the class structure of capitalist society and its effects upon the distribution of social resources between public and private uses, appears as the myth of an evil genius. "Were it so that a man on arising each morning was assailed by demons which instilled in him a passion sometimes for silk shirts, sometimes for kitchenware, sometimes for chamber pots, and sometimes for orange squash, there would be every reason to applaud the effort to find the goods, however odd, that quenched the flame. But should it be that his passion was the result of his first having cultivated the demons, and should it also be that his effort to allay it stirred the demons to even greater and greater effort, there would be question as to how rational was his solution. Unless restrained by conventional attitudes, he might wonder if the solution lay with more goods or fewer demons.

"So it is that if production creates the wants it seeks to satisfy, or if the wants emerge *pari passu* with the production, then the urgency of the wants can no longer be used to defend the urgency of the production. Production only fills a void that it has itself created."[22]

It is not the dependence effect as such which is responsible for the irrationality of consumer behaviour. For in every society wants are largely cultural acquisitions. The real problem is the nature of the social order which determines the content and pattern of wants. A society which fails to maintain the necessary complementarities between private and public goods and services drives itself even deeper into the accumulation of private amenities in order to compensate for the public squalor which this very process leaves in its wake.

The automobile becomes the true symbol of the North Ameri-

22 / Galbraith, *The Affluent Society*, p. 153.

can flight into privacy.[23] It has hollowed the cities and drained the countryside, melting each into the atomized living-space of suburbia; it is the instrument of urban congestion and rural uglification. At the same time, the automobile is perfectly geared to the values of technical rationality, private ownership, individual mobility, sex equality, and social rivalry – pre-eminently the values of the liberal ideology and the stock-in-trade of the corporate economy. The automobile is eminently the equilibrator of the tensions in corporate culture: it is a family headache and a family joy, an air-pollutant indispensable for trips into the fresh-air of the countryside, an escape mechanism from all the problems with which it is structurally integrated.

The role of the automobile in modern society makes it evident that we can no longer consider machines from the purely technological standpoint of the mastery of nature. We must take into account the interaction between machinery and the social relations between men not only in the context of machine production but in the wider context in which machinery patterns our style and ecology of life. Short of such an understanding, we find ourselves hallucinating the conquest of distance while all the time the road which opens up before us is the distance between a humane living-space and the little boxes which house our automobile.

But any criticism of the automobile is likely to be dismissed as quixoticism. For the power to respond to such criticism has been sapped through the cultivation of psychic identification with the

23 / Housing would illustrate the problems of over-privatization and the impoverishment of the public sector just as well as the automobile to which it must be related. The housing situation is especially illustrative of the tendency to privatize even explicitly public functions. "Public money totalling hundreds of millions of dollars has been advanced as National Housing Act loans for middle- and upper-middle-income families, to help them buy houses. But few lower-middle-income families and no poor families can get these loans. . . . many persons in Europe look on the Canadian system as socialism for the rich, private enterprise for the poor. The North American welfare approach to public housing singles out low-income tenants as conspicuous recipients of public bounty. It hives them off in ghettos for the poor. The European approach, on the other hand, treats housing as a public utility. It contains a big public sector, in which non-profit housing is provided to persons in a broad income range – not merely the poor. It also contains a large area in which private enterprise operates freely and profitably." G. E. Mortimer, "Canada's Leaky Housing Program," *Globe and Mail*, Toronto, Jan. 5, 1967, Women's Section, p. 1.

automobile as an extension of individual personality. Even where slightly less elongated extensions have been preferred by four-wheeled man, the apparent rationality of that choice actually only deepens the commitment to private as opposed to public transportation alternatives. The result is a chain-process in the privatization of other social resources integrated with the automobile culture at a time when more than ever we need to break that circuit.

The difficulty of intervention on behalf of the public domain is nowhere better seen than in the light of the potential hue and cry against interference with the individual's freedom to buy, own, and drive, wherever and whenever, that capsule which seals him off from physical and social reality while making him completely dependent upon them. Likewise, the course of public intervention in regard to the automobile is indicative of the impoverished conception of government in liberal society. The result so far is the confusion of the growth of public space with the extension of public highways which breeds more automobiles and accelerates the dislocation of urban spaces in favour of suburban locations. Commuting by means of private transportation becomes the only link between living spaces and working spaces. Finally, the rationale of this living arrangement is given a coherent projection through television advertisements in which the enjoyment of suburban values can be "seen" in the happy use of the automobile to take children to school, mother to the stores, father to work, and the dog to the veterinarian, without anyone even wondering how everything got so far away.

Alienation and the Sublimation of Politics
There is a trend in industrial society toward the interpretation of freedom and equality in terms of consumer behaviour rather than of political action about the nature and conditions of production and consumption. "Equality for the working-classes, like freedom for the middle-classes, is a worrisome, partially rejected, by-product of the demand for more specific measures."[24] In the context of corporate capitalism, the rhetoric of freedom and equality

24 / Robert E. Lane, *Political Ideology: Why the American Common Man Believes What He Does* (New York, 1962), p. 60.

no longer swells into a coherent political ideology as it once did as a strategy of bourgeois and proletarian emancipation. Just as the terrible freedom of market society has not always been tolerable to the middle class without escapes, so the working class response to market society has varied from class struggle to the becalmed acceptance of inequality softened by improvements to the social basement. This ambivalence in the response to the symbolism of freedom, equality, and reason must be understood in terms of the changing social contexts from which these notions derive their meaning and significance. Robert A. Nisbet has commented upon the changing contexts of individuality.[25] He observes that when we speak of "the individual" we are dealing with an ideal type or moral abstraction whose symbolic currency depends upon the existence of an institutional context which is favourable to its assimilation in everyday life. The liberal image of man, its possessive individualism, is the result of the imputation of the properties of market society to the interior life of the individual. The liberal theory of society and the individual was plausible just so long as the historical situation which liberalism presupposed effectively linked its vocabulary of motives with typical contexts of action.[26] However, once the evolution of market society moves in the direction of corporate society, the vocabulary of liberalism merely evokes lost contexts, arousing a nostalgia haunted by the loss of meaning.

The loss of a meaningful, social or public context for the ideals of individualism, freedom, and equality is reflected in the alienated and confused symbolism of David Riesman's *Lonely Crowd* or Paul Goodman's *Growing Up Absurd*. Each of these works confronts us with the paradox that society may be free without individuals being free. The liberal identity of individual and social interests, or, rather, the liberal perception of the challenge and opportunity offered to the individual by society, has withered away into a conviction of the absurdity of society and

25 / *Community and Power*, chap. 10, "The Contexts of Individuality." Compare C. B. Macpherson's discussion of "social assumptions," *The Political Theory of Possessive Individualism*, chap. I, II, III, VI.

26 / C. Wright Mills, "Situated Actions and Vocabularies of Motive," in *Power, Politics and People: The Collected Essays of C. Wright Mills*, I. L. Horowitz, ed. (New York, 1963), pp. 439–52.

the idiocy of privatization which is its consequence. For want of a genuine public domain, in which the political and social activities of individuals can achieve a focus and historical perspective, men abandon politics for the civic affairs of suburbia or the "bread and butter" questions of unionism. By shifting awareness toward improvements in consumption styles, these tactics deflect attention from the social imbalance which results from the pursuit of intra-class benefits that leave whole sectors of the population outside of their calculus. This tactic is further strengthened by the ideological acceptance of social improvement through the escalation effect of an expanding economy upon all classes rather than through any radical redistribution of class income or the extension of chances of individual mobility between classes.

As individual awareness is increasingly shifted toward a concern with consumption, economic knowledge is reduced to a concern with prices in abstraction from the corporate agenda which determines prices. The result is a loss of any coherent ideological awareness of the political and economic contexts of individual action. However, this does not represent an end of ideology. It is simply the nature of the dominant ideology of individualism shaped by the context of corporate capitalism. In order to break the tendency to monetize all individual experience, and in order to shift individual time perspectives away from short-term consumer expectations, it is necessary to institutionalize more universal goals of collective and long-term value. Such a requirement falls outside the pattern of instant satisfactions projected by the consumer orientation. The latter substitutes the thin continuity of progress for the solid accumulation of social history. The result is the paradox upon which Robert E. Lane has commented. "Is it curious," he asks, "that a nation that has so emphasized progress should have no sense of the future? I do not think so," he replies, for "progress is a rather thin and emotionally unsatisfactory continuity. It is the continuity of differences, the regularity of a rate of change, almost a rate of estrangement."[27] Any concern with social balance, institutional poverty, and waste, or the interaction between politics, economics, and culture presupposes a collective

27 / *Political Ideology*, p. 290.

and historical framework; but this is foreign to the liberal ideology of individual agency and its moralistic acceptance of inequality and failure within a natural order of social competition and private success.

In a society where individual interests are so privatized that people prefer private swimming pools to public swimming pools, common effort is likely to be viewed only as a substitute for private effort. Moreover, any comparison between public and private enterprise will be moralized in favour of the fruits of individual effort owing to the very real struggle involved in the acquisition of private pools, homes, and education. The loss of community functions resulting from the privatization of social resources makes individual accumulation appear all the more "rational." In reality, the individual is driven toward this pattern of privatization not from genuine choice but because he is deprived of alternatives whose systematic provision would require a public sector powerful enough to compete with the private economy. The provision of alternatives to the patterns of production and consumption in the corporate economy never gets beyond the platitudes of "variety" and consumer sovereignty which are virtually meaningless once attention is diverted from increasing the size of the goods basket to questions about the quality of a single item in it, such as bread.[28] The "efficiency" of private enterprise must be discounted by the loss of social energy involved in trying to choose a reasonable (unmagical, unwrapped, uncut) loaf of bread, and reaches an absurdly low point once the individual retreats to "home-baking," or, indeed, any kind of hobby which is a *substitute* for satisfaction in the private economy. The rise of para-social, political, and economic activities is an indication of individual withdrawal from "society." It is the expression of an abstracted individualism that is the ideological alternative to

28 / "I say we make the foulest bread in all the world. We pass it off like fake diamonds. We advertise it and sterilize it and protect it from all the germs of life. We make a manure which we eat before we have had time to eliminate it. We not only have failed God, tricked Nature, debased Man, but we have cheated the birds of the air with our corrupt staff of life." Henry Miller, "The Staff of Life," in *The Intimate Henry Miller*, with an introduction by Lawrence Clark Powell (New York, 1959), pp. 73–4.

political action on behalf of a world that men can have in common. This loss of a common world separates society into a corporate hierarchy and a multitude of individuals who are turned in upon themselves in the competition to maintain occupational status and at the same time other-directed in their attempt to rationalize their loss of community in the pursuit of the good life – family-style. Where there is no common world between working life and private life the individual's public life is reduced to shopping expeditions, church attendance, and movie-going, all homogenized to suit family-tastes, which are, of course, presensitized to the appeal of the "goods life."

It is in keeping with the liberal ideology of individualistic familism that tensions are personalized and at best call for individual therapy. Any attempt to relate private troubles to institutional contexts, which would suggest public or political action, is regarded as projection, the evasion of difficulties best tackled within the four walls of the home, if not in one particular room. The result is that men lack bridges between their private lives and the indifference of the publics that surround them. "Nowadays men often feel that their private lives are a series of traps. They sense that within their everyday worlds, they cannot overcome their troubles, and in this feeling they are often quite correct. What ordinary men are directly aware of and what they try to do are bounded by the private orbits in which they live; their visions and their powers are limited to the closeup scenes of job, family, neighbourhood; in other milieux, they move vicariously and remain spectators. And the more aware they become, however vaguely, of ambitions and of threats which transcend their immediate locales, the more trapped they seem to feel."[29]

It is the task of the political and sociological imagination to conceive men's private troubles in the contexts of public concern and to furnish bridging concepts which will enable individuals to translate their private uneasiness into public speech and political action. It must undertake to shift the contexts of freedom, equality, and reason away from the private sector and out of the

29 / C. Wright Mills, *The Sociological Imagination* (New York, 1961), p. 3.

household into a public domain which will constitute a genuine common world. And this is a task which must be articulated in a conception of government which is bold enough to seek understanding and responsible control over the human and social values generated but largely dissipated in the corporate economy which enforces the privatization of men's lives. Such a positive conception of government would help to create a public domain in which men share common assumptions about their moral and physical environment and exercise them in a concern for truth of speech and beauty of form in public places – places cleared of their present monuments to financial cunning and the fear of the future that wastes private lives.

5

The Regulation of
Canadian Broadcasting*

IAN M. DRUMMOND

IT IS DEPRESSING to see how many Canadian liberals and radicals are addicted to an odd mixture of vices. They love to scramble eggs while at the same time they are calling the kettle black. The egg-scrambling is the mixing and elimination of differences. Some of us think – or used to think – that national solidarity demands national homogeneity, and we were quite prepared to grind away at differences so as to achieve this great national goal. And some of us, I fear, believed that we must standardize in the interest of cheapness.

The kettle is the United States. While we Anglo-Canadians busily homogenize our own two-thirds of the country, we preen ourselves on our national diversity and criticize the United States for its melting-pot habits of mind. In fact, there seems to me to be much more variety in the arts and in the life of the mind[1] and much more tolerance for this diversity, in the United States than in Canada. Thus we have the unedifying spectacle of the homogenizers accusing an unhomogenized society of homogenization.

Given these national attitudes, there is a real danger that if any

*Some of this paper was first published in another form in the *Canadian Forum*, vol. XLV (Sept. 1966), and is reproduced here by permission.
1 / Though not in other things.

single group were to be given the financing, stimulation, organization, and control or regulation of any communications medium it would unwittingly impose a highly standardized pattern that would not properly accommodate performers, artists, or the consuming audience. Not maliciousness but unconsciousness would be to blame. Re-reading the reports of our special committees, select committees, unlabelled committees, and royal commissions, I am not encouraged to believe that in broadcasting this danger is at all remote. Again and again one encounters the obscurantism of the nationalists, the educators, the aristocrats, and the intelligentsia. In this sort of environment, broadcasting can safely be manipulated for national or cultural ends only if there is no unnecessary centralization of power. Therefore, we must try to invent some institutional arrangements which will provide the manipulation and the necessary assistance with minimum centralizing of power. Only by so doing can we protect ourselves against ourselves. In this paper I have tried to suggest a few of the mechanisms which we might adopt for the broadcasting industry. In thinking about the problems of regulating this industry, I have certainly had our national homogenizers in mind. However, my suggestions may interest even those who do not share my gloomy view of the Anglo-Canadian psyche.

Air Waves: A Scarce Resource

The regulation of Canadian broadcasting is an area of policy-making in which the influence of economics has been most conspicuously remote.[2] Economists have not been prominent on the numerous committees and commissions which have probed

2 / In Canada few people take economists very seriously. Undergraduates endure our courses, pass or fail our examinations, and eventually graduate, largely unchanged by our efforts. Politicians, who think us "too theoretical," are seldom seen in the company of qualified professional economists. The public at large, thinking it understands economic affairs because it has to make its living, prefers to treat the journalist as its economic oracle. The journalist, in turn, prefers to emphasize the "practical" – that is, the views which politicians already hold. The intelligentsia, confusing economic analysis either with business mentality or with an economic interpretation of events, heap scorn on the profession in lecture and common room. Some of the explanation may lie in the economist's failure to explain himself properly. But the present situation is not altogether the economist's fault.

the subject. None have testified before these bodies – at least not in their professional capacity. Yet broadcasting policy presents us with a classic example of *the* economic problem – the allocation of a scarce resource among competing uses, all good in themselves, under the guidance of some goals or purposes. The scarce resource is the broadcasting waveband, as defined by technology and by international agreement. The competing uses are approximately the various kinds of program services – local versus national, unifying versus diversifying, entertaining versus uplifting, and so on. As for the goals – well, what about the goals? What is broadcasting *for*?

On the subject of goals we have a plentiful literature but no consensus.

The intelligentsia seem to believe that Canadian broadcasting exists primarily for "higher" purposes – to unify the country, keep capitalism at bay, develop Canadian talent, repel American cultural influence, develop our interest in public and world affairs, and disseminate useful information. Sometimes, it seems, the question of audience appeal is thought totally unimportant. Better a good program with no audience than an unworthy program with a mass audience.

In the private communications industry, broadcasting is thought to exist primarily for entertainment. The intelligentsia sometimes say that the private broadcasters want to run their stations solely in the interest of their advertisers. This statement is neither accurate nor helpful; the private broadcaster knows that he cannot sell advertising time unless people are willing to watch or listen to his programming. Thus he must be concerned with entertainment. In broadcasting, as in other industries, the search for profit is a useful though not infallible guide; by following it, the broadcasters *are* tending to give the public what it wants.

But who is the public? And why does it want what it wants?

In fact, there are various kinds of popular taste, and various desires with respect to entertainment. Because the number of frequencies is limited, it is not always possible for a new firm to enter the broadcasting industry so as to cater to some particular group. If all the local radio channels are given over to teen-cult music, a sizable group may suffer acute frustration, yet there is no automatic mechanism to ensure it eventual satisfaction, because there is no automatic entry to the industry. If some channels are vacant, stations may choose to cater to such deviant tastes – so long as advertising revenue is sufficient to make it profitable. Advertisers will want to buy enough time on such a station only if they believe that the cost of doing so is justified in light of the increase in their own profits. This condition is likely to be met only in larger cities, and only when the minority taste is distinctive in some way which links its programming preferences with its buying preferences. For instance, an importer of Scandinavian furniture may find it worth while to advertise on the good music radio station but not on the teen-cult outlet. Further, there is no inherent stability in the situation. If the good music station decides that there is more money to be made in teen-cult music, it will change its programming[3] – as one Toronto station did in mid-1968.

It seems that, even if we say that the end of broadcasting is entertainment, we might want to regulate broadcasting stations, or supplement private stations by public ones, so as to ensure variety. But this conclusion follows only if we are prepared to deprive some people of benefits so as to give benefits to others. If we compel a radio station to broadcast "good music," when its managers would like to broadcast teen-cult music, we are giving the good music lovers a benefit at the expense of the teenagers, who are deprived of one choice. The intellectual may assert scornfully that the choice between a Beatle and a Rolling Stone is no real choice. But what he really means is that *he* thinks both are equally obnoxious. To a particular teenager, at a particular moment, there may be a real difference, and thus a real deprivation

3 / Some observers are inclined to expect stability in programming types, which would guarantee automatic variety at least in large cities. This stability will exist only if every broadcaster has canvassed all possibilities before settling on his first program type, if there is no later change in the taste balance of the region he serves, and if the "minority" audiences are sufficiently large and identifiable to yield the broadcaster sufficient profit by catering to them.

may be felt when the number of choices is less than it could be. As David Blank has recently pointed out,[4] the experience with pay television and cable television suggests that the mass public does want exactly this sort of choice – the choice between apparently similar programming patterns which the intellectual finds a meaningless choice.

If we want to regulate in the interest of "real" variety, we must be prepared to recognize and accept that the result is not without cost. Further, we should be clear-sighted enough to see that the cost will be borne by one group while the benefit accrues to another. The result can be called "better" only if we think that the happiness of the gainers outweighs the annoyance of the losers. Politicians are forced to consider this issue. Some of the rest of us, all too inclined to assume that we know what will make people happier "in the end," too often ignore the matter.

The Question of Public Tastes

In the preceding paragraphs I have been assuming that if we are to treat broadcasting as entertainment we must take public tastes as "given" data on which we must build but into whose origins we do not inquire.[5] Economists are accustomed to think in this way. But others are not.[6] Indeed, much of the past controversy over broadcasting policy has centred round the origin of public tastes. Are tastes what they are because people are people, because the

4 / "The Quest for Quantity and Diversity in Television Programming," *American Economic Review*, vol. LVI, no. 2 (May 1966), pp. 448–56.

5 / See, for example, Raymond Williams, *Communications* (Penguin Books, 1963).

6 / Here we should note the Prime Viewing Time Perplex. The intelligentsia say that there is really even less quality programming on television than there seems to be, because so much of it is at odd and inconvenient hours. Yet so long as tastes are taken to be fixed and unchanging, the person who has unusual and specialized tastes has no right to expect the rest of the world to arrange itself for his comfort. Concretely, suppose 95 per cent of the public wants Batman at 8pm and 5 per cent want Buxtehude. The 5 per cent have no justifiable complaint if Batman takes precedence at 8 and Buxtehude occurs at 1.45am. On the other hand, suppose tastes are *not* taken to be fixed. The intelligentsia could argue logically – if implausibly – that after continued forced exposure the majority will prefer Buxtehude.

media have a certain technological character, or because the
pressures of capitalist society create a certain pattern of tastes?
Can tastes be changed by regulation of broadcasting, by a new
technology, by the provision of a certain sort of programming, by
public ownership, or in any other way? Until McLuhan, the
participants in this debate have generally assumed that there is
an objectively given hierarchy of tastes – that some tastes are
objectively good and others are bad. Further, and especially in
Britain, they have often been influenced by that neo-marxist
argument which proceeds from capitalism through the profit
motive to the content of the mass media, finally arriving at the
debasement of the workers. Of course, it is disappointing for the
Left to discover that the workers are not interested in the same
things as the intelligentsia. Universal literacy did not produce a
universal uplifting of reading; increasing leisure did not cause
the WEA lectures to be crowded out; broadcasting did not produce
a mass audience for *Oedipus Rex* or Berthold Brecht. What was
wrong? Could it be that such things are inherently uninteresting
to some people? "Certainly not! What I like is *good*, and everyone
would like it too if only he had not been corrupted," this kind of
neo-marxist would answer. "The capitalists find it to their profit
to corrupt taste so that the people will consume the meretricious
products of their factories, thus preserving profits and staving off
the collapse of capitalism."

I cannot summarize this view without parodying it somewhat,
yet I know it has been influential. Of course, it reinforces two
other assumptions – that top people just generally know what is
good for the proles, and that it is my duty to re-educate you until
you agree with me. Such views lead logically to a state-owned
broadcasting system whose programming aims at education and
uplift, not primarily at entertainment; the programmers would
cherish the hope that the public will eventually like what is
offered to it, and meanwhile the broadcasters would enjoy the
plaudits of some opinion-makers and the encouragement of most
socialists. If the public does not quickly change its tastes, the
socialist can always point out that it is not enough to socialize
broadcasting, because capitalism can still exert its evil influence

through the remaining private sectors; the educator is accustomed to the fact that education is never easy or quick. The goal of the system is still entertainment, but it is, so to speak, entertainment in the long run after re-education through exposure.

There is no way of proving that the socialists and the educators are wrong about the source of public taste or about its malleability. On the other hand, they cannot prove that they are right. It seems unwise to model a national broadcasting policy on such unproven and unprovable assumptions. We of the intelligentsia do better if we admit that *we* demand more than entertainment, long-run or short-run, from the broadcasting system. In so doing, we imply that we are willing to impose the cost – the short-run public dissatisfaction with programming. Further, we must remember that – whatever their source, and however malleable they may be – mass tastes tend in the direction of the "low-brow" or "pure-entertainment" programming which the intelligentsia dislike. If we forget this, we render the entire Canadian broadcasting operation otiose, because most of our citizens can so readily get pure entertainment from across the border. I do not think it very sensible to prescribe a Toronto television programming pattern which ensures that 98 per cent of all Toronto television sets will be tuned to Buffalo. The waste of Canadian labour, capital, and air space would simply be too great, and the benefits too small.

What can we conclude about the goals we wish to set for our broadcasting system? It is perfectly sensible to treat broadcasting as pure entertainment which transmits what advertisers want. However, it is equally sensible to treat the industry in another way, recognizing that its main function is entertainment, but wishing to regulate or manipulate it to get more "true" variety, and to serve other ends than entertainment. Some of us may dislike the former system, but we must recognize that it *may* make the best use of the available frequencies. And so may the latter. I personally prefer the latter goals and in the following pages I shall assume that they are the model. But I do not think we can prove these goals to be better in any general way, and I wish that earnest reformers and publicists would stop trying. In any event, one must come down on one side or the other, before one can say anything about the regulation of Canadian broadcasting.

The Question of Ownership
Having opted for "entertainment plus," so to speak, I can now ask whether I have thereby decided who should own the broadcasting system. Need it all be state-owned? Can it be mixed? Can it be entirely private? Let us be more direct. Suppose the CBC did not exist. Would it now be necessary to invent it?

Before going farther we must sort out the several aspects of broadcasting – program production, distribution of programs, and transmission over the airwaves. These three functions need not be combined, and they have never been completely merged either in Canada or in the United States. There have always been some independent producers, and now there are many. Their program material is recorded on tape, which is then rented to stations, advertisers, or even networks. In the twenties and thirties, the distribution of programs meant networking stations through land telephone lines. Charlie MacCarthy came "live from Hollywood," and was broadcast simultaneously everywhere. Coaxial cables, microwave relays, and satellites now provide a vastly expanded networking system for this nation-wide or regional transmission. Yet the telephone and telegraph companies, not the networks, own the physical facilities for networking. And tape transcription has joined film and disc as a competitor in the distribution of program material. A station can get material from network links, film, tape, or disc, as well as from independent production in its own studios – under its own management, or by arrangement with an independent producer.

If we want broadcasting to serve national and cultural purposes, we want to make sure that certain kinds of program get produced, distributed, and aired. In principle, all these things could be done by a private broadcasting system, so long as a government agency exists to manipulate it through contract, subsidy, and rule. However, there are no obvious advantages to such an indirect scheme. It is more straightforward to have government bodies produce and distribute the needed programs.

Further, there is no good reason to exclude the provincial governments from these producing and distributing activities, so long as they do not displace the Dominion government but co-habit with it. At present, judicial decision excludes the provinces from the *regulation* of broadcasting but does not prevent them from operating stations or producing programs. Obviously the national government must continue to assign frequencies and to regulate the technical aspects of broadcasting. Further, unless the private sector can be trusted to handle the task, there must be some agency charged with responsibility for the production and nation-wide distribution of nationally significant programs. It is hard to believe that the provincial governments would create such an agency.

On the other hand, there is no reason for the government broadcasting bodies to own all the transmitting stations, or to manage them all. In thinly settled areas private stations do not pay, and government must run the station if there is to be any broadcasting at all. But in other areas, the government agencies could buy time from private stations and transmit programs. Besides, they could offer program material to the private stations. Private stations would pay for material when they chose to carry it, and they would be paid when the government agency required them to carry it. To ensure speedy and convenient working, the government body would probably need the power to "expropriate time." Private stations could hardly object, as they would be paid the going rate.

Furthermore, government agencies need not and should not be the only producers and networkers. Talent would be more likely to command its true value if there were several competitors bidding for it. Managerial quirks would be less likely to dominate programming. Writers, directors, and actors would be given a choice between the policies of the several managements. The more producers, and the more networkers, the more "true" variety.

The above paragraphs should not be read as a call for the abolition of the CBC. True, many CBC stations are now, strictly speaking, unnecessary, because private stations could provide the same programming in the same places if properly regulated and manipulated. But no harm is done by CBC transmitters, even though the circumstances which led to their construction are long past.

The CBC is, after all, a creation of the radio age. In the late twenties, many parts of Canada had poor radio reception or none at all. Radio waves can carry over great distances, but the existing private stations were too small, scattered, and weak to cover the country adequately. Hence the Aird Commission proposed in 1929 a nationally owned grid, with a few very high-powered transmitters. These would simultaneously claim Canada's property under international agreement and blanket the country with a good-quality signal. Private enterprise could not be expected to carry out a project of such size, scope, and uncertain returns. This fact was not the reason that the Aird Commission recommended public ownership. But we can justify its recommendation retrospectively in this way. After its creation in 1936, the CBC began to construct the Aird Commission's national grid. This task was barely completed before the television age began.

There is little sign that the CBC or the government noticed that the technology of television is radically different from that of radio. Television is transmitted on waves which do not follow the curvature of the earth. Therefore, before the satellite was perfected, no station could have a very long range, and many stations were needed to cover a country as large as Canada. So long as the television transmitter remains stationary, there is no point in thinking of a national high-powered grid which provides the basic national service.[7] Yet a modified Aird model was indeed applied. The CBC was to provide national programming, and to own the basic transmitters in large cities; private stations were to serve smaller cities and were to affiliate with the CBC network. In an effort to save public money while spreading coverage as fast as possible, private stations were not allowed to enter the great cities, and CBC stations were kept out of the private areas.

The result was entirely predictable. The public began to press for more variety in programming. Private broadcasters longed to enter the big cities and to form their own networks. Forced to be all things to all men, the CBC television network would have been unable to maintain the distinctive character of its programming even if it had wanted to, and even if funds had been available.

Eventually, in 1960, the government decided to license private

7 / Satellite transmission is another matter. But we can hardly blame the government for not foreseeing that development in the late forties.

stations in big cities; shortly afterward, it allowed a private network to appear. In my opinion, both governmental decisions were entirely proper, though both came several years too late. To repeat: the more stations, and the more networks, the better for the artists and the public.

At present, the CBC transmitters are important mainly because they strengthen the CBC's hand in the lobbying for public funds. Further, until recently they were certainly necessary for "true" variety – even though the CBC itself is still trying to be all things to all men.

Assigning Frequencies
Having decided that we can tolerate both private and public broadcasting stations, we can ask ourselves how many stations there should be, and how the scarce frequencies can be rationed among competing users.

One has the impression that in the past our regulatory authorities have tried to limit the number of licences, perhaps to protect the CBC audience and perhaps to protect the profits of private broadcasters. This note of limitation is sounded in the government's recent *White Paper on Broadcasting* (p. 10). But an economist, because of his professional interest in freedom of choice and his tendency to assume that businessmen generally know where profits are to be made, is inclined to say that there should be as many stations as the air will hold.

Yet it is not obvious how many stations there *can* be. Bad receivers, receivers of limited capacity, or high-powered transmitters all reduce the number of feasible stations. Government regulation could be useful here. For instance, Ottawa could insist that all TV sets receive both VHF and UHF. It could require all radios to pass a selectivity test. But government regulation cannot change geography or broadcasting technology. Further, we must work within the system of international agreements which assign some frequencies and station strengths to Canada.

Given these constraints, we have a choice between more or less clarity and more or less variety. The more stations, the worse the signal from any one station, other things being equal. In Britain the authorities have chosen to limit the number of services, partly in the interest of cheapness but chiefly in the interest of good reception. In American radio, the authorities have licensed so many stations that it is often impossible to get a clear signal from any station. However we Canadians choose to decide the matter, we must construct some sort of an answer as a guide to the licensing of stations. If the regulatory authorities have already done this, they have kept the answer to themselves.

Once we know how many stations there can be, we can assign the frequencies to users. The alternative tools for this rationing are administrative assignment and lease. For decades we have assigned the frequencies administratively. Now it is time to try leasing. Since broadcasting frequencies are scarce resources they command a conceptual price, whether or not this is collected. If the frequencies are used to make profits but no price is charged, the private users are receiving a subsidy from the public, which owns the frequencies. Such a subsidy is surely improper. Further, by pricing the frequencies the rationing board would be able to discriminate between high-payoff and low-payoff uses. The easiest way to price would be by auction. Each licence would expire every five years or so, and would then be re-auctioned. For the regulatory authority, the auction would be a great convenience, because there would be no need to carry out the kind of investigation which administrative assignment requires. The authority would simply announce the auction and give licences to the highest bidders.

The auction system could produce dreary results if each licence did not contain specific and detailed rules about the type of programming and the amount of advertising. The recent White Paper says, "quality standards cannot readily be made a condition for a licence," yet expects that "judgements about quality ... should carry a great deal of weight when an application for the renewal of a licence is being considered" (p. 11). But if we can say nothing beforehand, how will a station know that its current programming is measuring up? And what standards will be applied after the fact? If we can judge afterwards, surely we could formalize standards beforehand, incorporating guidelines into the licence. The Broadcasting Act (1968) appears to permit this sort of programming control. But at the time of writing, nothing has been done to fix the rules for preparing content or quality.

At the very least, one would want to confine each private licensee to the provision of a certain type of programming. Otherwise, as we have seen, "real" variety could easily vanish; all stations would tend to offer similar programming. Beyond this minimum, one might want to specify the standards of programming in greater detail.[8]

Defining Programming Standards
It is hard to mention the subject of standards today without sounding priggish at best or Edwardian at worst. One may even be accused of a print-bound mentality – though even McLuhan did not mean that the medium is all the message there is. But if we are to have "real" variety in broadcasting we must try to construct usable definitions of programming types. If we turn the problem over to an administrative board, like the CBC or the Board of Broadcast Governors, we are simply allowing the implicit views of the board members to define the terms which we are unwilling to define ourselves.

Of course we are plagued by problems of definition. What is "culture" or "art" or a "level of taste"? A libertarian economist is in a happy position. He can assert *ex principio* that what is produced is what ought to be produced. The rest of us must be less comfortable than the libertarian economist. Yet there is little point in talking about "high-quality programming" unless we are capable of saying what "high quality" is.

In Canadian broadcasting, at present, nobody fixes standards except for Canadian content. Yet there is a broad consensus about the fact that different stations broadcast noticeably different sorts of program. Until July 1968 the programming on Toronto's CHUM-FM was noticeably different from that of CHUM-AM, and both are still different from CFRB or CBL. We sense these differences if we do not yet define them. In Britain, the BBC long ago

8 / As is strongly urged by the Committee on Broadcasting's *Report* (Ottawa, 1965), pp. 106–9.

managed to define its Light, Home, and Third programs in terms which were meaningful for producers and listeners. The Americans have done something of the kind with educational TV. In Canada, the CBC once tentatively experimented with a qualitatively different service on its FM network. Educational television is also underway here. The evidence suggests, therefore, that we could say something useful about the sort of program which a station is to provide.

I think that the Canadian university intelligentsia have a reasonably clear, if private, idea of "suitable" broadcasting standards. At least in English Canada we like things to be homogenized. Some of us think we know what is best – in education, the arts, or television. Or we think we know what is true – even more dangerous. Naturally we want everyone to have the best, and since we admit only one best we end up with a standardized product and a standardized experience. Perhaps some of us feel threatened by the mere existence of difference. (After all, if Joe Weltschmertz does not agree with me, he might be right – and I wrong!) It sometimes seems that some Canadian intellectuals dream of a broadcasting system in which everyone is obliged to watch "elevating" programs.

But such a standardized broadcasting system would be intolerable. Moods and tastes differ. Further, it would be impossible. American programs are all too available in almost all our larger cities. So long as we do not jam signals at the border, we must face the fact that our citizens enjoy the freedom to choose not to watch Canadian broadcasting. If all available programming were of "elevating" standard we can be pretty sure that the masses would not tune in. Therefore, we must not set standards which merely enact the preferences of the intelligentsia. We must recognize that others want other things.

The obvious solution is to define levels or types of programming and to confine each station – public or private – within one level or type. With present broadcasting techniques it should be possible to operate enough stations in most areas to provide some real variety. In really big cities one could certainly allow three levels of radio broadcasting and at least two of television. When there are enough UHF television sets, and when satellite telecasting arrives, we could offer a really wide range of choice.

This solution would be more costly than a standardized system, because it needs more outlets and a great deal more programming. The more levels, and the more stations per level, the greater the social cost of the broadcasting system. This extra cost is a part of the cost of variety. It can be reduced, though not eliminated, by networking, transcription, and tape, which spread the production costs. That is, a system with a given number of stations and types of programming would spend much more on production if it could not use networking, transcriptions, and tapes. In this cost-saving we find the strongest reason for allowing private stations to form whatever networks and co-operative arrangements they wish.

Traditionally the CBC has tried to satisfy the different tastes of different people by "balanced programming" – for instance, hockey on Saturday and a string quartet on Wednesday. I doubt whether this is now a satisfactory arrangement, at least on radio. My impression is that most people now use radio chiefly as a casual accompaniment to other activities. No one plans to tune in on a particular program; people just turn the thing on and try what comes out (though there are exceptions, especially in the evenings, in rural areas, and among special groups such as farmers and small-boat operators, who need particular service broadcasts). A great deal of television viewing – especially in the daytime and late in the evening – seems to be treated in the same casual way. If people really do have this approach to radio and television, "balanced programming" will merely maximize irritation, because it will satisfy almost nobody at any particular time. If one "balanced station" is bad, two would be almost equally bad. It would be better to differentiate them by type, rather than force each station to carry some programs of each type.

When each licence requires the holder to provide a particular type or level of service, when licences are auctioned, and when there is a definite number of each sort of licence in a city, we may expect to find the private sector offering more real variety than it does today. A "Third" program licence would command a rather low fee, or no fee, because such programming would not be very popular. But in a big city a private entrepreneur might still make money on such a service. If he could, he would provide the service. There does not seem to be any chance of producing such a result under present licensing arrangements. A station may decide to offer such programming, but there is no incentive for it to do so, even if it would make *some* money by doing so, because *more* money can usually be made from a mass programming pattern.

Whatever kind of licence they hold, private stations should certainly be required to sell time to the CBC or to other publicly owned programming trusts. For many years the CBC has demanded air time from private stations in exchange for network affiliation. Usually this has not been paid for. The theory seems to have been that the private stations were discharging a national duty by carrying national programs. In effect, their sacrifice of profit was a sort of concealed licence fee. But this arrangement is untidy, and if licences were actually to be auctioned it would be illogical as well. If the private stations are paid the going rate when they carry such programs of national importance, they cannot complain when they are forced to do so. Normally such programs would consist of news, talks, and public affairs. However, the publicly owned agency should probably have the power to buy time for any purpose it thought proper.

To aid the private stations in the attainment of their programming standards, and to create a larger demand for Canadian talent, the CBC might develop a larger "program production service" which would rent tapes or network programs to private broadcasters. Private stations would pay for these programs when they chose to carry the material. Besides the CBC, the national government and the provinces could create and subsidize separate program production trusts, whose work would be available to the private sector. The result of such developments would be more work and more choice for Canadian performers, writers, and producers. If the programming material was sufficiently cheap and attractive, it would certainly be aired. The result would be roughly the same as the result of our present Canadian-content rules. But it would not produce the absurdities and sophistries which these rules now generate.

When renting programs from these program production services, private stations would be obliged to consider the terms of their own licences, but they could use the appropriate material as they liked, given their own desire to make profits. When the CBC or the programming trusts bought time from private broadcasters to air their own productions, they would also have to consider the terms of licences. Buying blocks of time at going rates, in principle they could then sell advertising space in these blocks of time. However, one doubts they would often do this.

Since most private stations now sell advertising spots and provide their own programming, such transactions would be possible only after some readjustment of the market for air time. However, even now some stations sell air time in blocks to advertising agencies, who provide both program and advertising. In the past, most American radio stations and networks operated in this way, at least during the evening. Reformers have often objected to the system because it delivered program content directly into the advertising agencies' hands. However, they could hardly object if the program production service of the CBC were to buy air time for the dissemination of culture or for the encouragement of Canadian talent. The same would apply to provincial government programming services.

One would not expect the services to be self-sustaining. However, their commercial revenue, from domestic and foreign program sales and from advertising, could be used to cover some of their outlays on production and on the purchase of air time, giving some financial flexibility. They would certainly need freedom to allocate their subsidies and commercial revenues between program production and the purchase of air time. The more funds Parliament and provincial legislatures give them, the less advertising they will need, the more time they will be able to buy, and the lower their charge for Canadian-content programming.

Financing the System
Suppose that these suggestions were adopted. The federal government would obtain a large revenue from the auction of broadcasting licences. It usually would spend a different amount from

this revenue on program production, on the purchase of air time, on networking charges, and on the operation of some broadcasting stations. All these spendings could be channelled, as at present, through the CBC. But the CBC would not have any advertising revenue, unless it chose to sell advertising spots when it bought time from private stations. Provincial governments would also spend on program production and perhaps on station operation – especially for educational broadcasting. Governments might spend more than they collected from broadcasters, or less. Government revenues from broadcasting would be determined directly by the expected profitability of each licence – and influenced indirectly by the federal government's rules for advertising and programming standards. Expenditures should be determined independently, by comparing the social valuations of broadcasting outlays and other government outlays. Thus government broadcasting revenues and expenditures will be equal only by chance. As for the private sector, it would get some revenue from the sale of air time to the CBC – and to program production trusts, if these are allowed to buy time and if they choose to do so. But the private sector would continue to rely on advertising revenue.

The problem of advertising is complicated. Advertising is needed for the support of the private sector, which in turn is useful if broadcasting people are to have a choice of employer. The more advertising we allow, the higher will be the bids for broadcasting licences. While advertising is annoying, a lack of variety also involves discomfort. The best plan would probably be to allow a level of advertising which encourages the private sector to take up all licences not required by the public sector. If bidders could accurately measure prospective revenues when bidding for licences, the result would be normal profits on all private stations, and sharp differences in the cost of licences. In the public sector, advertising should not be allowed on the "third program." If there is no advertising on this service, many people may turn to it so as to avoid another lecture on the state of their armpits. If one allowed the public "third program" to advertise, one would be foregoing this important incentive through which the public taste might eventually be raised.

Conclusion

The suggestions of this paper are these. First of all, the CBC should be preserved in roughly its present form, but it should offer a more specialized sort of programming on its own transmitters, and it should develop a large and autonomous program production service. Second, the federal government should give the CBC enough funds so that the national system could discontinue all advertising, and so that it could buy time from private broadcasters. Thirdly, the constitutional position of the provincial governments should be clarified so that they could operate program production services, stations, and networks, without encroaching on the federal power to issue licences and establish programming standards. Fourthly, there should be opportunity for parliamentary debate on the choice between clarity and variety in the assigning of channels, and on the question of programming standards; the regulatory agency should receive clear and explicit instructions on both matters. Fifthly, the regulatory agency should have the power to set the details of programming standards for individual licensees, and it should have the staff and authority to monitor all broadcasters – private, provincial, and national. Finally, licences should be allocated by competitive auction.

These suggestions imply a strengthened and somewhat altered CBC. They also imply a very strong supervisory commission, which would need more power to enforce compliance and to punish wrong-doers. The power to cancel a licence – the only power of discipline which the 1968 Broadcasting Act gives the Canadian Radio-Television Commission – is not enough. Cancellation is so drastic a punishment that it is in effect unusable. The commission must be able to impose fines, and it may need other powers as well. Here there may be constitutional problems. Can a federal agency impose such punishments merely because the distribution of licences is in the federal jurisdiction? I do not know the answers, but I think that where there is a regulatory will there is almost always a legal way.

Apart from the question of fines, the 1968 Broadcasting Act is well suited to my scheme. In it, admittedly, we find the regrettable concern with "balanced programming" which I have criticized above. However, in enjoining the CR-TC to enforce balanced programming, the Act does not compel *each station* to be balanced. The commission could differentiate the programming efforts of individual stations, as I have suggested, without contravening the Act, so long as the end result is balanced for the system as a whole. Further, the Act specifically gives the commission the power to fix quality standards, but says little about how to fix them. Therefore the sort of standards I propose would be consistent with the letter and spirit of the Act. Finally, the Act allows the commission to issue broadcasting licences and to fix the fees for them, but does not fix criteria for licensing, scales, or types of fees. It says only that licences are to be for a term of years. Hence the Commission could apply an auction scheme and issue five-year licences if it wishes. Further, it could issue as many licences as it wants. In short, it already has almost all the power and all the freedom to be a national regulator.

But can we reasonably expect that any regulatory agency will escape capture by the industry it regulates? In the public utility field the record is sufficiently dismal to give one pause. Unfortunately, though a regulatory agency and a mixed system of broadcasting may not work perfectly, neither may a monopolistic Crown agency. To a large extent we are faced with the choice between two imperfect instruments, and we can never be sure which is actually the better.

Fortunately, where an agency regulates many firms it is more likely to preserve a certain autonomy, because every firm has an interest in ensuring that all the other firms follow the rules, and because the firms, having divergent interests, may find it difficult to exert joint pressure for a change in the rules. Furthermore, thanks to the Canadian tradition of critical musing about broadcasting policy, we should find it easy to establish a genuinely impartial commission whose members are not in thrall to the private sector – or to the public sector. If the government makes bad appointments, of course, the commission will not do its work as effectively as it might. But gross derelictions of duty can be avoided if the commission is given a more detailed and explicit guide for its actions. Nothing is really solved by simply confiding the industry to a group of clever men. Here is the main and basic shortcoming of the 1968 Act. But by careful legislating we can perhaps protect ourselves against the worse effects of bad appointments. In any event, if a government were to make bad appointments, a single Crown agency would be at least as dreadful as a badly regulated mixed system, because it would be at least as badly led.

6

The Proliferation of
Boards and Commissions

PETER SILCOX

"WHO GAVE THEM the right to do that?" is a question often on
the lips of the citizen of all modern western democracies. Increasingly he finds himself subject to the dictates of bodies, usually
bearing the title "board" or "commission," whose right to regulate his conduct is far from clear to him. His lack of knowledge
about the composition of the board or commission, what precise
powers it has, and how it got them often makes him resentful of
its authority. The sum of this ignorance and these resentments is
the general feeling of dislike, distrust, and sometimes open hostility to boards and commissions – increasingly a feature of our
social life.

The activities of governments have expanded, are expanding,
and will go on expanding in all modern industrial states. It is
essential to understand three points about this expansion: it
involves all levels of government; the manner or means of expansion has varied in different areas of governmental concern; the
ambivalence toward the change felt by many governments has
affected considerably the form of administration adopted for the
exercise of the newly acquired powers. I shall say something
about each of these points in turn.

The expansion has taken place in two waves. In recent years, and in the forseeable future, the main burden will be borne by the lower levels of government, which are in most cases ill prepared to receive it. The first wave of expansion led to the involvement of national or federal governments in the economic sphere and in the provision of a comprehensive system of social services. From the Great Depression to the end of postwar reconstruction the government gradually assumed the responsibility for the general performance of the economy, including the maintenance of full employment and of economic growth. In the social service field, in which Canada and the United States have lagged behind other western countries, the government accepted the responsibility for maintaining a certain minimum standard of living and educational opportunity for all its citizens in all areas of the country. The second wave has been mainly concerned with the detailed regulation of economic and social life. In North America as opposed to England or Sweden the provision of specialist social services and attempts to improve the quality of life for the ordinary citizen have been mainly the work of provincial and local governments. The second wave has been mounting in the past decade and has yet to reach its crest. In Canada these two changes have taken place and have had a profound effect on federal-provincial relations. The second wave has proved the main force behind the "quiet revolution" in Quebec and the fundamental shift in the power relationship between the federal and provincial governments.

The lower levels of government in Canada as in the United States are ill equipped to tackle the much greater volume of more complex work that has come their way. Ontario has faced the typical problems created by the second wave of expansion: inadequate sources of revenue, inappropriate administrative structures, and the shortage of both specialist staff and professional senior administrators.[1] At the local level these problems have proved even more intractable, and progress in dealing with

1 / F. F. Schindeler, "Legislative-Executive Relations in Ontario," unpublished PhD dissertation, Toronto 1966.

them has been much slower, if it has occurred at all. As a result national governments have often attempted to deal with problems better left to provincial governments and the latter has taken similar action in relation to local government. These transfers have undesirable political and administrative effects. Most undesirable of all is the weakening of political control on matters of direct personal concern to local citizens and the decline in interest in local government that results. The most unsatisfactory arrangement from both these points of view is the delegation of powers in these appropriated areas to the semi-independent public agencies.

The expansion of government activities has not been a simple arithmetical process. The nature of the second wave leads to the situation where the direct provision of services or the adoption of complete responsibility for a given area of public concern makes up a much smaller share of the government business than it did when the operations of government were on a more limited scale. Licensing, planning, supervision, co-ordination, and approval are the words most often used in describing the new powers rather than the words provision and administration. These words have always been used to describe some of the government's work, but they now cover a substantially larger proportion of it than they did in the past.

These changes have had three important and interconnected results. First, the contracts between governments, government and non-governmental organizations, and government and the general population have all been made much more complex. Second, far more professionals and specialists have been brought into government and, because many of their activities are difficult for the layman to understand, the problem of political control has become more complicated. Third, new administrative forms, whose relationship to the normal departmental structure is difficult to work out, have proliferated.

Many of these changes have been brought about by political parties explicitly committed to the proposition that big government poses a threat to the best interests of society. This general view has also been shared by a large majority of the population, at least in North America. Despite these general outlooks popularly elected governments have gone on expanding their activities and there can be no doubt that they have done so, as they themselves claim, under pressure from public opinion. Practically every group in society demands government protection or assistance in its "special" case *despite* the fact its members share the general feeling of disquiet about the expanding role of government. This ambivalence has had an important effect on politicians when they have considered the best administrative structure for dealing with new governmental responsibilities. The semi-independent public agency has a number of attractive features for them. It can give the appearance of being a politically independent corporate body allowed to operate in the manner of the allegedly efficient profit-maximizing private corporation. This structure also has the advantage of making it easier to give interested groups a partnership role in the government's work. In general there can be little doubt that, whatever the realities behind the form, the use of this type of agency does appear to the public to depoliticize the government's role and also to some extent conceal the overall expansion of its power and influence.

These developments have made it progressively more difficult to identify the exact fields of a particular government's responsibility. At one extreme the federal (or provincial) cabinet accepts a clear responsibility for federal (or provincial) departments, not only on policy matters but also for detailed administrative operations. At the other extreme a small grant to a local YMCA might involve the contributing government to some limited extent in the provision of recreational facilities but few people would then hold it responsible for the general policies of the YMCA and even fewer for the efficient administration of that association's operations. Between these two extremes lie a large number of interventions by the government in social life and many organizations for which it accepts some degree of responsibility. It might be wise to think in terms of a continuum of responsibility with the department at one end and the YMCA in the above example at the other. Organizations do not always remain at the same point in the continuum. For example, in recent years Ontario universities have moved far closer to the departmental end of it.

Three types of government intervention and agency can be distinguished. First, departments directly under the day-to-day control and supervision of a member of the government. Second, semi-independent public agencies created and given policy goals by the government, which retains some control of the general size and shape of their administration structure. Third, government-assisted bodies dependent, often to a considerable degree, on government assistance and financial help but not created by an official government initiative; these have a much larger degree of control over their long-term aims and have considerable independence of outside control in organizing their internal organization and procedures. The line between groups two and three is a hazy one, as is to be expected in view of the nature of the continuum and the constant changes taking place in the areas of the government's activities, but it does turn out to be a useful division in practice.

It should be stressed that the degree of actual responsibility exercised by a government in any area of its concern can only be established as a result of actual investigation. Organizations in which government has an interest cannot be classified on the basis of purely formal criteria alone, such as statutory requirements and procedures which are often a very poor guide to the actual practices of government. Nowhere is this more the case than in the field of semi-independent agencies.

There are a very large number of semi-independent agencies in existence at both the federal and provincial levels in Canada. Most of them have been established in the past twenty-five years. As might be anticipated from what was said earlier the greatest number were established at the federal level between 1940 and the early 1950s while the most rapid expansion in the provinces has taken place since 1955. The best estimate I have been able to make puts the number at the federal level at fifty. The most notable group is of Crown corporations; a number of them like Air Canada and the CNR are as large or larger than the most important departments and others, like the War Veterans Allowance Board, are of more limited significance. The Report of the Committee on the Organization of Government in Ontario[2] put the number in Ontario at thirty-three in 1958. The best estimate for Ontario which I have been able to make puts the number of "ministerial agencies" at fifty in 1968. All these figures must be estimates because only an investigation of the entire field can identify such an agency. Some examples of Ontario semi-independent agencies are Ontario Hydro, the Hospital Services Commission, both employing large numbers of people, and the much smaller Ontario Highway Transport Board and the Ontario Racing Commission, both of which are enormously significant in their own limited areas.

Having attempted to sketch in the general circumstances in which the tremendous growth of semi-independent agencies has taken place, I want now to discuss in more detail their role in the framework of government. Their founders have given all kinds of reasons for setting them up. They range in sophistication from C. D. Howe's explanation of why he was establishing a particular Crown corporation, that that's the way they seemed to "operate around Ottawa,"[3] to the administrative-technical accounts found in textbooks on public administration. These latter explain that the semi-independent form is most useful when, first, the type of administrative flexibility associated with private corporations demands the avoidance of many of the administrative control procedures used in the departmental structure; second, the direct interference of politicians with the day-to-day operations is to be minimized; third, the co-operation of specialists prone to be unfavourably disposed to the idea of becoming civil servants is required; fourth, swift action is needed in areas in which the departments have no previous experience.

The most influential advocate of the public corporate form for nationalized industry, Herbert Morrison (later Lord Morrison of Lambeth), gave reasons of this sort for his preference. His case for the adoption of the semi-independent form for, say, the

2 / Report of the [Gordon] Committee on the Organization of Government in Ontario, 1959. This total includes Ontario Hydro.
3 / *Debates*, House of Commons, 1947, pp. 42–9.

government management of the British gas industry would run along the following lines. The gas industry will have to deal with and in some circumstances compete with private industry. It is most likely to be successful if it can adopt the personnel policies, accounting methods, processes for investment, decision-making and general profit-maximizing outlook of other large commercial undertakings. The day-to-day operations will be most efficient if political considerations are kept out of pricing policies, the location of large installations, and the timing of service extensions. Finally, the recruitment of applied scientists and managers with ability in related fields of private industry is likely to be hampered by the restrictions imposed by the civil service commission and the personnel management sections of the treasury. In summary then, successful commercial operations require a freer and more flexible environment than successful operations of the traditional type undertaken by governments. The same type of administrative-technical argument has also been used in the case of agencies whose functions might be described as being judicial or quasi-judicial in nature, although the greater freedom required in their case is of a different kind and for different purposes.

Students of the semi-independent agency and administrators dealing with it have been very impressed with this "objective" kind of discussion and it has dominated their consideration of its problems. Much too impressed, in fact. As a consequence in attempting to bring some order into the chaos of the new areas of government activity they have classified agencies according to administrative-technical criteria. Two standard criteria have been used: (1) type of activity, which has led to the establishment of subclasses such as proprietory, administrative, judicial, quasi-judicial, and so on; (2) the extent of direct government control as attested to by formal provisions establishing the agency: its freedom in raising funds and the security of tenure of its directors for example. This type of classification can be seen in the Canada Financial Administration Act 1951 and the Gordon Committee's report.

These classifications appear neat and definitive and they have a kind of non-political air about them acceptable to many public administrators. They are also almost useless if one is concerned with the question of how political power is exercised and the determination of the nature and extent of political responsibility. However, there is evidence to show these arguments often are in the minds of politicians establishing semi-independent agencies, but they are not as decisive as public statements would have us believe. The sceptical political scientist who investigates this area soon discovers that a far wider range of considerations, mostly of a personal and political nature, come to the fore. He is forced to remember that politicians have been at work. The political scientist discovers that within the department framework he can find branches and divisions who carry on activities of a commercial nature and that numerous ordinary civil servants are daily exercising judicial or quasi-judicial functions which seem no different from those assigned to semi-independent agencies. Then too, he discovers that all the formal protections for the independence of these agencies do not in practice protect them from the interference of politicians if a determined minister believes that the political credit of the government he serves is at stake. Formal prescriptions are a poor guide in attempting to determine who is responsible for the politically significant decisions taken in the area of concern of a semi-independent agency. If the political scientist is tactless and a little frustrated he may begin his questioning of one member of the board of a semi-independent agency, as one acquaintance of this writer did, by asking "How many times has the provincial premier phoned you at home at night to discuss decisions your board is about to make?"

All these considerations lead to the suggestion of a different or additional set of reasons why the semi-independent form is sometimes attractive to politicians and a very different system of classification that follows from it. The overall expansion of government activities has brought governments more regularly into contact with each other, with privately operated public service organizations, and with powerful pressure groups. Their partnership in particular areas has often been consummated in semi-independent public bodies. Partnership may be desirable for a number of reasons. It may lead to greater efficiency, allow a government to limit its financial commitment or general political responsibility, or it may be the necessary price for active co-operation and political neutrality.

These considerations have been of prime importance in the creation of many important agencies in the province of Ontario. The Ontario Housing Corporation will be using mainly federal funds supplied through the federal Central Mortgage and Housing Corporation. The co-operation of established and prestigious hospital organizations was important to the successful launching of the Ontario Hospital Services Commission. The Ontario Water Resources Commission's work involves constant contact with municipalities, in an area of traditional municipal responsibility, and with conservationist groups. In the labour relations field the wise government realizes its need to gain the active assistance of employers and trade unions if it is to influence collective bargaining and it can minimize the political risks by giving each side a share in the responsibility for arriving at decisions in particular cases where legislation is to be applied. The Ontario Labour Relations Board has members from both sides of industry as well as expert government nominees. In another important field doctors are much more likely to co-operate and much less likely to attack the government's health policy if they are involved in its implementation. No doubt the body set up to manage the projected Ontario medicare scheme will reflect these considerations.

The creation of a semi-independent agency provides the opportunity for a government to minimize its financial support for a particular service from general taxation. Often such agencies are given the responsibility of being as financially self-sustaining as is possible. Thus the collection of fees, charges, or contributions can be used to free the government from the financial burden. Contributions collected on a monthly basis by the Ontario Hospital Services Commission are quite clearly a simple poll tax, but they can be disguised as a form of insurance payment to an agency similar in appearance to a private insurance company. People in general are much less hostile to this kind of payment than to a simple poll tax or other regressive tax.

At a more immediately personal level a semi-independent

agency might be established to remove from the area of responsibility of a particular minister a new service which the cabinet
feels he is ill fitted to handle. One might also be established as a
separate empire for a particularly powerful government supporter
with a desire to press ahead in a given area. Who, for instance,
would be prepared to claim that Ontario Hydro would have been
organized in quite the way it was if Adam Beck had not had his
consuming interest in the field, and his own very special views
on what the best organizational form would be? The desire to
impress a special geographic area with the government interest in
it can sometimes be served by the creation of a development
agency directed by local notables. Establishing agencies free from
restrictions on hiring and firing partially makes up for the reduction of patronage caused by the merit system.

It now becomes possible to reconsider the question how agencies should be classified. The most relevant classification will
relate to the location of the effective political power to dictate the
policies of the agency, to alter its form, or to prescribe its internal
procedures. This criterion suggests that semi-independent agencies may be of three types. (1) Subordinate agencies: in relation
to which one government has the effective power to set the policies, appoint and replace the directing board or commission, dictate the internal procedures, and change the legislation governing the agency's organization and powers. (2) Government partnership agencies: in this case none of the above changes can be
made without changing the essential nature of the agency, unless
the approval of governmental partners has been given, even if
one level of government has statutory power over the agency.
(3) Government group partnership agencies: where the government is inhibited in exercising any binding formal powers over
the agency by the political requirement of satisfying the powerful
groups that any proposed changes are not inimical to their
interests. It might then be useful to classify agencies in each
group according to "type of activity" or other more formal
criteria.

This classification, like any other, is not a neat and tidy one.
Some agencies may be difficult to fit into it with any certainty,

and the same agency might be in different classes at different times. Its advantages are that it does take into account the question of where effective power to command the agency lies, and therefore where effective responsibility for its exercise should be fixed, and that it is not dependent on the purely formal criteria which are such a poor guide to the actual relationships between administrative bodies.

The conventional theory of the means for protecting the public interest assigns important roles to the government, the elected representatives of the people, and the group of individuals directing the agencies. The minister concerned has a number of tasks. It is his responsibility to lay down publicly the general role the government envisages for the agency and thus the general line of policy it must follow. He usually appoints board or commission members, and has final power of approval over investments, decisions, regulations, and procedural rules. With these responsibilities, and the knowledge gleaned from exercising them, the minister can ensure that the agencies' work is co-ordinated with those of his own and other government departments. He can also answer in public, and in the legislature in particular, for the agency in those fields where he has responsibility. The task of the board is to use its specialist knowledge to run the day-to-day activities in an efficient manner, and to make decisions within the general policies laid down by the minister with the public interest in mind and without reference to any political considerations. The guarantee that they will concern themselves with the public interest lies in the appointment of honest, intelligent men, whose independent position safeguards them from immediate political pressures. The role of the legislature is to oversee the government's exercise of its responsibilities by using numerous opportunities open to it under the procedures of the legislature. Members can question the minister concerned, debate the regular reports made by the agency which are tabled in the assembly, and scrutinize and debate all legislation concerning the agency brought before the house. The legislature might also keep a more detailed check on these matters through the work of legislative committees. The legislature's responsibility is, of course, to ensure that all activities of the agency are in conformity with the public interest, but its specific control is confined to the area for which the minister is directly responsible.

This is all very comforting to the average citizen. With all these varied groups hard at work to serve the public interest, the problems of co-ordination, public responsibility, and protection of the individual citizen's interests, all seem certain to be solved. But unfortunately it is not necessarily so. Immediately we begin to investigate the actual system, we find serious discrepancies between the theory and the practice.[4]

How do we define general overall policies? Do ministers always declare them? What assurances have we that the minister is satisfied with limiting his interference in the operation of the agency to those powers given to him under the legislation? Can we be assured that any powers of financial supervision, for example, will not be used to determine the scale and direction of day-to-day activities? In the case of agencies where more than one governmental level is involved, how do we know that the responsible representatives will agree on the general lines of development the agency should take? Is the minister knowledge-able enough and well disposed enough to other departments to ensure active efficient co-ordination of government policies? Where agencies involving co-operation with groups are con-cerned, is the minister more likely to be interested in pacifying important political interests than serving the public good? None of these questions can be answered in the affirmative with any confidence. But have no fear. Remember, the minister is dealing with politically disinterested boards and commissions, and the legislature has an alert eye on him.

Let us look at the boards and commissions and the legislature, then, for confirmation of this. First, the boards. The first thing we notice here is that there are a number of different categories of members, and one cannot always be confident of their inde-pendence. Some members are civil servants whose position or career prospects are directly dependent on the minister. Some are members of the legislature, although none seem to be mem-bers of political parties which oppose the government. Some have

4 / Schindeler, "Legislative-Executive Relations."

long records of political service to political parties or, to be more precise, to the party in power. Some are representatives of other governments or of non-government organizations. A minority are independent-minded experts with no political record. They are a very mixed bunch, and no board or commission is made up exclusively of one type of member. The one thing they have in common is that all were appointed originally by politicians and ultimately all of them can be removed by the same people who control the legislature, whatever kind of tenure they might have.

The performance of legislative assemblies in the exercise of the responsibilities assigned to them under the conventional theory has been studied in a number of jurisdictions. The general conclusions have rarely given room for complacency about the legislatures' effectiveness. The most common conclusions are that members are not well informed about the work of semi-independent agencies, because there is a paucity of information, the members are very busy and have no adequate assistance in researching areas outside their most immediate political concerns, or they are complacent purveyors of the conventional theory. The very existence of the conventional theory is often regarded as adequate testimony to its efficient operation. Then there is the fact that most legislatures have far too many detailed matters to consider, and the crowded legislative session leaves no time to discuss matters peripheral to the main concern of carrying on the continuous electoral forum. A poorly informed electorate can best be aroused by a concentration on familiar issues. Then, finally, if a group of members does show some interest, the government can use its control of the legislative majority to deny adequate sources of funds to run effective committee investigations and to limit the scope of committee activities. It is a constant source of wonder to the political scientist that the general public assumes that the government of the day is eager to allow the legislature a free rein to wander over the work of the administration. Nothing is further from the truth. The reform of parliaments is obstructed and impeded by governments who wish to get on with their executive operations, as free as possible from effective criticism.

The proliferation of semi-independent public agencies has led to three major problems which must be solved if the public interest is to be protected. First, the maintenance of efficiency requires that their activities be co-ordinated with those of other government bodies. Second, the protection of the right of citizens to have a say in how the government uses its powers requires that there be adequate opportunities for meaningful and informed discussion of their work. Third, the relations between the individual citizen and the agency must be conducted in such a way as to ensure that the former is aware of the reasons for decisions which affect him and is satisfied with the fairness of the procedures which have been followed. All of these problems occur in all public bureaucracies, but they are more acute in this sphere because physical and organizational separation from the departmental structure prevents the normal operation of the methods designed to overcome them.

The prime cause of these extra difficulties is the lack of readily available information on the exact relation of these agencies to the political executive and on their policies and practices. It is true that most of them are required to publish annual and financial reports, although some of them publish late or not at all. In addition, anyone familiar with such reports will readily agree that they are often singularly unhelpful in tracing the affairs of the agencies. Their most common characteristic is that they were written by someone who sought guidance from past reports on what to say. Then a related difficulty is the scarcity of experts outside the government service who have the time and the ability to understand and use information. These two matters are interrelated because busy administrators will not produce long and complex reports if they believe that no one is going to read and use them. Third, students of public administration ever since Max Weber have recognized the tendency of administrators to treat information about the work of their agencies as private property and to prefer administrative secrecy to full and frank disclosure. They often proclaim their faith in the conventional theories not out of ignorance but out of a desire to limit the outside interference in their work. Donald Rowat has dealt in some detail with the problem of administrative secrecy in a recent article and has shown that it is a basic element in Canadian administrative practice.[5]

It is essential to realize that the three problems arise from the same causes and that they are closely inter-related. For example, lack of co-ordination not only leads to inefficiency but also prevents constructive criticism, although criticism is necessary for efficient communication between agencies. The critic who is busy trying to find out exactly what governments are up to and who for lack of information is forced to discuss the work of individual agencies in isolation is unlikely to make constructive suggestions that will assist a government in planning its activities. In addition he will also aggravate his own problems, for his destructive criticisms will make public administrators more distrustful of him. In the past two or three years the province of Ontario has been engaged in many schemes to improve the quality and scope of post-secondary education. These have not been presented as part of an overall policy relating the assistance given through government scholarships to graduate students to prepare them for teaching careers (the Ontario graduate scholarships) to the recruitment of staff for the new Ontario universities and the province-wide system of community colleges. In the absence of such a comprehensive policy statement how can the government's critics analyse either scheme? In fact, they are forced to discuss each scheme in isolation and in the process they expose themselves to the charge that all they have to offer is a number of partial and destructive suggestions.

The relationship of the problems of making semi-independent agencies responsible to the public and protecting the individual citizen is even closer. It is impossible to judge if an individual citizen is being unfairly treated unless the aims, general policies, and procedures of an agency have been fully discussed and understood by a significant section of the public. Its conduct in individual cases can only be assessed against this general background. The failure to grasp this simple point has led to far too

5 / D. C. Rowat, "How Much Administrative Secrecy?" *Canadian Journal of Economics and Political Science*, vol. xxxi, no. 4 (Nov. 1965), pp. 479–98.

many cases in which there has been ill-informed criticism of particular agencies. The most common offenders are lawyers whose lack of knowledge of administrative law and experience in administrative practice does not prevent them from pontificating on the work of semi-independent bodies. Much of their criticism has concerned procedural aspects of the organization structure and they have given very little attention to the decision-making context and process. The fundamental problem is that of establishing that the citizen has rights that can be defended against the agency. Citizens have substantive rights only in relation to the general policies and laws approved by the elected representatives of the people. All the procedural safeguards in the world will not persuade a person who has come into conflict with a semi-independent agency that he has been fairly treated unless he sees the relationship of the decision in his case to the policies which the elected representatives of the people have prescribed for the agency. The more that is known about any agency the easier it is for the citizen to estimate how its operations might affect him and the general public to judge whether an individual has been treated fairly.

What changes then are necessary to ensure that the public interest is more adequately protected? The answer must, of course, vary with the type of agency; however, one major innovation is necessary which affects all of them. Far more studies of individual boards and commissions must be made and published. This means that academic investigators must be encouraged to take an interest in the field and their work must be facilitated by giving them free access to relevant material. If this is done, the complacency engendered by the conventional theory of control will quickly be dispelled. Disclosure alone will not deal with the problems I have outlined, but it is the necessary starting point in the search for solution.

Subordinate agencies are the first group we have to discuss. They range from departmental corporations, acknowledged in most cases to be part of the departmental structure, to quasi-judicial bodies with a reputation for their independence from political control. The one feature that these diverse agencies have in common is effective subordination to a minister, which means that a minister can get his own way over the policy the agency follows or the manner in which it is implemented without coming into direct conflict with powerful interest groups that have an institutionalized role in its work or with another level of government. The minister may in fact choose to give the subordinate agency a good deal of independence but he knows that he has the power to dominate, and so do those who direct the particular agency. Often this situation allows a minister to exercise power informally while stressing in public the formal limitations on his responsibility. For example, British ministers have often exercised a decisive influence in the affairs of public corporations managing nationalized industries although the formal means for doing so, the published directive, is practically never used. The essential point is that if a government creates a subordinate agency that it can control despite the apparent formal safeguards of its independence, then that capability must bring with it the ultimate political responsibility for the agency's operations.

In this situation it is clearly the responsibility of the legislature to see that the government acts in the public interest. The link between power and responsibility is as clear as it is in the case of government departments. Modern legislatures are ill fitted at present to undertake the work of checking the work of departments, let alone the extra work involved in doing the same for subordinate agencies. The need for reform to equip legislatures to carry out this task has been canvassed in many places.[6] The essential changes are not procedural: they are a willingness on the part of governments to make a clear statement of their policies and to lift the cloak of administrative secrecy, together with the provision of vastly improved facilities to the opposition for the collection of information and its expert assessment. On this last point it should be stressed that the odd extra typist and better research libraries are nothing more than token gestures; a massive bureaucracy cannot be shadowed by a boy on a bicycle. The essence of a democracy is the institutionalization of the role of the government's critics.

The most important single reform is the creation of a system

6 / B. Crick, *The Reform of Parliament* (London, 1964).

of small specialist committees of members sitting not for just one session but throughout a parliament, with an expert staff partially under the control of opposition members. A committee without expert staff for the minority party is like a bird without wings. It has no hope of checking on the work of departments bulging with specialists under the command of the minister. For the same kind of reasons a committee on commissions, with or without a staff, is bound to be of very limited value. How can such a committee carry out a useful investigation of dozens of unrelated semi-independent agencies, let alone check how successfully they have co-ordinated their work with related agencies? The work of any board or commission must be investigated at the same time as that of related departments.

In the case of government partnership and government-group partnership agencies the effective political power, and therefore political responsibility, of a single minister is less easily fixed. The independence of these bodies is real because it is based not on formal considerations but on effective political power. In this situation special procedures may be developed which will more effectively result in the protection of the public interest. Two methods commend themselves to this writer: the "watchdog" continuous consultative committee and the committee of investigation. In both cases the "watchdogs" must have teeth. They must be chosen in part by people other than the concerned minister and they must have a specialist staff.

The consultative committee should have a continuous existence; it should have a small, partly expert membership, the assistance of staff, the power to summon papers and persons, and the right to publish reports at will. It might facilitate its work if a central office of consultative committees was established. With these facilities it could provide, as legislative committees should in their areas of responsibility, a continuous commentary on the work of the agency and a centre where a citizen could take his complaints for discussion and if necessary for investigation. There might be some utility in attaching the office to that of the ombudsman, where that office exists. This would make the office's role more easily understood by the public and might lead to administrative efficiency by bringing together the staffs of offices with a similar role in the political system. It must be stressed, however, that the consultative committee should be concerned with general review as well as individual complaints.

An alternative or supplement to the consultative committee may be a periodic investigation by a small expert committee. Such an investigation if done on a regular schedule would have the advantage of being able to make a long-term assessment of the agency's work and of its success in co-ordination and dealing with the general public. In addition it might have some utility in checking the tendency of all administrative bodies to linger on in their old form long after it has ceased to be the most suitable one for the job.

The adoption of any of the suggestions made here for surveying the work of semi-independent bodies would bring protests from board and commission members, civil servants, and politicians enjoying the fruits of office. They would claim that investigation would impede the progress of their work and would threaten to undermine "our traditional system of responsible government." These pleas should be treated with the scepticism which might be shown toward a claim by the burglars' union that a reduction in the size of the police force would be a measure in the public interest. Semi-independent agencies are public bodies, spending public money and using coercive powers in the name of the protection of the public interest. This circumstance gives the public the right to know precisely how they are spending the money and using the power. Then too, isn't the essence of responsible government the right of every citizen to have the information necessary to judge how the government is exercising its responsibilities? The special control procedures suggested here might serve to dissuade politicians from using the semi-independent form. If this did happen it would have the desirable effect of reducing the complexity of the public bureaucracy.

The legislature, equipped for its task in the way we have recommended, together with the other committees, would publicize the work of semi-independent agencies and provide the information on which the public could judge the extent to which they are serving the public interest, however that might be conceived by different people. The individual citizen would know where to go to get advice from informed people and whom to complain to if he was dissatisfied by his treatment at the hands of an agency. There would also be a considerable impetus to co-ordination if there was a real chance that political capital might be made out of a government's failings on that score.

7

The Economic Council
as Phoenix*

GILLES PAQUET

Put down the bloody musket;
it's not a duck but an idea. PERCY ADAMS

THIS STUDY might be premature since one could hardly expect
any institution to crystallize fully within a few years. However,
since the Economic Council of Canada has already defined its
strategy and since we are in a position to sample its work, it might
be legitimate to raise some questions and to put forward some
suggestions as to the most appropriate lines along which the
Economic Council of Canada might be refurbished.

Modern Capitalism and Planning

The general idea of plan and planning is not new. Everybody
plans in one way or another. "Planning is something everyone
does who has any sense of tomorrow. A bum does not plan ahead;
that is what makes him a bum."[1] But before planning could

*Many thanks to my colleague, T. K. Rymes, for his disturbing com-
ments, during the period when this paper was written in the spring of 1967.
1 / H. S. Gordon in T. E. H. Reid, ed., *Economic Planning in a Democratic Society?* (Toronto, 1963), p. 39.

become important in our economic system, many myths had to be destroyed: first of all the myth of the invisible hand, which was guiding the economic system toward its optimum. Although little was known about the operations of this unseen hand, there was a belief that things would go better if the system was left alone. Another one is the myth of the neutrality of the state. This was a norm based on a rather poor understanding of the relationships between economic groups, social classes, and political structures. A third one was the myth of positive thinking. Indeed for a long time, and even nowadays, it has not been recognized that economics was not and could not be value-free. Some hiding behind scientific conventions like the Pareto optimum had a sterilizing effect on economic thinking.

These myths and many others were exploded by the cataclysmic experience of the 1930s. The invisible hand had failed, there was a need for a visible one to make sure that the system would run smoothly. This led the state to become more involved *explicitly* into the management of the economy. Very quickly, it became obvious that the state could not be neutral, i.e., it could not act always in such a way as to leave the different economic groups unaffected. In a hypothetical world made only of workers spending all their income on consumption goods and rentiers deriving all their income from clipping coupons, it is clear that the trade-off between fighting unemployment or inflation for the state represents a trade-off between satisfying one group or the other. Although any real world is not as simple, the problem remains the same. The state is forced to make some hard choices, to define its goals and strategies in full cognizance of explicit trade-offs.

Economics had mainly emphasized understanding until the thirties, when it became interested in forecasting. Economics was coming of age: it was becoming a therapy-oriented activity.[2] It was not sufficient any more for economists to state that they could not say anything. If many were worse off and a few were better off as a result of the 1930 crisis, there was no hesitation: the

2 / G. G. Granger, *Méthodologie économique* (Paris, 1955), partie III, chap. 2.

situation had to be changed even without the benediction of Paretian economics.

However, this metamorphosis of our economies and our view of them was still only partial. If the state was to intervene, why should its action be strictly *ex post* therapy? The logic of the visible hand was quite clear: the state should intervene not only to tinker with the functioning of the economy whenever the market system proves deficient or inadequate but rather it should streamline the very structure generating these deficiencies.[3]

This was the birth of the idea of planning in the Western economies. This idea was obviously embodied in various institutional frameworks and these differences in methods and institutions has revealed the many possible options covering a whole spectrum of viable solutions. Andrew Shonfield has recently examined these institutional features of the economic order in post-war modern capitalism.[4] This survey has shown that the idea of planning "so powerfully influenced by individual national styles"[5] has taken various forms which fundamentally constitute variations on a same fundamental theme. Moreover, it is quite clear from a rapid examination of the story that in most countries the interest in planning is a fairly recent phenomenon of the 1950s and 1960s.[6]

Canada went through this metamorphosis in the early 1960s. Some might argue that there were elements of thinking along this line much before the 1960s. Indeed H. E. English has examined briefly what some might consider as planning ideas and programs in Canada in the 1930s and 1940s,[7] but he emphasizes that not

3 / *Ibid.*, chap. 3 ("Planifier, c'est donc intervenir à l'échelle d'une grande unité économique, pour en aménager à la fois la structure et le fonctionnement"); F. Perroux, *L'univers économique et social* (Paris, 1960), introduction.

4 / *Modern Capitalism: The Changing Balance of Public and Private Power* (London, 1965).

5 / *Ibid.*, p. 221.

6 / A most interesting survey of the planning procedures and methodologies in the different countries and the time at which such institutions were introduced is available in J. Tinbergen, *Central Planning* (New Haven, 1964).

7 / H. E. English, "The Nature of Democratic Economic Planning," *Canadian Public Administration*, vol. VIII, no. 2 (June 1965).

until the early 1960s did "an epidemic of support for 'economic planning' spread through business and political circles in Canada."[8] The 1958–62 depression was certainly not a minor cause of the rebirth of interest in planning, as is shown by English's analysis of the steps leading to the Bill C-72 creating the Economic Council of Canada in the middle of 1963.[9] In fact, in 1962 and 1963, some seven provinces also created some sort of advisory councils more or less along the lines followed by the federal government.

A content analysis of this epidemic of literature in support of economic planning for Canada in the early 1960s would reveal the spectrum of opinions in Canada about the form that planning should take and about the difficulties to be faced in bringing about these new institutions. Although we shall not present here a complete survey of this extensive literature, it is important to mention a few warnings which have been issued right from the start and to enquire a bit further into the meaning of the words "economic planning" in those discussions.

Before the creation of the Economic Council of Canada, in the winter of 1963, the Canadian Institute on Public Affairs devoted its whole conference to the question of whether Canada needed planning. During this conference, a number of academics, businessmen, and labour leaders expressed their views, studied some of the problems of planning in a federal state, and examined various definitions of planning. It also presented what some thought to be the prerequisites of any adequate economic planning in a democratic state.

Three points were made time and time again. First, the problem of planning in a federal state where eleven governments or possible planning agencies would control part of the machinery is quite a challenge. It would certainly raise many more issues than in a unitary state. In the face of these difficulties, our planners would need to elaborate some machinery through which they could co-ordinate their activities.

8 / H. E. English, "Scope for Economic Planning in Canada," *Business Quarterly*, vol. 28, no. 3 (fall 1963), p. 51.

9 / H. E. English, "Economic Planning in Canada," in T. N. Brewis *et al.*, *Canadian Economic Policy* (rev. ed., Toronto, 1965), chap. 16.

Second, one of the blocks in the road to economic planning
which was often mentioned is that a challenge such as the one
implied by the construction of a planning machinery in a federal
state "can be met only after a drastic revolution has taken place
in the minds of the people."[10] Parizeau added: "It may be that
the Canadian economy will need to receive severe shocks before
we feel forced to get down to it." In the same vein, Clarence
Barber pointed to the fact that "native superstitions" might
explain much more than lack of research when it comes to an
understanding of policy: "I firmly believe that effective economic
planning is more likely to be handicapped in the future by deeply
ingrained prejudices about what governments should and should
not do than by our inability to determine what correct economic
policy should be."[11]

The third point has to do with the relationship between the
diverse meanings of the word "planning." It proved very difficult
for the participants to extract themselves from the confusion
cleared in the theoretical literature in the 1930s between *planning*
and *plotting*. The former refers to the steering of a macro-
organism toward its collective interest, while the latter refers to
the prospective thinking and conspiration of a subgroup in order
to mould the functioning of the system in such a way as to ensure
benefits for itself.[12] Although the point was not made explicitly
at the CIPA conference, this confusion proved a major source of
difficulties in getting a good understanding of economic planning.

Neither the difficulty of planning a federal state nor the
"native superstitions" nor the semantic confusion have been
eliminated. This explains in part why no serious discussion of
economic planning in Canada has really emerged. On the other
hand, it makes all the more important the few discussions that
seem to have been well organized. The experience of the Private
Planning Association has also been important: some of the most
cogent remarks on the problem of planning in Canada have come
from its various directors of research. We have already mentioned

10 / Reid, *Economic Planning?* p. 64.
11 / *Ibid.*, p. 73.
12 / H. Smith, "Planning and Plotting: A Note on Terminology,"
Review of Economic Studies, vol. III (1935–36), pp. 193–200.

some of the work done by H. E. English, but even more pertinent might be the "basic question" raised by Arthur J. R. Smith (later to become the Director of the Economic Council of Canada) at the CIPA Winter Conference of 1963: "Does a country have anything which can genuinely be called economic planning until it has a combination of three things: planners to suggest objectives; policies (including, if necessary, 'incentives' and 'compulsions') to achieve these objectives; and constant reappraisal of targets and techniques to assure progress towards accepted goals?"[13] This might serve as a most useful benchmark in assessing the work of the Council, for it defines, in conjunction with our previous remarks, the background at the time when the Economic Council appeared on the stage. It might explain the specificity of the Canadian metamorphosis, although it might also help to measure the distance by which the Economic Council of Canada is missing the mark.

A Primer on Economic Planning

In order to understand more clearly what are the limitations of the Economic Council of Canada, and to be able to make suggestions as to the ways in which it should be altered, we shall present a primer on economic planning. For as long as planning will remain a portmanteau word, there is little chance that we shall be able to comment meaningfully on the operations of a planning agency, or any proxy for it.

A plan is not a set of wishful statements; it is rather a set of logically ordered statements about the present and future states of the economy, the social and physical technology of the socio-economic system, the goals pursued, and the actions to be taken to achieve these goals under the constraints mentioned above.[14] By planning, we shall mean the implementation of the plan, i.e., the process through which the plan is transformed from a logical entity into reality. One would expect any good plan to make provisions for the "descent" of the plan, i.e., to deal explicitly

13 / Reid, *Economic Planning?* p. 55.
14 / H. Greniewski, "Logique et cybernétique de la planification," *Cahiers du Seminaire d'Econométrie*, no. 6, (Paris, 1962).

with the planning procedure within the plan. However, most of the time plan formulation and plan implementation are considered as two unrelated steps and this leads to magnificent constructs which remain for ever unimplemented.[15]

At the core of this problem of plan and planning is the relationship between planner and plannees. This relationship can best be analysed as a "dialogue" or exchange of messages between these two actors, or groups of actors. To understand this "dialogue," one has to know more about the way in which the plan is going to be formulated and about the way in which it will be implemented.

The views, impression, opinions, or stands of a population about any problem are formulated most of the time in an "unspecialized language." The patient coming to the doctor has no clue about his condition except that his belly aches. It is the role of any policy-maker who does not believe that there is a perfect automatic mechanism to integrate all these inarticulated messages and symptoms to make sure that these views and opinions are going to be registered and taken into account, and that the problem which they express in this inarticulate fashion is going to be translated into a language of problem-solution. Once this translation is done, it becomes possible to find a solution to the problem and to define procedures to implement this solution. It remains only for the planner to translate again this solution into a "language of persuasion" in order to "convince" the plannees to act in an appropriate manner.[16]

This informational view of economic administration partitions the problem into three segments: (*a*) definition of objectives and information gathering; (*b*) plan-planning; and (*c*) the descent of the plan.

(*a*) The elaboration of this logical construct which we have called "plan" requires first the collection of a certain amount of information about the present and future states of the world and

15 / A. Waterston, "A Hard Look at Development Planning," *Finance and Development*, vol. III, no. 2 (June 1966).

16 / M. W. Shelly II and G. L. Bryan, "Judgments and the Language of Decisions" in M. W. Shelly II and G. L. Bryan, ed., *Human Judgments and Optimality* (New York, 1964).

about the social and physical technologies defining a given economy. This information is not really available in this form anywhere. The planner is therefore forced to enter into some sort of dialogue with the plannees in order to obtain such information. This is done often without any explicit interviews of the plannees through the operation of the central statistical office which aggregates much relevant information for the purposes of the planning agency.

The planner, however, has to obtain some information also about the system of production possibilities and about the organizational and administrative structure of the economy. These will constitute more or less the rules of the game which the planner will have to keep in mind in determining the goals and the actions to be taken to achieve them. Any violation of the technological rules is not without cost and unless the planner has ways to introduce some "technological" changes, he will be bound by these rules. This is as true for the production process of steel as for the threshold of tolerance of consumers or workers.

A third type of information to be obtained has to do with the merit criterion which is to guide the planner's activity. These norms (in the very simple case) might be thought to be embodied in some objective function which makes it possible to order different possibilities as more or less desirable for the economy. However, the problem is not so simple. The planner is not simply registering a consensus in a neutral fashion. The planner has to recognize and to identify public wants which are not always explicitly perceived by the individuals in the population. Moreover, this recognition of public wants has to be done also in an atmosphere influenced by the interference of the plotting activity of many interest groups. It is not clear either that the planner or the state is not influenced in the identification of these public needs by its ideology. In the dialogue leading to the formulation of the norm to be used as a guide for action, the planner or the state is *generating* as much as *registering* the consensus of the population.[17]

Thus, it is in the interaction and in the consistency of these

17 / Ideology might be regarded as playing the same role in the public economy as publicity in the private sector.

three sets of statements which are translating the real world into a crude construct that the actions to be taken have to be decided upon. The planner, however, cannot decide as to the optimal path to be followed and the optimal strategy to be adopted without having translated these statements into a language of problem-solution.[18]

(b) Once the information has been gathered about the present and future states of the world, about the nature of the social and physical technologies, and about the public needs and wants, the problem remains to find a solution. This solution is a set of actions which will make the system as well off as possible according to the merit criterion extracted from the population and given all the constraints registered above. This requires that the problem be translated into a language of problem-solution. Indeed the planner's performance depends on his ability to translate the problems of the economy into a formal language. Some of the most popular formats have been the linear programming and input-output methods.

However, there is no assurance that there will always be a language of problem-solution within which the problems of the economy may be formulated and which would produce rational decisions. In fact, the problem as defined by the planner might be ill structured and might not lend itself to a formulation into any of the standard languages of problem-solution. This makes it impossible to generate a solution. Such conclusion is always very frustrating as demonstrated by Campbell's experience. "The attempt to express in the language of economics the typical features and problems of running the administrative economy effectively does not change them enough to provide fresh insight."[19] Campbell concludes by suggesting that "the specialists on the Soviet economy should take mass leave, and study cybernetics together for a year."

18 / For some examples of attempts to formulate the problem of planing into a "language of problem-solution," see R. Campbell, "On the Theory of Economic Administration" in H. Rosovsky, ed., *Industrialization in Two Systems* (New York, 1966); also B. M. Gross, "What Are Your Organization's Objectives? A General-Systems Approach to Planning," *Human Relations*, vol. 18, no. 3 (Aug. 1965).

19 / "Theory of Economic Administration," p. 202.

There is always a strong temptation on the part of the planner to force the problem into a simple programming language. However, it is neither always possible nor always suitable to put the plan-planning problem into an operations-research type of format. Very often one has to be satisfied with quasi-analytical methods[20] which, although less rigorous, are more adapted to the fluidity of the planning problem and constitute an improvement on the usual heuristic problem-solving methods.

The dangers of not resisting the temptation of reducing planning to programming, of reducing the fluidity of the *dialectical interaction planner-plannees* to a routinized problem-solving more or less adapted to the questions at hand have been emphasized by Pierre Massé.[21] Quasi-analytical methods ensuring the feedback of results into the problem formulation put the emphasis on adaptive processes. Instead of being considered in a static framework with known goals, the planned economy is perceived in a dynamic framework with qualitative and quantitative adjustments to innovation.[22] The decision upon any action is therefore not a once-for-all affair; it is the result of an "analysis" which is always tentative and it is subject to change. Planning appears therefore as much as a process-oriented activity as an outcome-oriented activity.

(*c*) However difficult it may be to come up with a set of rational actions, this is still not the end of the road. The planner still is left with the problem of providing for the descent of the plan. This entails a mixture of "bluff and deception," of persuasion proper, and of compulsion. But whatever mix is chosen, the conclusions reached in the language of problem-solution have to be translated into a language of persuasion which will ensure that the plannees are going to behave accordingly.

The planner has a wide-ranging arsenal of tools at his disposition. From forecasts which will reduce uncertainty about

20 / H. I. Ansoff, "A Quasi-Analytic Method for Long-Range Planning," in C. W. Churchman and M. Verhulst, eds., *Management Sciences – Models and Techniques*, vol. 2 (London, 1960).

21 / "Les principes de la planification francaise," *Weltwirtschaftliches Archiv*, Band 92, Heft 1 (1964).

22 / For a comparison between the two perspectives, see Alfred Kuhn, *The Study of Society* (Homewood, Ill., 1963), chaps. 38 and 39.

future states of the world and therefore enable the plannees to make better decisions, to incentives stimulating them to act in a given way, to coercive measures, the planner has to define a strategy specifying any mixture of these tools that he sees fit within the constraints of the technology.

Although there is always a temptation to believe that reasonable men should be easily convinced of what is good for them and for the country, many factors tend to show that it would be unwise to rely on persuasion in its usual sense to provide for the descent of the plan. The problem is to set up a signalling device which will ensure that plannees will do the *right* thing. This signalling device should not be limited to the attempts to convince the plannee that what makes sense in the language of problem-solution should make sense also in the unspecialized language of the plannee.

Very often, especially where "the tradition of problem-solving is weak," it is more appropriate to rely on the principle of the "hiding hand."[23] In order to obtain what is deemed essential from the plannee the planner will simply use whatever signalling device is going to produce this result. In some cases, it might mean that optimistic forecasts should be produced when in fact the future is grim in order to stimulate a counter-reaction from the plannee.[24] Although this manipulation of the economy by the planner might appear somewhat objectionable from an ethical point of view, it is simply the recognition of the fact that bluff and deception are part of the art of administration.[25] Even if no open support has been given to such an approach up to now, it would be easy to substantiate the fact that this has been going on for a long time. The problem is only to use this device rationally – not just to cover up for administrative inefficiencies.[26]

23 / A. O. Hirschman, "The Principle of the Hiding Hand," *The Public Interest*, no. 6 (winter 1967).

24 / "For instance planners can deliberately falsify forecasts and other signals in order to obtain certain desired reactions." See F. Martin, "The Information Effect of Economic Planning," *Canadian Journal of Economics and Political Science*, vol. xxx, no. 3 (Aug. 1964).

25 / Gross, "Objectives?" p. 195.

26 / A rational use of the hiding-hand procedure would imply that the planner takes into account the cost of being uncovered. This might create a crisis of confidence and it might lead the plannees to take defensive posi-

The Economic Council of Canada

How can one assess the operations of the Economic Council of Canada given the new twist of modern capitalism and given these rudimentary notions about the planning process?

First of all one must establish that these standards are pertinent. Indeed there has been so much double-talk on the part of the planners in the western world that it is not always too clear what they are trying to do. Shonfield has anatomized very well the difficulties of the planner in the western world: faced with the "traditional Western parliament, a non-expert body, by instinct non-interventionalist" and dealing with a plan which "is a living body of economic policy, adapting itself constantly to changing circumstances, sometimes undergoing drastic alterations in its component parts in order to secure particular objectives which come in time to acquire a new order of priority," there has almost been a "tacit consensus among the planners that it is, on the whole, best to bypass the parliamentary process."[27] The ambiguity of the goals, the vagueness of the methods really suggested and "the obfuscation of what is really going on" are all indications that planning "does not fit at all well with the existing structure of Western democratic institutions." This culminates in the question raised by Shonfield: "Who controls the planners?"

But despite all this vagueness, which is unnecessarily high in the Canadian case, it is clear that the Economic Council of Canada started its work as a planning body.[28] It is therefore not unfair to assess the performance of the Economic Council of Canada on the basis of our previous remarks, despite the fact that the personnel of the Economic Council would, in all likeli-

tions vis-à-vis the planner. Our objective is not so much to praise the hiding hand as to indicate that there are techniques to make risk-averters take risks and to make "projects appear less difficulty-ridden than they really are" and that these techniques have to be considered by the planner as part of his arsenal.

27 / *Modern Capitalism*, p. 230.

28 / The Chairman of the Economic Council of Canada described the Council's conclusions in its first annual review as ". . . a framework, a general strategy, a basic plan." See speech of J. J. Deutsch to Canadian Club, Toronto, Jan. 25, 1965, p. 6. This was brought to my attention by T. K. Rymes.

hood, no longer refer to their work as planning. This in itself is indeed worth noticing.

We shall discuss the way in which the Economic Council has dealt with each one of the three informational links suggested by our previous section. We shall make use of some of the critiques of the Council's work which have been published up to now in order to establish clearly that, if certain issues have been by-passed, it is not solely that they have been overlooked but that the Council has chosen not to regard them as sufficiently important to be worthy of discussion.

(a) The Economic Council has done a fair amount of work in collecting information about the present state of the economy. The gathering of information has often broken new grounds and it has on the whole been competent. The same cannot be said about the future states of the economy. Indeed the Economic Council has taken a very myopic view of its long-term responsibilities. One can hardly say that a five-year forecast is a sound prospective of the future. It is very surprising to find that while the Royal Commission on Health Services felt that it had to extend its time horizon until 1991,[29] the Economic Council was satisfied to look forward to 1970. This neglect of the future still constitutes one of the serious weaknesses of the Council's work.[30] Despite criticisms to this effect, the Council does not seem to be considering any serious study of the *futura*.[31]

The Council is, however, even weaker when it comes to the definition of objectives. Observers have raised questions right from the start about the foundations of the goals put forward by the Council.[32] It was quite clear from the beginning that the

29 / T. M. Brown, *Canadian Economic Growth* (Ottawa, 1964).

30 / This point was made in 1965 by S. G. Triantis in a critique of the first Annual Review. See his "Canadian Economic Development and Planning, 1963–1970," *Canadian Journal of Economics and Political Science* vol. XXXI, no. 3 (Aug. 1965), pp. 419 ff.

31 / In this connection see B. de Jouvenel, *The Art of Conjecture* (New York, 1967).

32 / "The staff of the Council would have made a valuable contribution and would have furthered the Council's purpose of seeking understanding of, and consensus on the goals presented, if it had explained the essence or content of some of these goals, as well as the reasons why, and the condi-

members of Parliament were not willing to spell out the national objectives.[33] Indeed as English points out[34] it would seem clear from the Prime Minister's statements that "the government hopes not only that the Council will help to spell out objectives and express them in more specific terms but that it will actually create a consensus in public opinion." This puts in the spotlight one of the important features of planning in modern capitalism, the role of the planner as politician.[35] As an "experiment to discern and implement a consensus on the political economy,"[36] the Council has been notoriously unsuccessful. It is not clear even at this stage that the goals put forward by the Council have even been accepted or supported by the government.

A surprising fact indeed is that there has been no serious parliamentary discussion of priorities among economic objectives and that the problem has not been taken up either by the Economic Council: it seems that in a typical Canadian way, this crucial issue has been by-passed and that most of the work done is an exercise on the pursuit of goals more or less artificially assumed.[37]

Another important deficiency of the work of the Economic Council is that it has not paid enough attention to the collection of information about the technology of the Canadian system. On the physical side this is only partly true, for there has been an

---

tions under which these goals should be pursued." Triantis, "Canadian Planning," p. 409.

33 / "Apart from expressions of general support for full employment and economic growth members of Parliament apparently did not feel equipped to detail the national objectives or to discuss an order or priority among them." English, "The Nature of Democratic Economic Planning," p. 129.

34 / *Ibid.*, p. 130.

35 / Shonfield, *Modern Capitalism*, pp. 234 ff.

36 / D. W. Slater, "Wine or Vinegar? The Canadian Economy and the Economic Council of Canada," *Canadian Banker*, vol. 74, no. 1 (spring 1967), p. 22.

37 / This is far from the back-and-forth dialogue between economically minded parliamentarians and politically sensitive planners which should preside over the definition of objectives. See Shonfield, *Modern Capitalism*, p. 235.

attempt to integrate the original forecasts of the first annual review into some sort of integrated framework. However, this is hardly sufficient for an agency which has the presumption of recommending what the "highest rank in the scale of priorities" is. The Council has been playing around at the aggregate level with data which leave something to be desired. It has made no effort to partition the economy along lines different from the standard analyses. The studies of the Council on the Canadian cyclical experience, on the contribution of education to growth, and on the trade-offs between pairs of targets have however made some contribution to our knowledge of the operations of the Canadian economy. On the social side, almost nothing has been done. The Council has paid no attention to the social technology defining the relationship between groups in Canada and about the thresholds of tolerance of each. This is in line with the relative neglect of the "equitable distribution of rising incomes" which was presented originally as one of the basic goals but which was really never given any weight in the work of the Council. Indeed an early diagnosis of Triantis about "the impression that non-regional inequalities of income are not a prime concern of the Council"[38] seems to be confirmed in the third review. In this last document, although the trade-offs between goals are discussed extensively, one would be hard put to find any reference to the relationship between these goals and the underlying social reality supporting it. This neglect of the underlying social reality and of the equity goal are indeed somewhat disturbing in the light of other activities of the Canadian government like the "war on poverty" and the priority given to equity by the recent report of the Royal Commission on Taxation.

The failure to take fully into account the importance of the social technology[39] has led the Council to unrealistic forecasts

38 / Triantis, "Canadian Planning," p. 417n.
39 / T. K. Rymes has questioned the assumptions of the Economic Council with reference to the "patience" of the consumers and the preference of society for future goods relative to present goods. See T. K. Rymes, "The Economic Council: Capital Employment and Growth," *Business Quarterly*, vol. 30, no. 4, (winter 1965), pp. 43 ff.

but more seriously to an important mishandling of the potentialities of incomes policies. Indeed the Council has discussed the problem in a rather odd way. Because Canada is not a unitary country with a tradition of considerable government intervention and because it does not have "readily available *corps intermédiaires* for implementation of the policy"[40] (i.e., because it is not easy, because it requires very imaginative adaptations of the general framework to the Canadian case, and because it demands a greater public accounting of the behaviour of economic power groups), the Council rejected the use of an incomes policy. Patience and the use of the standard tools – this is the recipe of the Economic Council.[41]

(*b*) One could complain bitterly about the lack of rigour and the lack of imagination of the Council in translating this information into a language of problem-solution and in generating a "solution" for the Canadian economic problem, were it not that we have emphasized above the great difficulty of doing so. The only thing that we can hold against the Council is that it does not seem to have spent much time attempting to perform the translation. This is a point where the great reluctance of the Economic Council to differentiate between its many roles has been rather costly.

There is nothing wrong about the many roles of the Council "as a researcher, an educator, a conscience, and an inspirer to action";[42] the problem is to make sure that the Council perceives clearly the complementarity of these roles and their specific function in the process of planning. The Council has not attempted to create a language of problem-solution and has used its many hats as a way out of this difficult problem. Such language cannot be borrowed from other countries; it represents a process

40 / Economic Council of Canada, *Third Annual Review: Prices, Productivity and Employment* (Ottawa, 1966), p. 159.

41 / *Ibid.*, p. 164.

42 / Slater, "Wine or Vinegar?" p. 22; this spectrum of roles of the Council was first emphasized by H. S. Gordon *An Assessment of the Role of the Economic Council of Canada and an Appraisal of its Second Annual Review* (Montreal, 1966). It is worth mentioning that for Gordon (p. 3) and Slater (p. 20) this spectrum of roles does not include planning.

which has to be defined in a way appropriate to the specificity of the economy and to its stage of development. Moreover, since the planning problem is not well structured and since the economics of planning is still in its infancy, in all likelihood quasi-analytical methods will have to be used. This contrasts with the apparatus apparently used by the Council which pinpoints problems but does not recognize the complexities of the development process. As Triantis puts it, in certain circumstances, "the maintenance of a flexible economy becomes an important goal for the medium run, perhaps as important as any of the other goals set by the Council."[43] Maintaining flexibility is a process-oriented activity and this is in sharp contrast with the outcome-oriented activities selected by the Council.[44]

Because of its lack of perspective and because of its refusal to adapt to the Canadian situation the planning problem faced by modern capitalism, the Economic Council has been unable to provide the political economy with a language of problem-solution. There is no reason to believe that there is a universal language which would be applicable to any situation and to any stage of development. As I have suggested elsewhere,[45] "it seems that the Economic Council does not fully realize that Canada's economic development has been and still is in part of the *extensive* sort, i.e. based on new investments and increases in the available labour force, but that the crucial issue is the transition to an *intensive* form of development based on technical change and productivity increases." Indeed the "incompleteness and waffling"[46] in the discussion of productivity by the Council is difficult to understand except in terms of its complete lack of a conceptual framework which would capture the Canadian economy as an inter-related whole. In the light of the poor performance of the Canadian economy on the productivity front, anything short of a major emphasis on the problem was bound

43 / Triantis, "Canadian Planning," p. 419.
44 / On the difference between process-oriented and outcome-oriented activities, see Ansoff, "A Quasi-Analytic Method."
45 / G. Paquet, "The Third Economic Review," *Canadian Forum*, vol. XLVI, no. 553 (Feb. 1967), p. 248.
46 / Slater, "Wine or Vinegar?" p. 20.

to be inadequate. In a recent exercise with the Verdoorn law, Nicholas Kaldor[47] has captured the problem in a most interesting way. Deriving from a cross-sectional study of the so-called advanced countries the relationship between the growth rate of productivity and the growth rate of total manufacturing production, Kaldor concludes that Canada was "one outstandingly bad performer" on the basis of what could be expected from productivity from the growth rate in total manufacturing production. Canada's rate of productivity growth "was only one half as high" as the expected figure.

Here is a very crucial deficiency of the Economic Council. For if it is rather easy to correct the faults in the data collection or gathering process, and if it is possible to eliminate the circumstances which make the definition of consensus and of meaningful goals rather difficult, it is not possible to tell the Economic Council how to perceive the problems of the Canadian economy in a proper way and how to translate these perceptions into a conceptual framework which will define the important issues to study. This would amount to telling the Economic Council how to do its job.

(c) Whatever one might think of the objectives chosen by the Council and of the conclusions and policy programs that it has arrived at on the basis of its studies, it still remains to implement these programs through some sort of *dialogue* with the opinion-moulders and the decision-makers in the system. Even within the confines of the mandate given to the Council, a whole arsenal of possibilities are open, from the spreading of information to public scolding. Very little of the possible scope for "persuasion" has however been used by the Council. Indeed it is not clear that the Council has ever perceived its role as "an inspirer to action." The Council has become an "instrument of public information," but it has never really engineered the construction of a language of persuasion which would tend to "convince" the government and the public of the advisability of following the Council's suggestions.

47 / *Causes of the Slow Rate of Economic Growth of the United Kingdom* (Cambridge, 1966), pp. 10 ff.

It is still not clear that the government accepts and supports the goals and targets put forward by the Council, and it is not clear that the Economic Council has attempted to "convince" the government any more than it has attempted to "convince" the public. The Council has been very reluctant to accept the fact that the planner has a political role. As Shonfield mentions in connection with Britain, "the combination of a politician with the pretensions of an independent expert is something which the British especially find hard to stomach."[48] This reveals a fundamental inadequacy of the western democratic institutions and it makes difficult the establishment of the crucial and necessary dialogue between experts and non-experts. In this sense the continental tradition is in advance of its time in accepting "the paid public official who slips into the occasional political role."

The problem has been faced more realistically in the United States where Congress provides a forum for a continuous dialogue between politicians and technocrats on a large number of issues, and where the migration of experts in and out of the parliamentary and administrative sides has made the "flow of power towards the executive"[49] less painful. In Canada the memories of the Coyne affair seem to have traumatized our technocrats, and this explains in part the reluctance of the Council to move into such a controversial role.

In its relation with the public, the Council has often taken the limitations of the planning techniques as an alibi to explain its inaction. In this connection, the discussion of incomes policy in the third review is very illuminating. The Council seems to be piling up the difficulties on the one side and the uncertainties of the benefits on the other, but nowhere does one find any attempt to produce imaginative solutions to circumvent these difficulties or to define the optimum signalling system which would provide an alternative to "periodic exhortations" and "public scolding," tools considered to be ineffective.

Too often the crucial problem of determining what is the optimal level of coercion to be used by the state has been hidden under incantations. Indeed the state "uses coercion to make us

48 / *Modern Capitalism*, p. 234.   49 / *Ibid.*, p. 236.

perform particular actions";[50] it is therefore not a matter of principle but rather the problem of an economic good which is rarely discussed in the literature.[51]

Indeed the selection of a system of instructions and incentives which would ensure the implementation of the plan at minimum physical, human, and informational costs defines the degree of centralization of the system. This choice constitutes the most important problem faced by any economy moving toward planning,[52] and it would be unwise to accept it as given. We have on the other hand no mechanism which would seem in a position to make such a choice: the insistence on the costs of coercion and on the uncertainties and difficulties of certain types of instructions and incentives is usually a technique to stick to the only tool that the conventional wisdom allows a democratic planner to use, the spread of information. Our contention is that "the spread of information" is neither here nor there unless we specify fully the nature of the messages to be sent to whom and the intention behind the sending of such messages. This in turn raises the problem of choice between alternative messages to obtain a given result. It is our contention that the Council has expressed a preference for broad-brush policies but at the same time has expressed great concern about "bottleneck analysis," and that it has rejected the use of incomes policy on grounds of likely ineffectiveness without imposing the same norm on the other instruments of policy of the government and of the Council. There are grave doubts about the effectiveness of monetary policy, but this has never been used as an argument to do away with it completely. The Council itself is greatly in need of some study of the effectiveness of the tools that it has used until now. Such a performance assessment might lead to drastic revisions of the Council's views on economic administration.[53]

50 / F. A. Hayek, *The Constitution of Liberty* (Chicago, 1960), chap. 9.

51 / An interesting exception is Francois Perroux, *Economie et Société* (Paris, 1960) where coercion is discussed as any other economic good or "bad."

52 / G. Paquet, "The Structuration of a Planned Economy," *Canadian Slavonic Papers*, vol. VII (May 1966).

53 / A most fascinating study of the performance of a wide-ranging system of instructions and incentives has been presented in J. Kornai, *Overcentralization in Economic Administration* (London, 1959).

Suggestions for Refurbishment

The Economic Council of Canada has been marking time. It was announced in the spring of 1967 that the chairman would leave the Council sometime in 1968. This meant that the Council was really stalled for one year. This raises two questions: Why did the chairman leave the Council during this period of construction? What sort of rejuvenated institution does the future hold in store for us? It seems, however, that this period of transition offers an appropriate opportunity to reflect on the possible forms that a refurbished set of institutions might take.

(a) Somebody has to discern a consensus. It is fairly important to recognize that the Economic Council of Canada does not seem to be equipped to do this. The dialogue between the Council and the public is non-existent: the chairman has been satisfied to issue his report every year and to spread the gospel at club luncheons. This is a monologue, not a dialogue. The Council sends the messages, but it does not wait for the answer. It is hardly satisfactory to know that the Council reads a few social indicators before making its suggestions.

What we need is a forum for all the individuals and groups in the system to meet and discuss the nature of the goals and objectives to be pursued. What we need is a Council of Social Values.[54] Up to now the closest thing that we have had to such a piece of social machinery has been the Senate Committees. For instance, the Special Committees of the Senate on Aging or on Consumer Prices have provided a forum for discussion on issues of great interest to the community. However, these Committees have had to work on a shoe-string budget and have not been able to call on as many experts as would have been required. It would seem that a refurbishment of the Senate in order to make it into a Council of Social Values providing a forum for discussion by individuals, groups, and technical experts on the goals to be pursued would provide for a much better apparatus to generate the goals and objectives of the planner.

54 / The suggestion of a Council of Social Values of a more restricted sort was put forward by Alvin H. Hansen, *Economic Issues of the 1960's* (New York, 1960), p. 91. It was also mentioned in the *Final Report of the Special Committee of the Senate on Aging*, Debates of the Senate, Feb. 2, 1966, Appendix, pp. 79–80.

This would provide the right sort of locus for the integration of information contained in economic reports, budget papers, and social policy statements. Such integration has already been forcefully demanded by Bertram Gross.[55] One of the important benefits of such machinery would be to reveal how the standard goals of the policy-makers are oriented to the social scene. Since the Economic Council does not seem to be either willing or equipped to deal with the formulation of the goals and objectives of policy, this new machinery would fill the gap.[56]

(b) Although our previous suggestion might be said to provide for some discussion of the goals to be pursued, it should be clear that this is not going to dam the "flow of power to the executive." It only represents a constructive effort to streamline the democratic institutions in order to make the dialogue between the public, the technocrats, and the government much easier. The Economic Council will have to agree to be a bit more cheeky: given the goals defined by the Council of Social Values, the Economic Council will have to *suggest* and to define the targets to be used as benchmarks by the policy-makers.

To do it, the Economic Council will then have to define a strategy of research. In order to do this, the Council will have to extend its time horizon beyond the next couple of annual reviews. Moreover, the arbitrary distinctions between short and long term will have to be eliminated. It is hardly conceivable that there should be a division of labour along this line since one of the most important elements of a sound planning activity is the interaction between short- and long-term perspectives, the long-term and perspective plans guiding the short-term activity and the short-term experience helping to correct the longer-term prospects. The suggestion, put forward in the third review, of an independent agency specializing in short-term analysis so as to relieve the Economic Council of this chore is misguided. What is required is not "an additional agency of short-term economic

55 / B. M. Gross, *The State of the Nation* (London, 1966).

56 / This institution would explicitly recognize the imperfections of the political system as a mechanism for recognizing and registering the public needs. See A. Downs, *Economic Theory of Democracy* (New York, 1957). It would provide a complementary channel of communication between the public and the state.

analysis, but for agencies and programs that rival and complement the Economic Council on its own ground."[57]

The Council would therefore have to lengthen its time horizon and to indulge in some prospective thinking. As we have mentioned above, there are ways to study seriously the *futura*. However, the Council will also have to accept the fact that it cannot import its institutions. There has been a tendency in Canada to borrow the jargon and to make pleas for the transplantation of Neddy or the French indicative planning into the Canadian scene. These choices have often been made by ideologues and uninformed experts. In fact the Council has to start pretty soon a serious research program which will explode these exhortations. By the same occasion, if the Council defines a strategy of research, it might be possible for it to make use of academics at least as much as academics have made use of it. Up to now, it has never been clear whether the Council chose the studies that *it* wanted done and which had some priority or whether it has accepted suggestions from academics of what *they* wanted done.

(*c*) Our new Economic Council would also have to accept a role as politician. This, as we mentioned above, is going to be rather difficult. However, it is difficult to imagine how the Council could avoid it. The Council will have to operate at the crossroads of the preferences of the population defined by the Council of Social Values, of the ideology of the state, and of the socio-economic technology of the system.[58] Pressured by the government, the public, and the plotters, the Economic Council will have to take a stand.

Up to now, the Economic Council has refused to take such a stand. Issues like tariffs and combines have not been touched. However, it is difficult to see how, after the report of the Senate Committee on Consumer Prices, the Economic Council could ignore the latter issue any more. The Council will need some courage and some imagination. It will have to utilize the whole gamut of instruments at its disposition in order to signal the economic agents in the right direction.

Earlier we insisted on the fact that this might mean that the

57 / Slater, "Wine or Vinegar?" p. 21.
58 / G. Paquet, "L'Etat et ses choix," *Maintenant*, no. 63 (mars 1967).

planner will become some sort of "hidden" and "hiding" hand. However, it means also that the Council will agree to establish a genuine dialogue with the different groups and with other research agencies. It will also have as its major function to "convince" the government and to "convince" the public that they should act in an appropriate way. Nothing short of a genuine dialogue will ensure the appropriate interaction between the parliamentarians, the technocrats, and the public.

It will be the role of the Council to engineer the redesigning of our society by gambling on new structures and by inventing a new network of relations between the population, Parliament, and the technocrats. The actual Economic Council of Canada is hardly the body to fit the job, but then what is the use of the Economic Council if it does not perform such a function and if it does not even tend to move in this direction?

Our criterion for judging the Council is simple – its performance. We require from the Council that it be a *harmonizer*. In the face of the preferences of the people, the ideologies of the state, and the schemes of the plotters, we ask the Council to resolve the conflicts and to go beyond these conflicts by producing new ideas and new solutions. This is not easy, but this is the only genuine "economic answer" based on the contention "that there is a rational criterion by which the actions of men and the institutions of society can be judged, that social progress has consisted in this criterion being more clearly conceived and more widely and consistently applied, and that the well-being of individuals and nations depends on reason playing an increasingly important part in the direction and control of social policies."[59]

As to whether a refurbished Economic Council supported by new ideas and institutions will do it, "my hopes are as good as your fears."

59 / A. Macbeath, *Can Social Policies Be Rationally Tested?* (London, 1957), pp. 3–4.

8

A New National Policy*

MEL WATKINS

> The old National Policy served Canada in its day,
> as an instrument of nation-building and a means of
> facilitating economic growth. The challenges have
> changed and a new National Policy is required. The
> nation has been built, but its sovereignty must be
> protected and its independence maintained. A diver-
> sified economy has been created, but its efficiency
> must be improved and its capacity for autonomous
> growth increased.

NATIONAL POLICY could mean simply the policy of a national
government. But in Canada, National Policy means the Canadian
system of protective tariffs as enunciated by Sir John A. Macdonald in 1878. Both historians and economic historians have,
over time, tended to broaden the term to encompass the set of
policies pursued by the Canadian government in the late nine-

---

*It will quickly become evident to the reader that this paper is
primarily about foreign ownership. Given my association with the Watkins
Report, it must be emphasized that the views expressed in this paper are
mine. I do not speak for the government of Canada or for any other
members of the Task Force which prepared the Report, though my own
views have benefitted greatly from my association with the latter.

The leading quotation is from Canada, Privy Council Office, *Foreign
Ownership and the Structure of Canadian Industry: Report of the Task
Force on the Structure of Canadian Industry* (Ottawa, 1968), p. 415,
known popularly as the Watkins Report.

teenth and early twentieth centuries in the interests of promoting
economic development – tariffs, railway subsidies and all-Cana-
dian transcontinentals, cheap land, and an open door to immigrants.[1] But few would deny that the tariff was central to the
strategy of promoting Canadian industrialization; certainly it has
been the prime issue in the debate over economic nationalism, or
economic independence, that reached an early peak in the
campaign of 1878 and has gone on ever since.

Among academics, a serious difference of opinion persists to
the present day about the efficacy of the National Policy.
Historians seem to be virtually unanimous in their view that the
tariff was an invaluable instrument of nation-building and that
economic nationalism was necessary to political independence
and the creation of a national economy. Economists, on the other
hand, have tended to imply at least that the National Policy, by
lowering the standard of living, weakened the material base on
which political independence must stand and on which continuing
economic growth must be based.[2] Economic historians, including
this writer, have not been fully identified with either camp. Their
most articulate spokesman on the tariff has vehemently attacked
it for its evil effects on the quality of Canadian life while nevertheless providing a rationale for it by arguing that it fulfilled its
mercantilist (but misguided) goal of creating a larger population
and aggregate income in Canada.[3]

There would be general agreement, however, that the National

1 / A key article in this respect is V. C. Fowke, "The National Policy –
Old and New," *Canadian Journal of Economics and Political Science*,
vol. 18, no. 3 (Aug. 1952), pp. 271–86; reprinted in W. T. Easterbrook
and M. H. Watkins, *Approaches to Canadian Economic History*, Carleton
Library, (Toronto, 1967).

2 / I have previously dealt with this difference in interpretation in
"Economic Nationalism," *Canadian Journal of Economics and Political
Science*, vol. 32, no. 3 (Aug. 1966), pp. 388–92, in the process of reviewing
an excellent documentation of the historian's position presented in Robert
Craig Brown, *Canada's National Policy, 1883–1900: A Study in Canadian-
American Relations* (Princeton, 1964). The boldest statement of the
economist's position is Harry G. Johnson, *The Canadian Quandary*
(Toronto, 1963).

3 / The reference is to John H. Dales. See in particular his *The
Protective Tariff in Canada's Development* (Toronto, 1966).

Policy, in terms of its relevance, is now a thing of the past. While there is still immigration to Canada, the great population-absorbing frontiers are closed. The railway is now the old technology and its potential for nation-building exhausted – though it may have untapped potential for urban and inter-urban passenger transport. The protective tariff clearly lingers on and is far from irrelevant to the contemporary economy and polity. Nevertheless, it is a remnant from the past in the important sense that the Canadian government has been consistently committed to multilateral tariff reduction since the Second World War as part of a broader commitment to multilateralism. Differences of opinion among Canadians seem largely to be with respect to the rate at which the tariff should be abolished, and the manner – unilaterally, bilaterally, multilaterally, or selectively by sector. The vanguard of the abolitionists has been the economists, while Ottawa has preferred to let other countries set the pace toward multilateral free trade and has been intrigued by selective arrangements, such as that with the automobile industry.

There are, then, no longer any hot advocates of tariff protection. In so far as tariffs are its content, economic nationalism is hardly a viable creed. But history does not stand still and so it is that the central issue of economic independence today, pro and con, is foreign ownership.

Now foreign direct investment – foreign investment that carries with it ownership and control – is not a new phenomenon in Canada. Indeed, its roots were firmly planted in the period of the old National Policy. The Canadian tariff segregated the Canadian market and induced industrialization behind its wall to serve that market. Foreign firms, previously exporting to Canada, now found it necessary to shift production to Canada. Specifically, Macdonald's protective tariff induced a spurt in branch plants, particularly American-controlled subsidiaries, in Canada. The call implicit in the tariff to bring forth entrepreneurship to meet new opportunities in the Canadian market fell frequently on foreign ears. In sum, the tariff created Canadian industry, but not necessarily Canadian entrepreneurship, and hence not necessarily industry under Canadian ownership and control.

162 / Agenda 1970

The full implications of this point have largely escaped attention by Canadian academics. Historians, including economic historians, have not addressed themselves in a serious way to the question of why the tariff created Canadian industries but not Canadian firms. Some credit for the existence of these industries must clearly be given to the expansive drive of American corporations; as they spread nationally in the late nineteenth century, some spill-over across the northern border was presumably inevitable. But to some extent those corporations flowed into a vacuum resulting from an entrepreneurial failure in Canada, a deficiency existing in spite of the St. Lawrence merchants who had emerged around the fur trade and who have been so much praised by Canadian historians.[4] Economists, in Canada and elsewhere, have judged the tariff in terms of its effects on economic efficiency and have had little of a convincing nature to say about its effects on economic growth. In particular, there has been a curious reluctance to recognize that national economic development – within the capitalist framework – requires domestic entrepreneurs, or a native bourgeoisie, to lead the process of growth.[5] While economic historians have generally been somewhat more realistic, Canadian economic historians have learned so much by focusing on the commodity – the so-called staple approach associated in particular with the writings of Harold Innis[6] – that other approaches, particularly the entrepreneurial, have never been pushed far enough to be credible alternatives.[7]

It is true that one of the most honoured themes of Canadian historiography, including economic history, has been that the

4 / See in particular, D. G. Creighton, *The Empire of the St. Lawrence* (Toronto, 1956).

5 / Two possible reasons for this bias of economists in general are, first, the mechanistic, non-institutional nature of neo-classical economics, and, second, the Marxist overtones of recognizing the critical role of capitalists in capitalist developments.

6 / See in particular his *The Fur Trade in Canada* (Toronto, 1930, 1956) and *The Cod Fisheries* (Toronto, 1940, 1954).

7 / The leading exponent of entrepreneurial history in Canada has been W. T. Easterbrook. See, for example, his "Long Period Comparative Study: Some Historical Cases," *Journal of Economic History*, vol. 17 (Dec. 1957), pp. 571–95.

state has played an important role in promoting and shaping Canadian economic development, that, as it were, the national government has played the leading role.[8] In this historical scenario, the deficiencies of private entrepreneurship have been compensated for by public entrepreneurship. But the point has clearly been exaggerated, as the extent of the actual reliance on foreign entrepreneurship attests. It would be more accurate to argue that a national government allied with the private élite was committed to use the state to create economic development, but not at the risk of weakening élite control; high tariffs and lavish railway subsidies expressed the limits of political action, while, significantly, education, particularly business schools, and freer banking – which might have facilitated the rise of new domestic entrepreneurs – were neglected. It can be argued that the Canadian government, rather than being praised for what it has done, should be chastised for what it has failed to do. More public entrepreneurship, in its own right and to stimulate private entrepreneurship, was needed to fill the vacuum which was created by the deficiencies of private entrepreneurship and which was filled by foreign, particularly American, entrepreneurship.[9]

The economist's critique of the tariff, and the old National Policy, needs to be re-examined in these terms. The problem with the tariff was not that it was too much, but rather that it was too little. Instead of creating a Canadian bourgeoisie capable of leading Canadian growth it tended to create only an emasculated bourgeoisie satisfied to manage a branch-plant economy.[10] The tariff, as it were, created "infant industries," but not "infant

8 / For the best development of this theme, see H. G. J. Aitken, "Defensive Expansion: The State and Economic Growth in Canada" in Aitken, ed., *The State and Economic Growth* (New York, 1959), reprinted in Easterbrook and Watkins, *Approaches to Canadian Economic History.*

9 / For a fuller development of this argument, though seriously deficient of hard research, see my "The 'American System' and Canada's National Policy," *Canadian Association of American Studies Bulletin*, winter 1967.

10 / This theme is brilliantly argued, albeit without new historical research, in Kari Levitt, *The New Mercantilism: The Case of Canada* (mimeo, 1968). A similar argument, in terms of barriers to entry of Canadian firms consequent on the entry of foreign firms, is implicit in Kenneth Wyman, *Non-Resident Control and the Structure of Canadian Industry: Case Studies* (mimeo, 1967).

firms."[11] And foreign firms, once attracted in by the tariff, had a vested interest in its perpetuation, while their very presence inhibited the emergence of Canadian firms.

To the extent that one is willing to accept the view presented here – that a successful national policy, including tariff policy, should have created Canadian entrepreneurship capable of dominating the Canadian economy – then the prime task of the old National Policy is yet to be completed. The burden of this paper is that this should be seen as the central task of a new National Policy, and that other aspects of policy, including tariff policy, should be framed in this light.

The Costs of an Emasculated Bourgeoisie

Let us now put foreign ownership at the centre of the stage. We must begin by recognizing that foreign ownership of Canadian economic activity is not simply a phenomenon induced by the Canadian tariff. This is true in two important senses. On the one hand, there is the straightforward fact of foreign ownership of much of Canada's resource industries.[12] These industries, being export-oriented, do not owe their existence or their ownership to the Canadian tariff. Rather, they exist because of Canadian endowments and foreign demand, and tend to fall under foreign control as a means to ensure access to the foreign market, that is, the owner of the firm is typically the buyer of its output.

The consequences of this, in terms of the thesis being argued, are very significant. Resource industries are, after all, the source of the staple exports which remain, down to the present day, the leading sectors and pace-setters in Canadian economic growth.[13]

11 / This point is implicit in a discussion for restrictions on foreign owners, rather than a high tariff, to induce Canadian entrepreneurship by Stephen Hymer, "Direct Foreign Investment and the National Economic Interest" in Peter Russell, ed., *Nationalism in Canada* (Toronto, 1966).

12 / For a comprehensive treatment of this phenomenon, see H. G. J. Aitken, *American Capital and Canadian Resources* (Cambridge, Mass., 1961).

13 / For a fuller development of this argument, see R. E. Caves and R. H. Holton, *The Canadian Economy* (Cambridge, Mass., 1959), part I; see also my "A Staple Theory of Economic Growth," *Canadian Journal of Economics and Political Science*, vol. 29, no. 2 (May 1963), pp. 141–58, reprinted in Easterbrook and Watkins, *Approaches to Canadian Economic History*.

Such is the role of foreign trade, particularly in the early stages of economic growth, in virtually all countries, that it can be argued that to permit widespread foreign ownership of export industries is seriously to inhibit the creation of a domestic entrepreneurial class and thereby to reduce significantly the possibility of auto-nomous national development.[14] Admittedly, the case for domestic ownership of export industries is one of degree, for there is no gainsaying that foreign ownership facilitates access to foreign markets, though at the loss of marketing flexibility in the long run. But at least in some cases, domestic ownership is likely to prove feasible – provided the attempt is made – and the major benefit, usually neglected by economists, of facilitating domestic entrepreneurship would thereby be reaped. The present high level of foreign ownership of Canadian resources strongly suggests that Canadian policy, both at the federal and provincial levels, has been insufficiently directed toward this goal.

The second important reason why it is wrong to attribute foreign ownership in Canada simply to the Canadian tariff is that it ignores the very significant institutional innovations that are represented by the evolution of the modern, and above all the American, corporation.[15] At the same time as the railway was creating a new potential for Canadian industrialization, it was also creating the American giant corporation capable of exploiting the national market shaped by the railroads. The proximity of Canada and the tendency of American businessmen to regard Canada as not a foreign country facilitated the spread of the American corporation across the Canadian border. The innova-tion of the corporation organized along functional lines in the late nineteenth century was followed successively in the twentieth century by the innovation of the multidivisional corporation

14 / From an analytical perspective, we need a "theory" of economic growth which effectively weds the Ricardian theory of comparative ad-vantage with the Marxian theory of the leading role of the bourgeoisie. Given the demonstrated efficacy of the staple theory in explaining Canadian historical development, an important topic awaiting serious research is the effect of different staples in facilitating, or inhibiting, Canadian entrepreneurship.

15 / See Alfred D. Chandler, Jr., *Strategy and Structure: Chapters in the History of the American Industrial Enterprise* (Cambridge, Mass., 1962, paperback 1966).

organized along product lines and the multinational corporation as an integrated entity producing in a number of countries. The latter has grown enormously since 1945, and most close students of this phenomenon are predicting continuing expansion.

To recognize these facts is to realize that no set of feasible Canadian policies could – or should – have tried to stop the entry of American corporations into Canada. The point is again one of degree. It is likely that the tariff acted to increase the extent of American ownership of Canadian manufacturing, but it is difficult to see how the absence of the tariff would have eliminated it. Rather, it would seem, along lines previously argued, that the basic determinants, from the Canadian side, were the deficiency of Canadian entrepreneurship and the failure to use public policy to encourage Canadian entrepreneurship and discourage foreign ownership.

It is, then, the combination of the Canadian tariff, Canadian resource endowments relative to American resource needs, and the entrepreneurial drive of the American corporation relative to Canadian entrepreneurial deficiencies which account for the present place of foreign, and particularly American, ownership in the Canadian economy. The extent of foreign ownership and control is too well known to require detailed presentation in this paper.[16] Suffice it to say that foreign corporations in 1963 owned more than half of Canadian manufacturing industries and almost two-thirds of mining and smelting and petroleum and natural gas, and that that ownership was predominantly American. Not surprisingly, the opening sentence of the Watkins Report reads "The extent of foreign control of Canadian industry is unique among the industrialized nations of the world."

In the language of the economists, foreign direct investment creates both benefits and costs for host countries such as Canada.[17] While the economic benefits resulting from our easier access to

16 / For the most recent detailed statistics, see Dominion Bureau of Statistics, *The Canadian Balance of International Payments 1963, 1964 and 1965 and International Investment Position* (Ottawa, 1967); for a summary of the present position based on DBS data, see Watkins Report, pp. 5–13.

17 / The cost-benefit approach pervades the Watkins Report.

foreign technology, capital, entrepreneurship, and markets are difficult to measure with precision,[18] it is clear that they are positive and have made a substantial contribution to Canada's present high standard of living.

But there inheres in the process of reaping potential benefits from foreign ownership a variety of costs. One of these, much emphasized by the Watkins Report, is a simple failure to get as large benefits as possible because of inappropriate industrial policy in Canada. In particular, benefits are emasculated by the absence of sufficient competition in Canada to keep costs and prices down. There is a large literature by Canadian economists lending support to the view that this phenomenon is primarily attributable to the combination of a high tariff and a weak anti-combines policy. The possibility that the cost *inheres* in foreign investment in so far as the American industrial structure is imported into Canada, with a consequent proliferation of firms of less than optimal size, is less frequently admitted. But the basic fact underlying these arguments that is almost never made explicit is the deficiency, quantitative and qualitative, of indigenous Canadian firms. Foreign firms are not compelled to be efficient by the presence of efficient Canadian firms, and barriers to entry from foreign firms are low because of the absence of established and viable Canadian firms. Rather, foreign firms occupy markets and create higher barriers to entry for domestic firms, thereby inhibiting Canadian entrepreneurship. In this sense, the major "cost" of foreign ownership is not the emasculation of benefits *per se* but the emasculation of the Canadian bourgeoisie.[19]

It seems almost redundant to add that political consequences inhere in this economic nexus. At the first level of analysis –

18 / For a heroic attempt to quantify benefits, see R. G. Penner, "The Benefits of Foreign Investment in Canada, 1950–56," *Canadian Journal of Economics and Political Science*, vol. 32 (May 1966), pp. 172–83; see also various sections of the Watkins Report.

19 / The essence of the situation is embodied in the Canadian-American Committee, where Canadian executives of American-controlled firms and their American "counterparts" preach to themselves – and to others silly enough to listen – the benefits of emasculation. It lies beyond the confines of the paper to explain why Canadian union leaders also participate in this farce.

again providing a basic theme for the Watkins Report and drawing particularly on the thinking of Stephen Hymer and Abraham Rotstein[20] – foreign investment implies control by large foreign-based corporations with a consequent tendency for the locus of decision-making to be outside the host country and to be more susceptible to the policy of the home government than the host government. Key decisions relevant to Canadians are made by Americans in board rooms in New York and conference rooms in Washington. But the basic fact is Canadian complicity in this arrangement consequent on the nature of a Canadian élite dominated by its emasculated business class. The Canadian bourgeoisie is fit only to live in a concessionary economy and the Canadian economy has explicitly taken on that character. Faced with the American interest equalization tax and American balance-of-payments controls on direct investment, Canada has sought "special status" at the cost of further diminishing its credibility as an independent country and further increasing its vulnerability to American retaliation – meaning chiefly American indifference to Canadian pleading – in the event of any Canadian initiative deemed unfriendly by Washington.

What kinds of economic policy have been proposed, particularly by Canadian economists, and, up to a point, practised, in the midst of these events? What may we already have by way of a new national policy? Essentially two things: monetary-fiscal policy and industrial policy. The former implies, following Keynes, the manipulation of the money supply and government spending and taxation in pursuit of the goal of full employment without inflation. While the Canadian government apparently committed itself to Keynesianism in the White Paper of 1945, its willingness to translate rhetoric into practice was slow and un-even. The major (perhaps only) contribution of the Carter Report of the Royal Commission on Taxation in 1967 may be simply that Keynes' *General Theory*, albeit as refined and emas-culated by (liberal) neo-Keynesians, has now been translated

20 / Hymer's work is summarized in his article in *Nationalism in Canada* cited in note 11; the same book contains a statement of Rotstein's position in his article "The 20th Century Prospect: Nationalism in a Technological Society."

into the Canadian vernacular. Unfortunately, the major contribution of the Economic Council of Canada in specifying the trade-off between the level of unemployment and the rate of price increase in Canada has been to show that the relevant variable is the performance of the American economy.[21] So far as pretensions to an independent monetary policy are concerned, Canada has been described as the 13th Federal Reserve District, and such are the constraints on fiscal policy that an increase in taxes to control inflation in Canada, as in the supplementary budget in the fall of 1967, is likely to leave Canadian prices unchanged, since the latter depend on the American price level, while at the same time increasing unemployment in Canada.[22] Monetary-fiscal policies remain important weapons to facilitate Canadian growth along the American growth path, but a neo-Keynesian National Policy – "let the price system work and lean against cyclical winds" – must not be confused with policies designed to create, or even maintain, Canadian independence vis-à-vis the American system. More bluntly, the capacity of the Canadian government to create jobs and keep inflation under control is negligible.

Canadians, aided and abetted by the Economic Council, have discovered a productivity gap between Canada and the United States – that is, that Canadians are on the average poorer than Americans – and have rationalized a set of industrial policies intended to rationalize Canadian industry in terms of its structure and performance: more and better education, particularly in management and vocational skills; more research and development; an effective anti-combines policy; and, above all, tariff reduction. Industrial policy, so conceived, has serious limitations, both of omission and of commission. Notably absent is any policy toward foreign ownership other than the open door. Even when we are faced with the hard fact that Canadian industry is a

21 / Economic Council of Canada, *Third Annual Review: Prices, Productivity and Employment* (Ottawa, 1967), and the Council staff study, "Price Stability and High Employment: The Options for Canadian Economic Policy: An Econometric Study," by R. G. Bodkin, E. P. Bond, G. L. Reuber, and T. R. Robinson.

22 / This is a one-sentence summary of a half-hour CBC TV interview of Professor Robert Mundell of the University of Chicago at the time of the supplementary budget.

miniature replica of American industry, it is steadfastly insisted that this results from the Canadian tariff and would disappear were the latter removed. The Economic Council has gone so far as to list *seven* factors which cause limited specialization within Canadian manufacturing without managing to stumble across foreign ownership.[23] Errors of commission, while less blatant, are nevertheless real. There is a failure to recognize that the neglect of R & D and of education are predictable symptoms of an emasculated bourgeoisie. There is a failure to see that a more vigorous Canadian anti-combines policy might inhibit the emergence of stronger Canadian firms able to challenge effectively the American-based giants and that, in any event, to move Canadian policy closer to American policy is not to guarantee real competition (the latter hardly being the most conspicuous feature of American capitalism).

Above all, there is a failure to recognize the limitations of tariff reduction as a policy weapon – for at least five reasons. First, in so far as the Canadian tariff has increased the population-sustaining capacity of the Canadian economy, the elimination of the tariff might reduce that capacity. To force emigration in the name of efficiency was widely practised by industrializing Europe in the nineteenth century but is curiously archaic as a twentieth-century policy. Second, to argue that lowering the Canadian tariff would increase competition in Canada *via* import competition is to ignore the extent to which the importers would be affiliates of Canadian firms whose pricing decisions are not predictable from assumptions of atomistic competition. Third, the tariff is an instrument of government policy and as such has virtue – that is, no government faced with a number of goals unthinkingly abandons a policy instrument. Economists advocating free trade, free capital movements, and, following Carter, a neutral tax system[24] may be (unintentionally) weakening the

23 / *Fourth Annual Review: The Canadian Economy from the 1960's to the 1970's* (Ottawa, 1967), pp. 155–56.

24 / For a critique of the Carter Commission (Royal Commission on Taxation) *Report* in these terms, see Stephen H. Hymer and Melville H. Watkins, "The Radical Centre – Carter Reconsidered," *Canadian Forum*, June 1968.

capacity of the federal government, already hamstrung by the constitution, to pursue certain national objectives. Fourth, while tariff reduction would provide some incentive to rationalize Canadian industry – indeed, in some cases at the risk of otherwise perishing – it does not in itself provide the means, be it capital, entrepreneurship, or planning, necessary for rationalization. Finally, while the tariff facilitates rationalization, given the existing extent of foreign ownership, it must do so within multi-corporations and in a manner appropriate to their mode of operation. When foreign-based firms rationalize their Canadian operations, the decisions will be made in head offices outside Canada, and a pattern of specialization is likely to be adopted that will require more parent company control for the indefinite future. This point provides an answer to those people who sense that free trade must have political costs, but have difficulty speci-fying the channels of political influence. If fewer decisions are made in Canada by Canadians, *that* is a political cost – and this could very easily happen under free trade unless there is a strong national government.

There is undoubtedly a case for rationalizing the Canadian tariff structure, but only as part of a broader national policy. In general, the set of monetary-fiscal policy and industrial policy now widely supported in Canada have not interfered with, but rather have probably facilitated, the recent drift toward continentalism.

Although free traders have had too easy a time in this country recently, it is nevertheless true that a new national policy must centre on foreign ownership rather than the tariff; the beginning, but hopefully not the ending, would be to implement the proposals of the Watkins Report – if not its letter, at least its spirit. There is a need to increase the economic benefits from foreign ownership – by rationalizing the structure of Canadian industry, by proper taxation, by Canadian participation in ownership (including minority shares). There is a need to decrease political costs by setting up Canadian legal and administrative machinery to coun-tervail the intrusion of United States law and practice with respect to trade with certain communist countries, anti-trust procedure, and balance-of-payments guidelines and controls imposed on direct-investment firms. Above all, however, the burden of this paper is that things must be done to promote domestic entrepreneurship, private and public, the creation of the Canada Development Corporation being an obvious first step.

To come to terms with foreign ownership would cause Canadians to view other policy objectives and instruments in a more realistic light. The present obsession with increasing Canadian productivity might be exploited, but "rationalization" should be recognized for what it should be – that is, "economic planning" – and the existence of alternative modes of rationalization recognized. There is no need for Canadian industrial policy to operate solely within rules imposed by the multinational (American) corporations. If the object of the exercise is to rationalize Canadian industry *under Canadian control* – and the economic and political arguments for the latter are strewn throughout this paper – then rationalization causing each Canadian firm to specialize vis-à-vis its American parent, thereby locking the Canadian industrial structure more tightly into the American industrial structure, must be spurned in the interest of promoting mergers within Canada which would create Canadian-based giants capable of surviving in a world of American-based giants.[25]

Other instruments of policy would also fall into perspective. Further special exemptions from United States monetary and commercial policies should be avoided if at all possible. Tariff reduction should be seen as part of a policy of economic planning rather than as a chapter in the theology of economic liberalism. And anti-combines policy should be revised in such a way as not to inhibit Canadian firms from growing to challenge American firms, at home and abroad.

Just as the old National Policy had extra-economic implications in terms of nation-building, so would a new National Policy of the sort being sketched here. The failure to limit American extraterritoriality via the medium of the American subsidiary

25 / It might then develop that American extraterritoriality via American anti-trust law, by inhibiting American-owned subsidiaries in Canada from participating in such rationalization programs, will have to be recognized for the serious problem that it is.

constrains the exercise of an independent foreign policy in Canada and thereby limits an essential component of modern nationhood. Canada will be in a most anomalous position should Ottawa succeed in diplomatic recognition of China while our major corporations which happen to be American-controlled face formidable obstacles from Washington in trading with China; it would be intolerable to have a major Canadian initiative in the direction of co-existence diminished in this fashion.

It would be dangerous to pretend that the problem of national unity could be solved in Canada by coming to terms with foreign ownership, but there is good reason to believe that unity would be fostered, not hindered, by so doing. It is inherent in the nature of foreign power to divide and rule and American corporations are not able to escape from this compulsion. Regions within Canada are understandably concerned to get their fair share of foreign-controlled industry and hence to compete among themselves to the extent of their *laissez-faire* policies. Only a *national* policy is feasible, and to make common cause against foreign encroachments can be a satisfying component of nationalism. Nor is it unrealistic to argue that Quebec, as it enters a more advanced stage of capitalism, would find Canada a more attractive country to which to belong if Canadian capitalists could be taken seriously. For the new generation of French-Canadian technocrats and capitalists, it would seem important to have Canadian institutions, private as well as public, in which they can not only speak their own language but pursue their own industrial ambitions.

It has become customary to view the political dimension of policies toward foreign ownership as meaning that independence would create costs in terms of lowering the standard of living. But the dichotomy between political independence and economic benefits may be false – at least in the long run. The extent of foreign ownership of Canadian economic activity has meant the creation of a branch-plant economy in Canada. A branch plant is not where the action is, in terms of new products, technologies, and ideas; and neither is a branch-plant economy. Insufficient attention has been devoted to the inherent limitations, in terms of potential for economic growth in a world of constant innovation, of a branch-plant economy. A distinction is sometimes made by economists concerned with the poor countries between economic growth (rising per capita income within an existing institutional shell absorbing foreign technology but not generating its own) and economic development (the institutional transformation of the economy as a precondition for autonomous and sustained growth). Considerations of this type have led Kari Levitt to label Canada as the richest underdeveloped country in the world. Development would consist of substituting a native bourgeoisie for a foreign-dominated bourgeoisie.

But the most important political dimension of a new National Policy would be the simple need to assume the burden of the old National Policy of "defensive expansion"[26] vis-à-vis the United States. As the American industrial system has evolved into the military-industrial complex, the threat to survival, both personal and national, has crossed new thresholds. "Defence" must mean what it says, rather than be an antiseptic word for complicity. "Expansion" must mean not rising standards of living at any political price, but rather the nurturing and sustaining of Canadian institutions and values that may bend but not necessarily break in the face of America's erratic swings from remaking the world in its own image to withdrawing into the isolation of fortress America and leaving the rest of the world to go it alone. The latter possibility is rapidly becoming a probability and Canada may shortly have to assume the burden of its own destiny by default.

Realities

It has not been the intention of this paper to insist that a new National Policy should ignore all matters that do not relate to foreign investment. It is right to care about poverty, housing, and pollution. But the term National Policy had already been appropriated to describe economic independence and it seemed legitimate to build on that tradition.

Nor has it been intended to exaggerate the efficacy of a new National Policy. It is central to this paper that multi-national

26 / The term is H. G. J. Aitken's; see note 8.

corporations do run the "free world" and that talk about the *independent* power of the technocrats is more a future possibility (not necessarily desirable) than a present reality. To know where the power lies is to know that it will be difficult to do much about it. Nevertheless, it seemed better to search for possibilities rooted in our history rather than play at being blind men or engage in flights of fancy.

Nor, finally, has it been intended to come down too crudely on the side of Canadian capitalism. It is necessary, however, to "tell it like it is." Canadian reformers have been hung up too long by refusing to recognize that their dislike of the Canadian establishment (to use their euphemism) only plays into the hands of the American establishment. A capitalist is also a citizen and liberals who argue that a capitalist is merely a capitalist are vulgar marxists unwilling to face the reality of nationalism. Canada is committed to the capitalist path of development, and, in the final analysis, Canadians should prefer home-brewed capitalists over alien capitalists. If Canada is to be a capitalist country – and the prospects for change in this respect are hardly part of the agenda for 1970 – then a case can be made for a *Canadian* bourgeoisie whose competence and initiative are of a high order.

To argue for a policy of Canadian independence is not to neglect the urgency of social reform for Canada. The tasks of redistributing income, alleviating poverty, disposing of the benefits of the new technology in a more democratic way – none of these are precluded by focussing on economic independence. Indeed, it is difficult to see how Canadians can humanize the operations of an economy over which they have lost control. What does it mean to argue that Canadian social reformers should forget about economic independence so as to focus more clearly on the welfare state[27] when Ottawa appears to lack the simple capacity independently to create jobs and control inflation?

And to suggest that Canadian nationalism is a good in itself is not to praise nationalism but rather to insist on the need for protection from American fall-out: "[A] strong Canadian

27 / This is the favourite gambit of Carleton University economists in letters to Ottawa newspapers.

nationalism capable of reversing the absorption of this country in the United States is an essential first step towards the emergence of the kind of Canada that could possibly make some small contribution to the realization of the anti-nationalist ideal [of the establishment of the federal republic of mankind]. Canadian sovereignty is not being eroded by the republic of mankind; it is being eroded by the American Empire. A Canadian elite which permits increasing integration of this country with the United States, whether or not it does so under the cover of well meaning cosmopolitan slogans, will be serving not the interests of humanity, but those of the most powerful and possibly the most dangerous nationalism in the world. The point of Canadian nationalism is not to preserve a sovereign Canadian nation state for ever and ever no matter what, but to preserve it so long as the only unit capable of absorbing it is a larger and more terrible nationalism."[28]

28 / Gad Horowitz, "Trudeau *vs* Trudeauism," *Canadian Forum*, May 1968.

9

Centrifugally Speaking: Some Economics of Canadian Federalism

DAVID M. NOWLAN

PUZZLES HAVE SOLUTIONS, problems don't; problems have responses, and one man's response will inevitably give rise to another man's objection. No anodyne logic from an economist's armoury of professional devices will obliterate the fact that we in Canada are faced with a problem in our desire to secure some appropriate distribution of fiscal responsibilities among our various levels of government. As political, social, and economic pressures build, a piecemeal alteration in the distribution of these responsibilities takes place; this has happened in the past and will continue to happen in the future. While no disgrace should be attached to such piece-by-piece economic evolution (I confess that I distrust visionary reconstruction), we have now got what one large newspaper has called a "confused web of federal-provincial relations in the fiscal field." If we wish to avoid compounding this confusion, we should be talking, thinking, and arguing about the respective fiscal responsibilities that should fall on the federal, provincial, and municipal governments in Canada.

The current confrontation between Quebec and Ottawa has tended to obscure the fact that this problem is confederation-wide. I have no illusions that economic theory can provide an ultimate rationale for any particular distribution of power, but it can be of some help in setting goals against which our piecemeal manoeuvring may be assessed. Theory is as theory does; and theory does deal with abstractions and ideal forms. The trick is to see if these abstractions can be put to work for us.

It will quickly become evident, however, that I do not stick to my last and confine my remarks to accepted theoretical considerations in the economics of federalism. My view is that the economic responsibilities of the provinces, in both fiscal and monetary matters, should be greatly increased, and I am writing as much about this view as I am about economics. One desirable consequence of such a shift in responsibilities would be the diminished role Ontario would have in influencing the economic policies of the country. The massive economy of this province has tended to dominate federal economic policy, a current example being the move afoot to slow down the inflow of foreign capital. This of course would have little impact on an established industrialized area with easy access to Canadian savings, but it could severely harm the economies of the less developed hinterland provinces.

It is generally agreed that over the last ten years or more the economic role of the provinces has been increasing. Statistics on expenditure by various levels of government confirm this general agreement, but the extent of the shift is sometimes exaggerated. Of the total expenditure on goods and services by all levels of government, the federal government accounted for roughly 53 per cent in 1955 and only 35 per cent in 1964. Provincial-government expenditure rose from 18 per cent of the total to 23 per cent over the same period. However, if defence spending is excluded from this total, the federal share fell from 25 per cent to 21 per cent between 1955 and 1964, and the provincial share also fell, from 28 per cent to 27 per cent; the share spent by municipalities increased. Of course it is completely open for discussion what is the best way to measure relative federal-provincial economic power or influence. If transfer payments, in which educational expenditures play a large role, were included, the increasing role of the provinces would again be shown.

In what follows, I have divided my comments into three parts. The first deals with the theory of public spending and its bearing on the division of spending responsibilities among the various levels of government; the second deals with interprovincial income transfers and their impact on resource allocation and economic growth; and the third section is a comment on the potential role of the provinces in income stabilization policy. My discussion is focussed on the economics of federalism, a focus that takes as given the various political or fiscal units in Canada. This avoids the rather barren land of the pure theory of fiscal decentralization.[1]

Federalism and the Theory of Public Spending
Goods and services the use or consumption of which by one individual does not diminish the amount available to others are defined as public goods; a public park is a simple example. It is with these kinds of goods that the theory of public spending deals. The basic theorem, which was established by Professor Samuelson,[2] is that a decentralized market mechanism, a competitive market for example, is not capable of providing the best or efficient levels of public goods. This means that whenever such public goods exist a competitive market will not allocate resources in the best way.[3] If an efficient allocation of resources is our overriding goal, we are left with the prescription that public goods

1 / The homogeneity assumptions needed do not make very good fertilizer, as may be seen in an essay such as that of Charles M. Tiebout, "An Economic Theory of Fiscal Decentralization," in National Bureau of Economic Research, *Public Finances: Needs, Sources and Utilization*, (Princeton, 1961).

2 / "The Pure Theory of Public Expenditures," *Review of Economics and Statistics*, xxxvi (Nov. 1954).

3 / Formally, a best or optimal allocation of resources exists when no one person in the economy can be made better off without some other person being made worse off. To be quite strict, the theorem does not apply to public goods that have a zero cost to the society. These a competitive market would allocate efficiently; they would be free.

ought to be provided free of charge, presumably by the government for reasons mentioned below. The government should provide for general use parks, roads, emergency hospital care, national defence, museums, welfare services and so on, taking care not to exclude the agencies now in the United Appeal (except that the provision of YMCA services to businessmen might be left in private hands). The private market, which requires payment for goods and services, could not efficiently provide these goods; nor could they be provided by voluntary subscription, even if the benefits were then made freely available to society, because each individual would be inclined to undercontribute and society as a whole would have less than optimal amounts.

The actual level at which public goods and services should be provided is in general indeterminate without specifying some desired distribution of income.[4] This is where the government enters. By deciding the extent to which public goods will be provided to the public, governments at all levels must take an implicit or explicit stance on the appropriate distribution of income; there is, I assume, no other body to which we would be willing to delegate this responsibility.

To carry this line of thought one step further, I assume – or perhaps it is a definition – that the government distributes income in a socially desired fashion. If this is accepted (the only way to dispute it would be to provide a more generally accepted definition of a socially desired income distribution), it follows that if resources are allocated efficiently or optimally between the private and public sectors, there is no meaning in asking whether the appropriate (i.e. the socially desired) amounts of public goods are being provided. It is only when the allocation is inefficient that it can definitely be said that public goods are available in inappropriate amounts. Inefficiency of this sort will exist any time public goods are provided by the free market or by subscription, even if they are also provided by government. Thus, the basic public-spending theorem may be used to criticize the

4 / In other words, there are any number of different ways in which the available resources may be allocated efficiently, each one corresponding to a different distribution of income among members of the society.

government for not providing certain services that are being provided by the private sector but it cannot be used to press for an increase in or the establishment of services that are not provided privately. Of course it is open to any individual or group to lobby for additional amounts of government-provided goods or services whether the initial public-private distribution is efficient or inefficient.

The theorem is occasionally wrongly used in its reverse form. Nothing that has been said should be taken to imply that it is inefficient for the government to provide non-public goods.

It is possible to make this comment on public goods with some confidence only because the related policy goal, an efficient allocation of resources, is likely to be widely accepted. But now, even with agreement that government ought to provide public goods, the problem of dividing public-spending and revenue-raising responsibilities between the various levels of government in a federal country is much less tractable partly because the range of defensible goals is broad and partly because more than one government becomes responsible for income redistribution. Arguments favouring any given division of responsibilities may be based on considerations of national unity, constitutional absolutism, administrative efficiency or efficiency in resource allocation; or they may rest on straight paternalistic grounds. Intermingled with such more substantive principles are emotional or philosophical biases, which appear primarily as either a desire to have more centralization or a desire to have more decentralization of government functions; a centripetal bias versus a centrifugal bias. In using these labels I short-change a considerable body of writing that attempts to rationalize one or other of these positions.

A centripetal bias is manifest in the general belief that public-spending responsibilities should rest primarily with the federal government, and should be delegated to lower levels only if warranted on the ground of some substantive argument. The centrifugalist, on the other hand, argues that such responsibilities should automatically fall on the lowest level of government, unless an acceptable case can be made for moving a responsibility up one level. These biases are important primarily when the application of some substantive principle to a particular case produces a less than completely decisive outcome.

In a search for some substantive ground on which to base the allocation of public-spending rights and responsibilities among the federal, the provincial, and the municipal governments in Canada, it is natural for the economist to turn first to the already introduced notion of efficiency and to ask what might constitute an efficient allocation of these spending responsibilities. Approaching the problem this way, we may make at least an initial advance; the argument, it turns out, is in part analogous to the logic leading to the recommendation that public goods (as defined) should be provided by the government. Now, instead of having a government and a private market, we have three levels of government.

Consider this example. Part of Ontario's highway network benefits residents of other provinces. The highways provide both access routes to Ontario centres and through-routes for western residents travelling to eastern Canada and for eastern residents travelling to western Canada. If Ontario decided to charge tolls to non-residents (something in addition to gasoline taxes which introduce a general element of inefficiency affecting both resident and non-resident) for the use of through-highway routes, then some non-residents would decide not to use this Ontario service, a service which could in fact have been provided to any individual non-resident completely free of any cost to Ontario. Resources would not be allocated efficiently and this would provide an argument for having a higher-level government (the federal government) responsible for providing a highway route through the province free of charge to all Canadians.

To generalize would be to argue this way: any time a non-resident could or does benefit from, but must pay for, a provincial service that costs nothing extra to provide, resources are allocated inefficiently and this inefficiency provides an opportunity for arguing that the federal government should take over responsibility for the service. Similarly, if a municipality charged non-residents of that municipality for the use of a service that costs nothing extra to provide, one could argue that the province should take responsibility for the service and provide it free of charge to all provincial residents. The logic of this argument is the same as the logic behind the prescription that the government (*a* government, we would now say) should expand its provision of any public good that is being sold in the private market.

This particular form of the efficiency criterion for the distribution of spending responsibilities has, however, limited application. In the first place, there are few services provided, or likely to be provided, by lower-level governments (a province or a municipality) for which non-residents are charged more than residents; and secondly, an alternative to moving the responsibility for the service up one level of government is simply to abolish the discriminatory pricing against non-residents. If this latter alternative were followed, we would have public goods provided (possibly free, but at least at an equal cost to all Canadians) by a government and, as I have previously argued, there appears to be no question whether appropriate amounts of these goods or services are being provided; we take for granted that the government is providing the right amount.

But, now that we are dealing with three levels of government, can we take for granted that any one government will provide the appropriate amount of a public good or service? Consider first the efficiency aspect of this spending. With only one government to contend with, we could reasonably assume that if a group of citizens were willing to pay for the extra cost of providing additional levels of a public good but the government did not respond to this willingness, then the private market would provide the good or service. This would indicate an inefficient allocation of resources and policy could be guided accordingly. If the government were the only agent who could legally provide this service, then pressure by the citizens could be brought to bear on the government. But, to revert to the highway example, if Manitobans wanted a better through-highway in Ontario, and were willing to pay the extra construction and maintenance costs, they would have no way of pressuring Ontario into providing this better service. The Manitobans are economically disenfranchised, at least with respect to the provision of highway services in Ontario. This leads to inadequate amounts of Ontario-provided through-highways. Resource allocation is inefficient. Inefficiencies of this sort could exist any time the services provided by a lower-level government benefit without cost residents of another jurisdiction. Thus we do end up with a widely applicable efficiency criterion for the distribution of spending responsibilities.

The efficiency criterion of the previous paragraph can be strengthened by considering the income-distribution aspect of spending by lower-level governments. To take the highway example once again: if expenditures on through-highways in Ontario benefit other Canadians, why should other Canadians not bear part of the tax burden needed to finance these highways? The distribution of spending responsibilities will be inequitable (which is not the same as being inefficient) if a lower-level government is charged with providing a service that benefits residents of other jurisdictions as well as its own. Thus we can add an equity criterion to the efficiency criterion in setting up a substantive principle to guide the distribution of spending responsibilities.

In summary, if the spending of any one provincial government benefits without cost the members of another province, the spending has external or spill-over effects, and to get an efficient and equitable allocation of spending the federal government ought to take over responsibility for that particular good or service. In an economy with a hierarchy of governments we might usefully subdivide the general category of public goods into "federal-public" goods, "provincial-public" goods, and a residual category of "municipal-public" goods. Provincial-public goods cannot efficiently and equitably be provided by municipalities acting in their own interests and federal-public goods cannot efficiently and equitably be provided by provinces acting in *their* own interests.

On this basis, therefore, the federal government should clearly be responsible for such federal-public goods as national defence spending, harbour construction and maintenance, the publication of statistical material, and the administration of at least some aspects of external affairs, to mention only a few broadly dispersed functions. For reasons of administrative efficiency as well as spill-over effects, the federal government might well carry out desired public research in various scientific and technical fields. However, the spill-over argument is scarcely capable of providing justification for federal spending, including grants-in-aid (conditional grants) to lower levels of government, on, for example, parkland, local construction projects (or even national-linkage construction projects beyond a certain point), ARDA, and other regional planning projects, hospitals and technical or educational facilities. The external effects of provincial or municipal expenditures on such items are probably not absolutely nil, but I would judge that they are sufficiently small, and the goods or services sufficiently basic, that each lower level government would be as likely as the federal government to provide optimal levels of output. Such a conclusion betrays my centrifugal bias; a centripetalist might rule in favour of federal control whenever the least amount of spill-over was suspected.

A serious practical obstacle may arise in the attempt to persuade all governments concerned to accept federal responsibility even for goods or services that are clearly federal-public. The obstacle is that interprovincial income redistribution (or inter-municipal redistribution, if provincial-public goods are being considered) operates through, in part, the spending pattern of the federal government. This does not invalidate the notion that, to bring about efficiency in allocation, all responsibility for federal-public goods should fall on the federal government; but it does mean that a particular province may not favour the federal take-over of a federal-public service, because interprovincial income distribution may be altered to its detriment. In fairness to the centripetalists, I should also emphasize what is frequently neglected, that the spill-over argument in no way stands against a higher-level responsibility for what is clearly a lower-level public good.

Shared-cost arrangements between Ottawa and the provinces for joint provision of public goods may easily lead to inefficient overall amounts of such goods. Each level of government tends to regard the cost of a shared-cost program in terms of its own outlay; no decision-making body oversees the total expenditure. This will generally lead to the overprovision of a shared cost good or service, the distorting effects of which may partly be the underprovision of other provincial-public or federal-public goods. If there were only one body responsible for and paying for the regional provision of highways or medicare, it is possible that, with unchanged government expenditure in total, outlays on these items would decrease and more resources would be devoted to the public support of, for example, education, research activities or housing. With the partial vision of shared-cost programs eliminated, this allocation of resources would necessarily be more desirable.

The argument that shared-cost programs are desirable because they help establish various services at levels considered appropriate by the federal government is really an argument for the outright federal provision of the service. Such shared-cost programs influence the marginal or last dollar spent by the provinces, and not only, if at all, the initial dollars spent. It follows that the federal government is encouraging spending right up to the total level of service ultimately provided. If this is desirable, it clearly is even more desirable that the provinces leave the field to the federal government alone. The establishment of regulations imposing on the provinces a minimum level of service is a slightly different matter and may be defended on paternalistic grounds, about which I comment below.

An independent argument may be made for the federal provision of public insurance schemes such as unemployment insurance, old-age pensions, workmen's compensation, medicare provisions (if this is treated as an insurance scheme), and so on. If payments and benefits are uniform throughout the country, people can move more easily from province to province, and such freedom of movement is a desirable component of nationhood.

Aside from the economic aspects of the issue, there are other substantive points to be considered in a discussion of the distribution of spending responsibilities. These I raise and comment on very briefly just to show my own biases and not because I feel that they can be dealt with adequately in a few paragraphs.

In considering federal versus provincial responsibilities I generally disagree with centralizing arguments based on grounds of paternalism ("Ottawa knows best") or administrative efficiency. There seems little reason to suppose that the federal government can judge better than the provinces the nature and level of provincial-public services that provincial residents want. In considering the possibility that some governments might be more astute or effective in providing public services, Professor J. S. Dupré has suggested, as an example, that provincial discrepancies in the level of youth-allowance payments and loans to university students "are not likely to be tolerated" by provincial residents.[5] Not only are safeguards of this sort likely to exist if a maximum degree of decentralization occurred but also we would probably find a wider range of public services being introduced, perhaps in single provinces at first and then more widely if they appeared to be successful and desirable. I find it hard to believe that the central government would have more imagination and initiative than the ten provincial governments combined. If cross-Canada homogeneity in public services is what is desired, Professor D. V. Smiley offers reassurances here. With the decentralization of responsibilities, he argues that "as elites concerned with particular public amenities become more influential, the expectations throughout that society about the appropriate levels of particular public services will become more homogeneous."[6]

When it comes right down to the question whether or not the provinces have civil servants or politicians that are sufficiently competent to handle increased fiscal responsibilities, it seems to me that one cannot settle the question by pointing to past inefficiencies or incompetences. In any case the past record, especially in recent years in fields such as economic planning, is not by any means one-sidedly in favour of the federal government. The presumption for the future surely must be that the brilliant civil servant and the enlightened politician will go where the power lies.

Bases of administrative efficiency or paternalism as support for

5 / Canadian Tax Foundation, *Report of the 1964 Conference* (Toronto, 1965), p. 214.
6 / *Ibid.*, p. 221.

provincial control of municipal-public goods, such as welfare services and educational facilities, are, I think, much stronger. In a small municipality particularly, there may well be major gaps in representation on governing bodies; and this gap may be sufficient to require some paternalistic overseeing. I see no harm in being arbitrary in this matter,[7] in pushing, within limits, for decentralization down to the provincial level and centralization up from the municipal level.

Arguments for federal control in certain fields based on the ground of national unity leave me unconvinced, mainly because I fail to understand the meaning of the ground. Such arguments frequently seem to be no more than definitional declarations: "If Quebec takes sole responsibility for these spending fields, national unity, as we know it, will not survive." This is not a direct quotation from any person, but I think it captures the essence of a lot of talk; and it clearly does not provide us with any insights into the problem.

Unwavering devotion to the letter of the constitution does not really form a rallying point for discussions of spending responsibilities. On such responsibilities, the constitution provides for divisions on such general grounds, and leaves so much open for negotiation, that there is little support on which to hang an argument. But when notions of provincial financial independence and financial responsibility[8] are combined with fixed concepts, derived only partly from the constitution, about the division of revenue-raising rights between federal and provincial governments they lead automatically to a stance on the division of spending responsibilities; there are simply no residual degrees of freedom. It is clear that independent positions cannot be taken on both spending responsibilities and taxing rights within a framework of fiscal responsibility. If taxing rights are believed to be fixed, this determines within limits the revenue-raising powers of the various

7 / Aside from the merits of this case, being arbitrary is a convenient way to delay the day when one is computer-programmed out of a job.
8 / These are terms used by R. Dehem and J. N. Wolfe in "The Principles of Federal Finance and the Canadian Case," *Canadian Journal of Economics and Political Science*, vol. xxi (Feb. 1955). The limits within which financial or fiscal responsibility might operate are commented on in the next paragraph.

levels of government and this in turn leads to the view that the provinces, to take the current example, cannot undertake more spending, except through federal grants, because they have not got the revenue-raising capacity.

Some form of fiscal responsibility certainly should be imposed on the provinces. Although the desire for provincial income redistribution and the desire for full-employment policies are good reasons why a provincial dollar spent need not be matched by a provincial dollar raised, each province should be faced with the full opportunity cost of providing additional public goods or services; i.e., the resources used for providing them should be provincial except when the province raises outside loans or receives grants from the federal government that are intended to redistribute provincial income. But to achieve an efficient alloca-tion of resources, it is vital, I believe, not to assign taxing rights until after spending responsibilities have been decided upon, and even then the taxing arrangements should be flexible enough to leave the provincial and federal governments with the freedom to decide the levels at which they should exercise their respective spending responsibilities. Tax rental agreements result in un-necessary revenue rigidity; the 1962–67 federal-provincial fiscal arrangements provide a desirable departure from previous post-war agreements. The present tendency in Ottawa to try to come to some agreed division of the income-tax revenue between the federal and provincial governments is similarly undesirable. Ottawa's view that this division is related to the amount of control it can exercise over aggregate demand seems to me unfounded, since this control operates through absolute changes in revenue and spending and it makes no difference whether a given absolute change in spending or in taxes is 8 per cent, say, rather than 5 per cent of the total federal-government revenue.

Income Transfers, Resource Allocation and Economic Growth
Income redistribution between governments must be set by a higher-level government. It follows from the arguments of the previous section that if an efficient use of resources is to be made, transfers of money among the provinces should be in the form of unconditional grants; but, of course, this is not the only form

of provincial income redistribution. Much federal-government spending has a differential regional impact and to this extent is also a redistributive device. Such redistributive spending is not inefficient, but I have argued that it should not be undertaken except on federal-public goods or services.

Under most circumstances it is generally agreed that lump-sum income transfers among individuals do not result in an inefficient resource allocation. But where the transfers are among regional governments, the possible inter-regional migration of factors of production such as capital or labour may lead to overall national inefficiency in the allocation of these factors. The question then arises: Do attempts on the part of the federal government to equalize provincial incomes necessarily result in such inefficiency?

Professor Anthony Scott, in what turned into a debate with Professor James M. Buchanan,[9] argued that income transfers from the rich to the poor provinces in Canada impeded the movement of factors from areas of low marginal productivity, such as the Maritimes, to areas of high marginal productivity, such as Ontario. Buchanan argued that efficiency in resource allocation was best achieved by providing in all areas the same "fiscal residual," which he defined as benefits received as a result of public spending less tax costs incurred. The fiscal residual is clearly a rather hazy concept, but in broad outline I agree with Buchanan's position, even though dissenters have recently forced him to backtrack somewhat.[10]

The argument against Scott is this. Factors of production, men and capital, move from region to region in response to the prospect of greater total benefits or income. This income consists

9 / See A. D. Scott's articles "A Note on Grants in Federal Countries," *Economica*, vol. xvii (Nov. 1950), "The Evaluation of Federal Grants," *Economica*, vol. xix (Nov. 1952) and "Federal Grants and Resource Allocation," *Journal of Political Economy*, vol. lx (Dec. 1952); and J. M. Buchanan's "Federalism and Fiscal Equity," *American Economic Review*, vol. xl (Sept. 1950) and "Federal Grants and Resource Allocation," *Journal of Political Economy*, vol. lx (June 1952). John F. Graham in his book *Fiscal Adjustment and Economic Development* (Toronto, 1963) deals with this controversy at some length.

10 / See his comments in NBER, *Public Finances: Needs, Sources and Utilization*.

of two parts: money returns to the factor, which are assumed to bear some relation to marginal productivity, and services or goods provided by the public sector. To the extent that a rich region can provide higher levels of public goods relative to tax costs, resources are drawn to the region independently of marginal productivity criteria. Since efficiency in the allocation of resources requires factors to be used where their marginal productivity is highest, different provincial levels of the fiscal residual may encourage inefficient interprovincial allocation. So our desire for an efficient allocation of resources would lend support to transfers designed to equalize provincial revenues, quite aside from the fact that some degree of equalization is likely to be a federal goal in any case. The same argument may be used to support inter-municipal income transfers by the provincial governments. The tendency of industry to locate in rich urban areas, where the level of public services relative to tax costs is high, may result in inefficiencies (heightened by the many external diseconomies to an overcrowded community of having industry locate in it) that could be overcome by subsidies to poorer or smaller municipalities, with such subsidies being used either to increase the level of public services or to reduce the local tax rate.

Scott's argument has considerable currency, however, and for this reason it should be looked at more carefully. He begins with the implicit assumption that we know beforehand the desirable direction for factors to move, i.e., the direction that will lead to a more efficient allocation. Implicit in the argument of Buchanan is that we do not know this. At first glance, this latter position might seem untenable; surely it is obvious that marginal products are higher in Ontario than in the Maritimes, and that, at the very least, Ontario and not the Maritimes should form the major Canadian growth area. Frequently such a view is based on one or both of two propositions: that the regions most rich in natural resources are those that can most efficiently employ additional factors of production (this roughly is Scott's contention) or that economies of scale in production exist, and resources should therefore be channelled to established and relatively large industrial areas. The validity of the first proposition depends, first, on the relationship between the natural-resource endowment and the current use of other productive factors (a natural-resource-poor area might have a relative capital shortage, for example) and, second, on the nature of the industry under consideration. That all growth is related to natural-resource endowment is a position of geographical determinism that, unfortunately, comes easily to Canadians bred on the staple theory of economic growth. In fact, the production of natural resources is a notoriously bad indicator of economic maturity; the *consumption* of natural resources is a good indicator, but an area can consume such resources without producing them. The second proposition, that relating to economies of scale, is in its baldest form generally founded on a misunderstanding. If such economies exist this does not constitute a basis for recommending the transfer of resources from small producing units to large. To say that economies of scale exist is only to say that *average* unit costs will fall with an increase in output. For any industry, even when different firms in different locations use the same technology, the smaller firm might have lower *marginal* costs and efficiency might therefore be enhanced by moving resources from larger to smaller units.

These points strengthen the case for, or at least weaken the arguments against, increasing interprovincial equalization payments above current levels. Until the 1962–67 federal-provincial tax agreement, equalizing transfers were made on the basis of provincial per capita revenues that would result from the application of a standard tax rate on personal income, on corporation profits and on inheritances. Under the current arrangement there is a belated, half-hearted recognition that other sources of revenue should be taken into account: 50 per cent of the per capita three-year average of revenues from natural resources are now counted in deciding the level of equalization payments. A backward step was also taken, however, in that these payments are now made on the basis of the average per capita yield for all provinces rather than on the basis of the per capita yield of the richest two. The importance of natural-resource levies for some provinces is shown in data compiled by Marion Bryden in a recent Canadian Tax Foundation study: for the year 1963, 29.4 per cent of Alberta's revenues (excluding intergovernmental transfers) came from these levies, as did 10.1 per cent of Saskatchewan's revenues and 12.5 per cent of British Columbia's revenues. The Canadian average was 6.6 per cent. Small taxing bases force poorer provinces into higher levels of regressive consumption taxes. Across Canada, provinces in 1963 raised 28.7 per cent of their revenue from consumption taxes; in Newfoundland the percentage was 58.6; in Prince Edward Island, 47.8; in Nova Scotia, 41.1; and in New Brunswick, 39.2.

As well, the poorer provinces should, I think, be concerned about the drain of savings to richer, more developed regions. It is difficult to pin down a case for concern about this movement and all too easy to say that it indicates a gratifying mobility of funds in search of higher returns. Studies of the availability of capital in the Atlantic provinces have concluded that it is not, in general, more difficult for any given class of borrower to obtain funds in that area than in other provinces, and these findings have tended to produce some complacency. But the wider issue is not whether current borrowers can obtain funds, but whether steps should be taken to encourage greater entrepreneurial initiative, and hence an even greater demand for capital, in some of these areas.

I have already indicated some reasons why an outward flow of capital is not necessarily an efficient response to marginal productivity differentials. Given the conservative nature of the institutions through which these funds are channelled (and I am thinking now especially of life insurance companies and the chartered banks), one might present an even stronger case for suggesting that more risk capital should be directed to the less well-developed provinces.

I would not, however, press these arguments to include income-equalization payments to all subprovincial underdeveloped regions. The provinces provide a useful arbitrary geographic area within which attempts might be made (by the provinces) to reallocate resources in what was considered to be an efficient manner. Federal operations on resource allocation among subprovincial units leave me most unimpressed. The subsidies provided to coal producers in Cape Breton and gold producers in Northern Ontario have been nothing short of ridiculous. It is not clear that expenditures on ARDA and other federal regional redevelopment schemes are in the overall interest of the provinces in which such expenditures are made. Recently, officials from thirty-five western Ontario municipalities protested, with justification, that the federal-government designated-area scheme discriminated against their communities by not including them. In this federal scheme, eighty-one areas were designated on the bases of unemployment figures and average income levels as qualifying for grants and tax concessions. If the money for these projects was available to the provincial governments, those governments could spend it in accordance with some pre-planned design for provincial growth and we might see the end of indiscriminate support of areas with little long-run economic potential. My general position is that grants to bolster low-growth or low-income areas should be made on a provincial basis in the form of equalization or special non-tied transfers, and that incentive resource mobilization should be planned by the provinces on an intraprovincial basis.

Income Stabilization
In both the United States and Canada the bald, unadorned view that the federal government alone is responsible for counteracting cyclical income fluctuations seems to meet with little argument. As long as this is the general attitude, the provincial governments are unlikely to press for greater responsibilities in this matter because to assume them is rather invidious in an era when the desire to stamp out price increases weighs more heavily than the desire to eliminate unemployment, which means that tax increases will appear to play a larger role in government policy than tax cuts. Indeed, complete federal responsibility might be justified if unemployment and income levels across Canada moved together, if full employment in one area was matched by full employment in all other areas, and if federal action had an equal impact in all areas.

It appears to be the case, however, that a regionally differentiated fiscal policy is frequently called for. If industrial employment is taken as a current indicator of provincial business cycles (no better indicator is available at the provincial level), it may be seen that between provinces the provincial cycles are frequently out of phase. Moreover, it is well known that even where provincial cycles are in phase, the unemployment level may vary greatly between the provinces. Because Ontario is so large and so rich the situation prevailing there dominates the aggregate Canadian data on which federal economic decisions are based. This is hardly a desirable situation for the Atlantic provinces this year, Quebec that year or the Prairie provinces some other year; it is a situation that strongly suggests that the provinces should take over from the federal government a large measure of the responsibility for contracyclical policies.

If provincial responsibility in this regard were strengthened at least one desirable side benefit might accrue. Of the eleven governments acting to stabilize income and employment at least one might recognize what Ottawa seems to neglect – that in the interests of efficiency in resource allocation it is primarily, if not entirely, taxation levels and not government-spending levels that should be altered. If a government takes a stand, in some period with full employment, on the appropriate levels at which government goods and services should be provided then it is inappropriate to alter these in order to fend off inflation or deflation;[11] instead, taxation levels should be increased or decreased, the idea being that if the government is successful in its policy the desirable or previously determined distribution of output between the public and the private sectors will be achieved. If a decision is made to cut government expenditure when inflation is anticipated or add to government expenditure when a falling off of economic activity is expected, you end up with too little or too much government participation in the economy. The argument also applies to situations where the economy is inflated or deflated, but then the overriding desire to get back to some appropriate level of aggregate demand may warrant a contracyclical alteration in government spending.

11 / I suspect that an alteration in the level of government spending is popular partly because generations of policy advisers have been brought up and continue to be brought up on textbooks of elementary economics that lay great stress on the demonstration that the multiplier effect of a dollar of government spending is greater than the multiplier effect of a dollar change in tax revenues.

We have finally reached the point in public understanding of fiscal policy when even financial-page columnists concede that there might be something in the notion that budgetary deficits should be run by the government in economic slumps and budgetary surpluses when the economy is peaking.[12] With more governments participating in discretionary fiscal policy, the public might come to realize that even this is not an accurate statement of post-Keynesian fiscal policy. The role of the fiscal policy is to adjust appropriately aggregate demand, and this may well dictate that budgetary deficits be run in economic peaks as well as slumps if in these peaks demand is still not sufficient to bring about a satisfactory employment level, as seems to be the case in most of the Atlantic provinces.

Although my remarks have related to fiscal policy, there is no reason why provincial governments should not be encouraged to pursue an active monetary policy as well. To this end the provinces should have access to the Bank of Canada. The flexibility of provincial-government economic policy would be enhanced if they were permitted to engage, where the central bank deemed it was warranted, in a bit of inflationary financing.

It should be made clear that while I am pushing for a far greater degree of autonomy for the provinces in the taxation field, I recognize that it is necessary for the rate of progressive taxation to be generally uniform throughout Canada. Progressive taxation is a device for the redistribution of personal income and if it initially differed significantly from province to province there would be a tendency for the tax structure of all provinces to be pulled down to the structure of the least progressive; otherwise the high income earners would tend to leave the provinces with the most progressive tax structures. A similarity in tax structure would not imply that tax rates for any given income level would be equal; these could still vary, but their variation would be related to the degrees of government spending.

12 / The most convincing demonstration I can think of to show just how far these columnists have come is to point to Fraser Robertson's column in the Toronto *Globe and Mail*, Feb. 16, 1966.

10

The Flexibility of
the BNA Act

BARRY STRAYER

THE MODERN POSITIVE STATE must manifest itself in legislative action. Its legislature must be free to choose among a wide
range of techniques for furthering the social security of the
majority and curbing the anti-social tendencies of the minority.

Can the positive state coincide with a federal state where
power is divided among several legislatures? Are effective welfare
or regulatory measures possible in such a state where no single
legislative body has complete authority? Dicey and many of his
contemporaries would have answered in the negative. For him,
federal government meant "weak government." Power divided
was necessarily power diluted. A federal government could not
effectively interfere with the economy.[1]

We could cheerfully ignore for present purposes such nineteenth-century concepts of federalism, were they not still the
source of a substantial part of the national folklore. Unfortunately, we still have many politicians who see the British North
America Act as a serious obstacle to almost any new governmental venture. One suspects there are also judges who accept as

1 / A. V. Dicey, *Introduction to the Study of the Law of the Constitution* (10th ed., London, 1961), pp. 171–4.

an inarticulate premise that large-scale invasions of private rights could never have been authorized by the Fathers of Confederation.

In the long run the true test of any constitution is its workability. Does it provide a suitable vehicle for solving current social problems? The use of this test should not be thought to imply certain preconceptions as to a supposedly inevitable need for centralization or a long-run dilution of minority rights in favour of national hegemony. Changing needs may as easily dictate decentralization in some fields or special arrangements for the preservation of cultural values. The real objective of a federal constitution should be to ensure that matters best managed at the local level are susceptible to local control, and matters best managed at the national level are susceptible to national control. To reach this objective, the constitution must have a large degree of flexibility built into it in some manner. An attempt will be made in this essay to examine the Canadian constitution to see what elements of flexibility it does contain. Particular emphasis will be placed on the possibility for new legislative action to meet current problems.

Formal Constitutional Change
It has been frequently suggested in recent years that what Canada really needs is a completely new constitution. Politicians both federal and provincial have urged a complete rewriting of the British North America Act. It is argued that only such an extreme step could bring the constitution into line with current needs.

This approach to constitutionalism is unlikely to succeed. First, it is predicated on the assumption that once we get a new constitution that is "right" (i.e., in accord with current needs) thereafter our problems will be solved. But no constitutional solution can be "right" for all time. It would be more to the point to try to ensure that the constitution will be flexible enough to serve our needs as and where they may appear.

Secondly, it is quite optimistic to suppose that under current conditions one could achieve a consensus on a substantially different constitution. While we continue to have constitutional problems in Canada, conditions are yet far from chaotic. There are too many people, both public and private, with vested interests in the BNA Act as it now stands and with too little incentive to abandon evils of which they know for those of which they know not. After all, the American constitution was not drafted until the Articles of Confederation had clearly failed; the BNA Act did not appear until government under the Union Act, 1840, had reached an impasse.

The Federal-Provincial Constitutional Conference held in February 1968 did decide that a study of possible changes in the constitution should be made. Intergovernmental machinery was established for this purpose, contemplating a systematic and sustained effort at constitutional reform such as we have not seen since Confederation. Yet the Conference emphasized seven possible areas for study, not a complete rewriting of the constitution. Admittedly, these seven areas – official languages, fundamental human rights, the distribution of powers, federal institutions such as the Senate and the Supreme Court of Canada, regional economic disparities, a constitutional amendment procedure, and machinery for federal-provincial consultation – are very extensive. The third, the distribution of powers, is potentially all-important. It was a significant achievement even to reach agreement that so many possible changes should be jointly studied. But at that time there was no decision on any particular change, and it is predictable that a consensus on any specifics will be slow to develop.

The fact that it is once again necessary to discuss a constitutional amendment procedure should remind us of the difficulties inherent in significant formal constitutional reform. It has long been generally accepted that we should devise a method of amendment which would enable us to effect constitutional changes, *within Canada,* as the need may arise. This would enhance our sovereignty – seemingly impaired by the need to seek amendments from Westminster for important changes – and would also build in a potential flexibility which would assure us of a constitution responsive to future needs. This is a more modest approach to constitutional reform, emphasizing permanent machinery for formal change rather than immediate wholesale change itself. Unfortunately, the path to constitutional reform by amendment is beset with difficulties.

The existing system of amendment – if one may call it that – is legally flexible. All that is required is a simple enactment at Westminster. By convention, amendments are made in response to addresses by the Canadian Senate and House of Commons. The provinces have no status in this procedure. Yet in spite of this, since 1867 there has been only one amendment (giving Parliament power over unemployment insurance) which has actually diminished provincial legislative power and none depriving Parliament of power. This reflects the political difficulties involved in formal transfers of jurisdiction.

If we do in fact achieve a Canadian amending procedure it is likely to create further obstacles to change. Serious efforts to devise such a procedure began in 1935 and have continued sporadically ever since. We still have no all-embracing Canadian amendment procedure in the vital area affecting distribution of legislative power. The closest we came to it was the Fulton-Favreau formula[2] which was actually approved unanimously by a federal-provincial conference in 1964. But even it failed of adoption by all the provincial legislatures. Assuming that this formula most closely represents the maximum amount of agreement possible, the future of formal amendment is dismal indeed. The Fulton-Favreau proposal would have given the provincial legislatures a considerable voice in internal changes within the government and Parliament of Canada and would have given each provincial legislature a veto over any change in the distribution of legislative powers. To give such a power to each provincial government would be extremely hazardous; to give it to each provincial legislature could be disastrous. The constitutional amendment which could survive this process would be innocuous indeed.

There is a lesson to be learned from all this. Formal constitutional change, either by wholesale revision or by amendment procedures present or future, is a difficult means for adjusting

2 / See the White Paper, *The Amendment of the Constitution of Canada*, (Ottawa, 1965), pp. 110–15.

constitutional norms to meet social, economic, and political realities.

The Potentials of the BNA Act

We will probably have to continue to run our governments within the general framework of the BNA Act. Ideally the Act could be improved by a number of amendments, but we can still make it serve important social ends in its present form. For those who accept the philosophy of the positive state, the most important thing is that there be effective governmental power located some place within the state. In the federal positive state, we would wish for a large measure of flexibility of action as between Parliament and the legislatures. The federal government should have power to act where there are clear advantages in centralized control and when such action becomes politically feasible. Otherwise the provincial governments should be free to operate programs and regulate activities at least as long as the federal government is unwilling to do so. Using these criteria we should examine the BNA Act as it now stands to see if it provides this degree of flexibility.

The most flexible constitutional device in federal structures is that of concurrent powers. The United States and Australian constitutions provided for large areas of concurrent powers, but the BNA Act on its face did not appear to do so. In both the United States and Australian constitutions the pre-existing states continued on as before union, except for the few powers taken away from them. These constitutions conferred specific powers on the federal legislature, but this conferral did not *ipso facto* deprive the states of power. There were specific limitations on state action such as that against state tariffs on goods entering or leaving a state.[3] In addition there were matters implicitly beyond state power, for example the power to legislate for the borrowing of money on the credit of the nation as a whole. Such a power could obviously only be exercised by the federal legislature on which it was expressly conferred.[4] Apart from these areas expressly or

3 / US Constitution, art. I, s. 10; Australian Constitution s. 90.
4 / US Constitution, art. I, s. 8; Australian Constitution s. 51(iv).

impliedly withdrawn from state jurisdiction, in the United States or Australia the state legislature can legislate on any matters on which the federal legislature can. If both the federal and the state legislature should enact laws on the same subject and their laws are inconsistent, the state law is invalid. This leaves ample scope for state experimentation in the absence of federal initiative.

The BNA Act made very little specific provision for concurrent powers. The most conspicuous examples appear in sections 95 and 94A. Section 95, in the original Act, conferred concurrent powers on Parliament and the provinces in the fields of agriculture and immigration. Each could legislate, but in the case of repugnancy of federal and provincial laws the federal law would prevail. Section 94A, added in 1951, gave Parliament a power which it was thought to be lacking previously to legislate on old age pensions. This is a concurrent power, provincial jurisdiction in this matter being assumed, but here provincial legislation is to prevail in case of inconsistency.

The most important set of concurrent powers, however, are those with respect to direct taxation. Section 91 [3] of the BNA Act gives Parliament jurisdiction for "the raising of money by any mode or system of taxation." This obviously embraces both direct and indirect taxes, imposed in any fashion Parliament sees fit. The provinces are confined by section 92 [2] to "direct taxation within the province in order to the raising of a revenue for provincial purposes." The exact limitations on these powers are yet to be completely defined but the effect on the ordinary taxpayer is quite clear: either level of government is entitled to impose on him direct taxes such as income taxes, consumption or use taxes, or property taxes. There is no inherent limit on the amount each can take from him, save the practical limitation that he cannot be forced to give more than he has. In case of conflict in the process of collection, the government of Canada apparently can be given priority where the taxpayer's assets are not sufficient to pay both tax bills.

Out of this area of concurrent taxing powers has come the series of federal-provincial tax agreements. While the history and significance of these have been ably discussed in many other places,[5] suffice it to say that they have been invaluable in reconciling spending needs with fiscal realities.

Concurrent taxing powers are closely associated with concurrent spending powers. There may be some limit on provincial spending power (the direct taxation power being given only "for provincial purposes"), but the courts have yet to strike down any spending scheme on this basis. The federal spending power appears to be unlimited, provided that a spending scheme is not combined with a system of regulation which would otherwise be beyond federal powers.

These concurrent powers of getting and spending have been largely responsible for making Canadian federalism workable. They have permitted the federal government to maintain more effective control over the economy, to provide directly or indirectly for certain basic standards of social security across the country, and to equalize in some measure the revenues of the various provinces. Thus they have been a means of maintaining effective government in the face of social conditions vastly changed from 1867 when the original division of taxing powers was made.

Concurrency of fiscal powers has largely distracted attention from the distribution of legislative powers as otherwise provided in the BNA Act. Whereas thirty years ago the battle-lines of federalism were largely in the courts, today they are in federal-provincial conferences. We have come to accept much of the earlier constitutional jurisprudence as eternally valid. We have frequently sought to avoid its worst effects through intergovernmental agreements or have used it as an excuse for legislative inaction. In the process constitutional law and constitutional lawyers have been pushed farther into the background.

The argument to be made here is that there is still a legitimate role for lawyers and judges in making the constitution a vehicle of effective government. The more places in which useful legis-

5 / See *e.g.*, J. S. Dupré, "Tax Powers versus Spending Responsibilities: An Historical Analysis of Federal-Provincial Finance" in A. Rotstein, ed., *The Prospect of Change* (Toronto, 1965), p. 83; Moore, Perry and Beach, *The Financing of Canadian Federation* (Toronto, 1966).

lative power can be found, the more chance there is of legislation forthcoming. Even in those areas where intergovernmental agreements prevail, it is the constitution as judicially interpreted which largely fixes the bargaining powers of the respective parties. It will also be argued that the BNA Act is displaying new potential for development which should augur well for the positive state.

It is true that, through judicial interpretation, the original scheme of distribution of legislative power soon became a barrier to effective government. Whether or not this was the expectation of the Fathers of Confederation, the Judicial Committee developed a very rigid approach to the application of the two great sources of legislative power – section 91 for Parliament and section 92 for the provincial legislatures. The various heads of jurisdiction came to be regarded as "watertight compartments" of powers conferred on one level of government to the exclusion of the other. Legislation was rigidly characterized as pertaining to a federal head of jurisdiction or – more commonly – to a provincial head, and little regard was paid to the context in which it was enacted. Yet even as this trend dominated judicial review during the first eighty years of Confederation, there was another concept developing which has since provided the means for a more dynamic constitutionalism. This concept recognized that in one context Parliament could pass legislation which, in another context, a province might also enact for a purpose justified by one of its own heads of jurisdiction. This principle required for its application a judicial willingness flexibly to characterize similar legislation, ascribing it variously to federal or provincial heads depending on the context in which it was to operate. Thus overlapping or concurrency of legislative activity was permitted, though in case of actual conflict between federal and provincial laws the federal would prevail.

The real potential of this "overlapping and paramountcy" approach did not become apparent until after the Second World War. Since that time the courts have allowed large areas of legislative overlapping. They have achieved this by taking a liberal approach to characterization of legislation, finding for most pieces of impugned legislation a legitimate compartment in the distribution of legislative powers.[6] The inarticulate premise appears to be that if a legislature has seen fit to tackle a problem not otherwise looked after by some other level of government, its legislation should be upheld if at all possible. Along with this approach, the courts have taken an extremely narrow view of "conflict." Only rarely will the Supreme Court of Canada now find that federal and provincial legislation in the same area actually conflicts. A few examples will best illustrate this trend.

The development and rapid growth of highway traffic in this century has created problems never foreseen by the Fathers of Confederation. Highway traffic involves problems of construction and maintenance of roads, the qualification of drivers, the suitability of vehicles, and the regulation of traffic in motion on the roads. The courts have been unable or unwilling to force all of these problems into one of the "compartments" of section 91 or section 92 of the BNA Act. Instead in a series of decisions in the last thirty years they have recognized legitimate interests of both levels of government in this field. The provinces are able to exercise powers in relation to "licensing" and "local works and undertakings." Parliament can impose certain controls in the exercise of its "criminal law" jurisdiction. The results have been in marked contrast to the earlier concepts of "watertightism."

For example, the Criminal Code of Canada penalizes those who drive with "criminal negligence" or are guilty of "dangerous" driving. Highway traffic laws in most provinces create the offence of "driving without due care and attention." Provincial laws have been challenged in the courts on the basis that they are "criminal law," a matter exclusively for Parliament, and that in any event there is a conflict between the two kinds of legislation making the provincial legislation inoperative. Nevertheless the Supreme Court of Canada in two recent cases has upheld such provincial laws. Refusing to characterize them as "criminal law" the Court has also found that they do not conflict with the Criminal Code because they deal with a lower level of negligence. From a

6 / See, for example, W. R. Lederman, "The Concurrent Operation of Federal and Provincial Laws in Canada," 9 *McGill Law Journal* 185 (1963).

practical point of view, this means that since Parliament has not gone far enough in regulating lesser degrees of wrong-doing on the highway, the provinces have been allowed to fill the vacuum. Concurrency of powers brought other surprises for the automobile driver. The Criminal Code, to be sure, prohibited him from driving while intoxicated, but it also assured him that for the purposes of prosecution under the Code "no person is required to give a sample of ... breath. ..."[7] But if he lived in Saskatchewan and was suspected of drunken driving, he would discover that the provincial Highway Traffic Board could suspend his licence for up to ninety days if he refused to give a sample of breath; and this law was applied with the blessing of the Supreme Court of Canada, which sanctioned it as a "licensing" provision. Once convicted, the same driver might find that not only could his licence be suspended under provincial law but the magistrate might also issue an order under the federal Criminal Code prohibiting him from driving anywhere in Canada!

The regulation of public sales of corporate securities is another area where the courts have been willing to permit a concurrency of legislative powers. Parliament has largely confined its regulation to a few Criminal Code sections prohibiting the publishing of fraudulent prospectuses, the use of mails for fraudulent promotions, and stock exchange manipulation. These apply to transactions in all shares, while other legislation lays down special requirements for the sale of shares of federally incorporated companies. The provinces, on the other hand, have set up extensive regulatory legislation and machinery. In many instances provincial regulations overlap federal laws: for example, for the same transaction one might be convicted under the Criminal Code of publishing a fraudulent prospectus, and under provincial law of filing a false prospectus with the provincial securities commission.

In other cases the provinces have successfully entered fields which Parliament could enter if it chose to do so – such as the

7 / At the time of writing, proposed amendments to the Criminal Code are before Parliament which, if adopted, could require the giving of samples of breath.

regulation of share transactions which appear to be interprovincial or international in scope. It is hard to distinguish this kind of regulation from abortive provincial attempts thirty or forty years ago to regulate all sales, including interprovincial sales, of grain or other natural products. At that time the courts struck down such legislation as an invasion of the exclusive federal jurisdiction over "regulation of trade and commerce" because interprovincial sales were involved. Now provincial regulation is permitted, in the absence of any federal measures.

Again one may speculate that the courts have permitted the provinces to fill a regulatory void. Parliament has provided no comprehensive legislative or administrative control over securities transactions. Provincial measures, wider in scope and emphasizing prevention of frauds rather than mere punishment, have proven more effective in preventing fraudulent transactions. Concurrent powers have been attributed to the provinces by the courts in such a way as to validate provincial efforts to protect the investor.

The Supreme Court has given another boost to concurrency, in the field of "interest." This subject, specifically assigned to Parliament by section 91 and at one time jealously guarded from provincial interference, now appears to have a provincial aspect as well. In 1963 the Supreme Court upheld an Ontario statute which permits a court to revise the terms of a loan contract where the cost of the loan appears excessive and the transaction harsh and unconscionable. In effect, the province can now in exercise of its "property and civil rights" power over the contract authorize the scaling down of excessive interest charges. Parliament could achieve the same result. Either could probably compel proper disclosure of interest rates to the borrower.

A related example may be drawn from the banking field. Section 91 of the BNA Act assigned to Parliament jurisdiction over "banking" and the "incorporation of banks." This was an exclusive jurisdiction, also at one time ardently defended by the courts. Nevertheless the banking system created under Parliament's authority has not adequately filled the nation's banking needs. Its lack of flexibility and the conservative restraints imposed on it have created a demand among Canadians for other kinds of banking services. As a result, a host of "near-banks" such as credit unions and trust companies have been established under provincial legislation. To a large extent these operate outside federal control, yet many of them carry on what is really "banking" business. The Porter Royal Commission on Banking and Finance recognized that a large portion of these institutions would fall within federal jurisdiction over banking. It also appeared to concede, however, that in the absence of federal regulation they could continue to function under provincial legislation. This assumption of a concurrency of regulatory power over bank-like institutions has yet to be refuted by the courts.

A number of less obvious examples of the trend to concurrency might be cited. The foregoing should be sufficient, however, to illustrate this point: that most of the provincial initiatives for legislative reform during the last twenty years have been upheld by the courts by means of an increasingly flexible technique. This technique involves a liberal characterization of legislation by which provincial statutes are attributed to some head of provincial jurisdiction and not to some head of jurisdiction within the exclusive federal domain. At the same time, the courts have skilfully avoided any finding of conflict as between the impugned provincial law and existing federal statutes. The net result has been a marked departure from the concept of "watertightism" that prevailed until the Second World War. In political terms, as the federal momentum for legislative activity – the attempts at centralization during the thirties and the extensive economic measures during the Second World War – slowed in the postwar period, many of the provinces became laboratories for experiments in social legislation. The constitution has not proven to be a barrier, even though some of the experiments have occurred in areas at one time thought to be exclusively within the federal sphere.

It would nevertheless be wrong to assume that the trend to concurrency has significance only for the provinces. There is much in this development which could support federal legislative innovation. The fundamental significance of concurrency is, after all, a recognition that both levels of government have a right to legislate, barring some conflict. Concurrency is the antithesis of "watertightism," and it was the latter approach which defeated a host of federal measures: anti-hoarding and anti-profiteering laws after the First World War; conciliation laws and the regulation of strikes and lock-outs in all industries regardless of connection with some specific head of federal jurisdiction; the regulation of interprovincial marketing inextricably linked with intraprovincial marketing; the creation of national labour standards with respect to holidays, minimum wages, and hours of work; a system of unemployment insurance; the control of the insurance business; and others. The tendency was to ascribe such matters to provincial heads of jurisdiction such as "property and civil rights" and "matters of a merely local or private nature." Along with this aggrandizement of provincial heads went a narrow interpretation of federal powers such as those with respect to "peace, order, and good government" and "the regulation of trade and commerce." If the courts can take a flexible approach in the characterization of provincial legislation, there is no reason why they should not now be equally ready to ascribe federal legislation to a federal power instead of condemning it as interference with a matter inherently and immutably preserved to the provinces.

In fact there are indications that the legislative potential of Parliament has also been increased by modern judicial techniques. There was a long period from the end of the nineteenth century to the end of the Second World War when Parliament was precluded from exercising its general "peace, order, and good government" power in areas also covered by provincial heads such as "property and civil rights." Only in times of emergency – mainly war – could the federal power be so exercised. Since 1946 the tendency has been more readily to characterize federal legislation as pertaining to "peace, order, and good government" even though it may deal with activities and relationships which in another context might be within provincial jurisdiction. Similarly, the federal "trade and commerce" head which had at one time been whittled away to almost nothing has been used as an independent and vital source of federal power. Most significantly, it has been relied on to support grain marketing legislation even where that legislation may on occasion deal with transactions which are purely intraprovincial in scope. Our courts have started to see that which became obvious to American courts twenty-five years ago – that local trade may be so inextricably linked with interprovincial or international trade that the control of the two latter necessarily requires the control of local trade as well.

Armed then with the precedents of liberal characterization of provincial legislation, and encouraged by the trends in the construction of federal powers, we may be permitted some optimism with respect to the future of effective government in Canada. It follows from this that we should treat with scepticism our politicians' use of the constitution as a pious excuse for legislative inaction. Scarcely a day passes that a politician somewhere in Canada does not deny responsibility for a problem on the basis of the British North America Act. At times these protestations are justified, but frequently they are not. It is at least time that we started examining them more critically. Otherwise it will be this defensive use of the constitution, rather than the constitution itself, which will substantiate Dicey's dictum that "federal government is weak government."

It will be useful to speculate concerning potential legislative power in a few foreseeable problem areas. Since provincial initiatives have already been taken in many of these fields, the emphasis will be on the possibility of effective federal measures.

In the advancement of social security measures, the federal government has two main avenues available. It can, if it wishes, confine itself to making grants to support provincially operated schemes. If it wishes to maintain certain minimum standards and to ensure honest and effective use of the money it may attach conditions to its grants. As long as the provinces have the option to accept or refuse the grants, there is no constitutional obstacle to acceptance of federally imposed conditions, even though these conditions may restrict a province in the exercise of its jurisdiction over the matter involved. Conditional grants for hospitalization insurance or for medicare are obvious examples. The constitutional propriety of this device is now generally accepted, though recent federal proposals indicate a political trend away from the conditional grant or shared-cost program. But should a future federal government wish to promote social welfare through conditional or unconditional grants, the possibilities would be limited only by fiscal and political considerations.

A possibility for more direct federal action lies in the field of social insurance. Unemployment insurance and the Canada Pension Plan have demonstrated the possible advantages of national contributory social security measures. The constitutional background of these schemes requires examination, however. Hopes for federal action in the social security field were largely shattered by the 1937 decision of the Judicial Committee of the Privy Council in the *Employment Insurance Reference*. The Employment and Social Insurance Act, 1935, part of R. B. Bennett's "new deal" legislation, was the forerunner of present unemployment insurance legislation. It was held invalid because it interfered with contracts of employment – the employer and employee each had to "contribute" to the fund – and because it created a system of insurance. These matters were deemed to be inherently related to "civil rights" and within provincial control. A constitutional amendment in 1940 solved this particular problem, but the Judicial Committee's opinion has deterred other compulsory, contributory, federal social insurance measures. The government apparently thought it would preclude even a non-contributory federal old age pension, and obtained a constitutional amendment in 1951 before introducing such a scheme. A further amendment was made in 1964 before the contributory Canada Pension Plan was enacted. In the meantime it has been assumed that in the absence of constitutional amendment the proper federal role in other insurance programs (such as those for hospitalization or medical care) is one of cost-sharing only.

With the trend to concurrent jurisdiction and the tendency to widen important federal powers such as "peace, order, and good government" the *1937 Employment Insurance Reference* should be reassessed. It was at best only an opinion on a reference to the court, not a judgment in contested litigation. As an opinion it is not binding on subsequent courts. Any modern court which is capable of the refinements recently used to uphold provincial legislation should be able to distinguish the 1937 opinion. Federal social insurance schemes, carefully framed so as to provide nation-wide guarantees against financial misfortune, should be supportable as matters of "peace, order, and good government." No longer need we confine "peace, order, and good government" legislation to times of grave crisis. Compulsory premiums in partial support of such programs could be upheld, either as "taxation" or as mere incidents of inherently valid legislation. The nexus with "taxation" is as plausible here as recent constitutional justifications for some of the provincial legislation described earlier.

Admittedly, the current trend is away from direct federal operation of social security schemes. Whether this is a sound trend, or a long-range trend, is another matter. We may at some future date wish to reconsider the need for direct federal action. An adequate medical care insurance scheme may never be realized otherwise. Other possibilities come to mind, such as federal drug insurance or federal insurance covering loss of income through sickness. These are constitutionally possible.

There are also substantial federal regulatory powers now obscured through disuse. In some areas, provincial regulation has been available but inadequate with respect to problems essentially national in scope. In other areas the provinces have been precluded from exercising powers which were exclusively federal but dormant.

As we have seen, the regulation of trading in corporate securities has been almost entirely provincial. Yet the questionable practices in this field are frequently carried out on an interprovincial or international basis. With ten separate regulatory agencies there is not the consolidation of information or the means of enforcement which is needed for effective control of this business. In the United States the Securities and Exchange Commission effectively regulates major interstate transactions in securities. Ample support for federal regulation in Canada of interprovincial transactions could be found in Parliament's power over "trade and commerce." Considerable federal control over intraprovincial transactions could also be asserted, either as an incident of interprovincial regulation or in exercise of the "criminal law" power.

The need for effective control of air, water, and land pollution is rapidly becoming apparent. We are told that while the federal government may exhort and advise, this is essentially a matter for the provincial legislatures. It is assumed that property rights, including provincial rights in water and land, are the only matters at stake. If this view is persisted in it is unlikely that we will have effective pollution control. It is obvious that various substances carried by air or water can readily move from one province to another. Assume that province X is upstream from province Y on an interprovincial river. Province X is determined to attract new industries and is reluctant to impose onerous conditions such as the purification of industrial wastes dumped into rivers. What protection will province Y have if federal action is not available? An obvious basis for federal regulation can be found in the "criminal law" power. This power supports an elaborate system of regulations and penalties with respect to food and drugs and the sale of narcotics. If purity can be required for food and drugs, why not for air and water? The only limitation on the criminal law power is that it must be exercised to suppress some danger to the public. The danger from pollution is obvious. In addition, federal control could be related to the "peace, order, and good government" of Canada.

Another potential problem related to water is maldistribution of resources among the provinces. While Canada is rich in water, much of it is in uninhabited areas. Eventually it will be necessary to undertake major diversion systems to move water to the places where it is needed. Federal authorities have so far taken the position that public water resources (the property of the provincial Crown) and private water rights are exclusively within provincial power. On this assumption it will be difficult indeed to develop long-range plans for sound water use. Again there are legitimate grounds for federal intervention. The guarantee of a safe and adequate water supply for the whole of Canada is surely a matter of "peace, order, and good government." This will become more obvious as localized water problems become acute, but even now our jurisprudence does recognize a constitutional relationship between the ounce of prevention and the pound of cure. Thus early action would be justifiable. Also, if diversion projects were undertaken, they could be declared by Parliament to be "works for the general advantage of Canada" and thus under federal control. Or where they continued from one province into another they would for that reason alone be within federal jurisdiction.

New measures for the protection of the consumer could also be introduced by Parliament. Uniform packaging and labelling legislation is of the same genus as pure food laws. It protects members of the public from the evils of confusion and ignorance as to what they are buying.

In the related field of interest disclosure and the control of loan costs, Parliament can also call in aid its jurisdiction over "interest" and "banking," though to the extent that it would prevent deception such legislation would also have a "criminal law" basis. In the new era of concurrency, the fact that some jurisdiction here has been conceded to the provinces should not prevent Parliament from asserting its own independent powers.

Parliament might also perform a useful function by curtailing trading stamps. Existing Criminal Code prohibitions are not complete and leave ample room for the use of stamps. Federal officials have in the past argued that further control is a matter for the provinces and some provinces have taken suitable action. But the validity of these provincial measures might still be questioned, particularly as they relate to interprovincial trade in stamps. Parliament could easily amplify its legislation to deal with this problem.

The demand for safety control in automobile design is rapidly increasing. The advantages of national standards here are obvious, particularly from the standpoint of the manufacturer. If it had the inclination Parliament could surely enact certain minimum requirements and provide penalties for breaches. This would be analogous to pure food and drug legislation, a proper exercise of the "criminal law" power. If Parliament can send to jail the man who drives while drunk, it can surely penalize the company which produces a car that is a menace on the road.

These and other opportunities for regulatory measures are available to Parliament should it care to take them. It should also be noted in passing that federal and provincial regulation of economic activity is not limited by constitutional guarantees of individual rights. The British North America Act distributed virtually all legislative power among Parliament and the legislatures. Those who have tried to read some guarantee of "life, liberty, and property" into the Canadian constitution have had little success. The Canadian Bill of Rights, it is true, purported to guarantee such rights against any federal interference except by due process of law. But the narrow construction placed on the Bill gives little likelihood of effective protection. The implication in our present constitution is clear. If Parliament or a legislature wishes to take collectivist measures otherwise within its powers, it will be no legal obstacle that individual rights are thereby prejudiced. Should a constitutional Bill of Rights as proposed by the federal government at the February 1968 Constitutional Conference be adopted, this situation could change. In the federal proposal, however, possible difficulties with substantive due process were noted and some suggestions made as to how legislative supremacy could be preserved in essential areas of regulation.[8]

Conclusion

It has been suggested here that the Canadian constitution is sufficiently flexible to permit effective government at whichever level required. It must be admitted, of course, that many of the proposals are contrary to widely held assumptions about the existing distribution of legislative powers. If these proposals are sound, how are they to be realized? It is submitted that the first requirement is for politicians who will continue to pursue effective government, more willing to find the means than to find a reason for inaction. Second, there must be a spirit of experimentation in

8 / See the White Paper, *A Canadian Charter of Human Rights* (Ottawa, 1968), pp. 19–20.

the field of legislation. Desirable measures should be passed, even at the risk of a judicial finding of invalidity. Third, in the courts the judges and lawyers should ensure that new legislation is considered in the contemporary context, with all facts available as to the problems it was designed to cure and its probable effect.

Much of this may seem unrealistic and irrelevant at a time when the tides of provincial autonomy are running strong and when the problems of biculturalism affect so many decisions in federal-provincial relations. Nevertheless, enough has been said to show that our constitution can sustain strong government at either level. As the political centre of gravity moves back and forth between the federal government and the various provinces the necessary legislative power can be found. In the meantime the practitioners of "co-operative federalism" should reassess the assumptions upon which they bargain. And Canadians generally should critically examine the protestations of politicians who plead the constitution as a justification for inertia.

11

What Happens
to Parliament?

RONALD BLAIR

WHILE THEOLOGIANS dispute the death of God, political scientists
(and others) lament the demise of Parliament. It appears that
nothing is sacred – not even the profane. If the gospels of parliamentary supremacy and ministerial responsibility are proven
worthless, in what are we then to place our trust? To the tradition-
alist, Lloyd George's flat assertion that "Parliament has no control over the Executive: it is pure fiction" sounds like heresy; yet
Mackenzie King permitted himself to say much the same thing,
only more ambiguously.

But since political diagnosis still remains more art than science,
the student of government may be permitted to maintain a certain
scepticism about such judgments. There is much confusion in the
vast literature on parliamentary decline and reform. If Parliament
has declined, has this decline been in its absolute power or in its
power relative to the power of the executive? Is the decline in
efficiency, or in public interest and esteem, or in the behaviour of
members, or in all of these? In any event, what is meant by "Parliament"? And is there a decline in the case of other democratic
legislatures, not merely parliaments such as the Canadian or the

British? For example, in a surprising *volte face* many British writers now find various aspects of the United States Congress eminently praiseworthy. Probably none would agree today with Woodrow Wilson's pronouncement in 1885 that "Unquestionably, the predominant and controlling force, the centre and source of all motive and regulatory power is the Congress." But equally probably, most would enviously agree with the verdict of a contemporary American scholar that "it is certain that Congress has always shared in the real powers of government and therefore in the responsibility for making decisions. And Congress is the sort of representative institution it is, precisely because it is a real governing body."[1] Yet it is commonplace for American writers to lament the attrition of congressional power, and the chief Washington correspondent of the *Times* of London has recently concluded that the British House of Commons is not only a more powerful, but also a more democratic and more modern, institution than Congress.[2]

Of course, there will always be those who refer back to a golden age of parliaments, as of everything else. Such individuals can point to the decline in public subscriptions to Hansard as evidence of the present sad state of affairs. The information that people once paid significant sums of money to have the opportunity of sitting in the galleries at Westminster gladdens their hearts.[3] There is a familiar ring to the opening sentences of Bryce's chapter on "The Decline of Legislatures," written almost half a century ago: "Every traveller who, curious in political affairs, enquires in the countries which he visits how their legislative bodies are working, receives from the elder men the same discouraging answer. They tell him, in much the same terms everywhere, that there is less brilliant speaking than in the days of their own youth, that the tone of manners has declined, that the best

---

1 / Theodore J. Lowi, "Representation and Decision," in T. J. Lowi, ed., *Legislative Politics U.S.A.* (2nd ed., Boston, 1965), p. xii.

2 / Louis Heren, *The New American Commonwealth* (New York, 1968).

3 / Andrew Hill and Anthony Whichelow, *What's Wrong with Parliament?* (London, 1964), chap. 1; A. Aspinall, "The Old House of Commons and Its Members (*c.* 1783–1832), I," *Parliamentary Affairs*, vol. 14 (winter 1960–61), pp. 13–25.

citizens are less disposed to enter the Chamber, that its proceedings are less fully reported and excite less interest, that a seat in it confers less social status, and that, for one reason or another, the respect for it has waned. The wary traveller discounts these jeremiads. ..."[4] Nevertheless, Bryce did believe that a decline had occurred generally, although not in the cases of Australia and Canada, where "we cannot ... talk of a falling off, for the level was never high. Corruption is rare, but the standard both of tone and manners and of intellectual attainment is not worthy of communities where everybody is well off and well educated, and where grave problems of legislation call for constructive ability."[5]

We must beware, then, of those who harbour delusions that members of Parliament should actively govern the country, or that political parties are instruments subverting the parliamentary system of government, or that cabinets and civil services consist universally of aggrandizing despots. Even so, there remains a widespread belief that the balance of power in parliamentary government has tilted dangerously far in favour of the executive and that the House of Commons no longer exercises effective control over executive actions. Although concern is often expressed about the weaknesses of the Commons in the performance of other functions, it is the lop-sided nature of executive-legislative relations that is held to be the crucial defect of contemporary parliamentary government. And while there are numerous interpretations of what effective "control" by the House of Commons should involve, whether it be the power to make and unmake ministries, or more simply the ability to secure adequate information and hold effective debates on government policies, proposals for parliamentary reform all seek to redress the balance to some extent.

It is the object of this paper to provide some perspective on this assessment of Parliament, and this will involve two rather distinct lines of inquiry. The first of these deals with constitutional evolution in Britain, since it is still commonly assumed that in the mid-

4 / James Viscount Bryce, *Modern Democracies* (London, 1921), chap. 58.
5 / *Ibid.*

nineteenth century the British parliamentary system provided a model of "balanced" government where the House of Commons maintained a proper degree of control over the ministry. Since that time, it has been argued, there has been a steady erosion of the Commons' power, until today it is a mere "rubber stamp," subject to the dominance of a prime minister, supported by his colleagues, his party, and the civil service. I am not concerned with the historical authenticity of this analysis, for while it is quite clearly an exaggeration in terms both of the past and of the present, its significance lies in the degree to which it has become an acceptable stereotype, despite the criticisms levelled against it.

The second line of inquiry concerns the applicability of this view of British constitutional development to Canada. It is clear that political institutions and practices in Canada, whatever their origins may have been, are now markedly different from those in Britain. The existence of a federal form of government by itself profoundly modifies the wholesale application of British constitutional theory, but in addition there are great differences in other areas, such as the party system, the form of the cabinet, the committees of the House of Commons, the office of the Speaker, and so on. Yet the assumption remains that, except for a federal form of government, parliamentary government in Canada remains a close approximation of that in Britain and, with a blithe disregard for reality, academics (and journalists) accept uncritically the validity of analyses of British government for Canadian government also.[6] Writing in the *Canadian Forum* in 1930 Underhill

6 / It is difficult to overestimate in this connection the influence of R. MacGregor Dawson's *The Government of Canada* (Toronto, 1947; 4th ed., rev. by N. Ward, 1963) which has established an enduring ascendancy. Dawson gave little attention to federalism apart from the formal constitutional aspects, and in his treatment of political institutions not only did he focus exclusively on the federal level but also he laid stress on the British constitutional legacy and assumed the validity of this for Canadian government. Of course, no one was more aware than Dawson himself of the Canadian divergences from the "Westminster model," but he never really dealt with the problem of reconciling theory and practice, though his work remains unexcelled in other respects.

A good specific illustration of this point can be found in a report in the Toronto *Globe and Mail* on June 7, 1968, of a paper delivered by Professor Edward McWhinney to a meeting of the Learned Societies of Canada at

offered his own prescription to bridge this gulf between theory and practice: "We in Canada are suffering from a literary theory of our constitution. It prevents us from realizing how British institutions when transplanted to America actually work, and it is high time that we shook ourselves free from it. Perhaps a good preliminary step towards this end would be to place Burke and Bagehot upon a Canadian Index."[7] The latter part of the paper, therefore, will deal with this constitutional "credibility gap" and an alternative interpretation of the Canadian pattern of development will be suggested.

I

The "classic" era of British parliamentary government is usually taken to correspond to the period between the Reform Acts of 1832 and 1867, although the year 1846 separates two rather different phases within this period.[8] In a speech in 1893, the eighth Duke of Devonshire, a distinguished Liberal statesman, extolled the features of this form of government: "Parliament makes or

Calgary. Professor McWhinney, according to this report, would appear to have heaped a Canadian constitutional Pelion on a British Ossa when it would have been more appropriate to have steered a prudent course between Scylla and Charybdis.

7 / See R. MacG. Dawson, ed., *Constitutional Issues in Canada, 1900–1931* (Toronto, 1933), p. 135.

8 / Again it should be stressed that no attempt is made here to present a historically valid account; rather, I outline the stereotype. However, it does seem that this stereotype is valid in some respects, though not all. J. P. Mackintosh in *The British Cabinet* (Toronto, 1962), chap. 3, gives an admirable account of the mid-nineteenth-century situation, but his analysis of contemporary developments tends too much toward the "prime ministerial domination" thesis. Eulogies of the classic period are many: for example, Lord Campion, "Parliament and Democracy," in Campion et al., *Parliament: A Survey* (London, 1952), and M. J. C. Vile, *Constitutionalism and the Separation of Powers* (London, 1967), chap. 8. A recent work by Ronald Butt, *The Power of Parliament* (London, 1967) contains (chap. 2) a vigorous attack upon this interpretation and the author appears to endorse Lord Salisbury's description of the period as a "formless chaos." An article by G. W. Jones, "The Prime Minister's Power," *Parliamentary Affairs*, vol. 18, (spring 1965), pp. 167–85, is a most able critique of the more extreme expositions of the modern period. A useful collection of short readings on the subject is H. V. Wiseman, ed., *Parliament and the Executive* (London, 1966).

unmakes our ministries, it revises their actions. Ministries may make peace or war, but they do so at pain of instant dismissal by Parliament from office; and in affairs of internal administration the power of Parliament is equally direct. It can dismiss a Ministry if it is too extravagant or too economical; it can dismiss a Ministry because its government is too stringent or too lax. It does actually and practically in every way directly govern England, Scotland and Ireland."[9] The contrast suggested by this passage is not only with the later period, but also with an earlier one, since before 1832, "if the authority of the Cabinet and of the prime minister had not yet taken their familiar shape, the position of ministers in relation to parliament was in some ways stronger than it became in the later years of the nineteenth century."[10]

Yet it is an easy matter to misunderstand both the theory and the practice of that era. The concept of parliamentary supremacy, the underpinning of the classic theory, is far removed from that of *gouvernement d'assemblée*. Ministerial responsibility never at any time (disregarding the experience of the Long Parliament) meant that ministers were the absolute creatures of the Commons. Legally it was the King-in-Parliament that was supreme, and in practice the King-in-Parliament in the middle of the nineteenth century consisted of the government of the day and the House of Commons. This classic theory postulated a delicate balance between these two elements. It could be claimed that there was attained, to a remarkable degree, a "balance of separation and unity, of harmony and functional differentiation, of control and collaboration. ..."[11] While some ministers were members of Parliament (the remainder were peers), their number was extremely small in relation to the total membership of the House. And while the ministry had to possess the confidence of the House and respect the law, this did not mean that the Commons interfered in strictly executive functions or sought to deal with every matter of

9 / Quoted in A. H. Birch, *Representative and Responsible Government* (Toronto, 1964), p. 73. The Duke's comment may be due to the fact that at this time there was an Indian summer of the classic phase.

10 / E. L. Woodward, *The Age of Reform* (Oxford, 1938), p. 23.

11 / Vile, *Constitutionalism*, p. 222. I have found Vile's argument of considerable assistance in writing this paper.

Ronald Blair / 223

government. Against the power of the Commons to withdraw its
confidence from the ministry, the latter in turn exercised the pre-
rogative powers of the Crown, notably, in this respect, the power
of dissolution.[12] Thus while the ministry could not exercise domination over the other members of the House, neither was there
any prospect of the House absorbing the ministry. In short, the
ministry maintained its autonomy, but could be removed if it lost
the support of the House.

This pattern of balanced government suggests the unwisdom of
identifying the two elements in functional terms as "legislature"
and "executive." It was generally accepted that the executive
power and the power to *formulate* and *initiate* laws were united
in the ministry, although it was quite clearly limited in its exercise
of these powers. Therefore, the basic functional differentiation, as
J. S. Mill correctly suggested, was between governing, on the one
hand, and the control of government, on the other.[13]

To many, though not all, contemporaries, this form of government appeared to be highly successful. The complex, and paradoxical, mechanism of autonomy and interdependency of the two
parts permitted both functions to be performed in a generally
satisfactory manner. Power checked power, but not so as to create
a stalemate. And while in many respects the scales were weighted
in favour of the Commons – to Stockmar, it was the "absurd,
usurping house of commons" – the balance was not unduly lop-
sided, at least not in the period up until 1846.

In retrospect, it is clear that the conditions required for this
kind of governmental arrangement were very difficult to secure
at any time and even more unlikely to endure for an extended
period. Classic liberal parliamentary government was prized by
the middle and upper classes, who were in general agreement,
whatever their party labels, about the desirability of a relatively
limited role for government. Few would have taken exception to
Palmerston's famous comment before the opening of Parliament

12 / But see Mackintosh, *The British Cabinet*, pp. 87–90.
13 / Mill's argument in chapter 5 of *Representative Government* is as
convincing today as when it was written. It is important to note, moreover,
the continued acceptance in British writing of the necessity for a strong
and stable government.

in 1864, when he was asked about the contents of the Queen's Speech and replied in a satisfied manner: "Oh, there is really nothing to be done. We cannot go on adding to the Statute Book *ad infinitum*. Perhaps we may have a little law reform, or bankruptcy reform; but we cannot go on legislating for ever."[14] As long as these classes alone exercised political power the system was reasonably secure and they could accept the necessary restraints in maintaining its successful operation. Thus ministers did not seek to employ their powers to coerce the House, nor did the House attempt to govern the country directly. In a word, under the conditions of a limited franchise there was a consensus among the governing class about general political values. The line of social division between the parties was horizontal, not vertical: "Beneath each banner proud to stand / Looked up the noblest of the land." The most obvious weakness was that it was "a synthesis of opinions and interests which left out about ninety per cent of the nation."[15] Within the House itself there was a unique combination of independence and party loyalty. This was due to many causes, such as the number of political groups in the Commons, the lack of cohesion of party leaders, and the degree to which control over members was exercised by interests in their constituencies as well as by party leaders. In any event, the state of the parties and the nature of party discipline were of crucial importance in providing "balanced" government. In this hey-day of parliamentary Blue Books members displayed the power to extract whatever information they sought from the ministry.[16] Despite the complaints of some leading politicians about the lack of discipline, members succeeded in staying on a "straight and narrow path"[17] between too little party discipline and too much.

14 / Quoted in Woodward, *The Age of Reform*, p. 163; and cf. Sir Sidney Low, *The Governance of England* (2nd ed., London, 1918), p. 53.

15 / Campion, *Parliament*, pp. 17–18.

16 / There is no intention of idealizing all back-benchers as assiduous and intelligent members. An embittered Peel once described them as men "who spend their time in eating and drinking, hunting and shooting, gambling, horse-racing, and so forth." Quoted in Woodward, *The Age of Reform*, p. 105.

17 / This phrase is the title of a novel by Honor Tracy and is derived, the author claims, from a sentence in an Irish sermon which is peculiarly

In the former case, "there would be nothing to prevent the meddling of a faction-ridden legislature in the day-to-day business of government"; in the latter, "the ordinary members of the legislature would be subordinated to the Cabinet."[18]

II

This precarious equilibrium did not last, although public figures such as Gladstone and Morley continued to assert its continued existence.[19] Academic writers also gave the system their stamp of approval, most notably Dicey, whose *Law of the Constitution* had a profound and enduring influence. However, while the conventional wisdoms were widely accepted until after the First World War, there were some individuals who detected a significant change in the balance of power between the two elements of Parliament by the turn of the century. Sir Henry Maine observed that the cabinet was "manifestly the English institution which is ever more and more gaining in influence."[20] The American scholar A. L. Lowell laid stress upon the growth of executive power in Britain and described the legislative press as one in which "the cabinet legislates with the advice and consent of Parliament."[21] In succeeding years commentators increasingly laid stress upon the "incapacity of the House of Commons to perform its work,"[22] the strictness of party discipline, the growth of the power of the cabinet and especially of the prime minister, and the development of a vast and expert bureaucracy. While it is improbable that the phrase "mere executive power" was ever appropriate in Britain, the tilting of the balance in favour of the executive steadily became a subject of scrutiny and of concern. By the early 1960s the picture presented of "parliamentary" government in a distinguished

---

appropriate in this context: "What we have to do, my dear brethren, is stay on the straight and narrow path between right and wrong."

18 / Vile, *Constitutionalism*, p. 223.

19 / But see n. 9 above.

20 / Sir Henry Maine, *Popular Government* (2nd ed., London, 1886), p. 115.

21 / A. L. Lowell, *The Government of England* (new ed., New York, 1919), vol. I, p. 326.

22 / Ramsay Muir, *How Britain Is Governed* (London, 1930), p. 322.

study is hardly to be reconciled with the classic liberal theory: "Now the country is governed by a Prime Minister, his colleagues, junior ministers and civil servants with the Cabinet acting as a clearing house and court of appeal. Despite the number and strength of the various pressure groups, governments with a definite will to act and popular backing have a wide field open to them. Governments are restrained not so much by Parliament or by the opposition as by their own desire to keep in step with public opinion and to increase their strength. This development has come about not because of any conspiracy by civil servants or because there is any desire to abrogate old customs, but simply because the country wants it."[23]

While such a conclusion is open to some question, nevertheless a great change had occurred, and the causes of this transformation were overlapping and interdependent. First, political justice was secured to a reasonable degree with the steady extension of the franchise until it became universal. Then the demands of the new electorate led to the ascendancy of social justice as a political value and this resulted, in turn, in an immense increase in governmental activity and a greater trend toward "collectivism." The expansion of the role of government was in any event well-nigh inevitable, given the complex problems, both domestic and international, of modern society.

In turn, there were changes of great magnitude in the political order itself. The extension of the franchise caused parliamentary parties to be converted into mass parties, and this involved an immense development of party organization. Increasingly, party leaders acquired the power to discipline back-benchers, for the size of the electorate now required candidates to secure the support of the party organization. For members of Parliament, failure to support the party leaders in the Commons would lead to a withdrawal of party support at the following election.[24] Perhaps the most trenchant early analysis of this loss of independence by ordinary members was provided by Ostrogorski when he

23 / Mackintosh, *The British Cabinet*, p. 524.
24 / There is increasing evidence that even in Britain this is a gross oversimplification.

described the increasing domination of party caucuses over back-benchers. Parliamentary leaders, he wrote, were becoming party dictators and conducting general elections as "personal plebiscites," appealing directly to the electorate in each constituency, over the heads of the candidates. The balance in Parliament was thus being "destroyed in favour of the leaders."[25] The significance of this development has been stressed by a Canadian political scientist: "The elevation of political party leaders to the rank of legitimate or constitutional rulers is not merely revolutionary in practical politics, it amounts to a constitutional revolution and is tantamount to the inauguration of a new state form, the party state."[26]

In the early 1880s the increased volume of government business, coupled with the problem of obstruction by Irish Nationalists in the House of Commons, led to major procedural changes which reflected the growing ascendancy of party leaders. Friedrich has suggested that "The rules of procedure constitute a pattern which is shaped by the main business before the Parliament,"[27] and in the 1880s, "the government (Cabinet) came to rely more and more upon popular as contrasted with parliamentary support, the party organization and the caucus supplanted parliamentary control. Therefore, the problem of procedure became how to insure to the government adequate control over parliamentary work. Closure and various other devices for expediting parliamentary business were adopted to deal with the problem."[28]

Another consequence of the demand for increased state activity was a vast enlargement of the bureaucracy which gave, and gives, the constant support of expert opinion to the prime minister and his colleagues.[29] Indeed, the continued growth of the positive, regulatory state has made a mockery of the distinction between

25 / M. Ostrogorski, *Democracy and the Organization of Political Parties* (London, 1902), vol. I, pp. 215 and 608.

26 / H. McD. Clokie, "The Modern Party State," *Canadian Journal of Economics and Political Science*, vol. XIV (May 1949), p. 143.

27 / C. J. Friedrich, *Man and His Government* (New York, 1963), p. 498.

28 / *Ibid.*, pp. 498–9.

29 / See R. C. K. Ensor, *England, 1870–1914* (Oxford, 1936), p. 124, for the parallel development of democracy and bureaucracy in Britain.

"politics" and "administration" upon which so high a value was placed at one time. Again, back-bench members (and, indeed, the opposition front bench) are increasingly unable to challenge this expert opinion and the ever greater use of discretionary power.

In these ways, critics charge, the balance between the two elements has tilted steadily in favour of the government side and, within the government, in favour of the prime minister. Charges of "cabinet dictatorship" have become commonplace and more recently the prime minister has been likened to a latter-day American president. While the language of the classic parliamentary system continues to be used, its meaning has changed: "Ministerial responsibility is now little more than a formal principle used by ministers to deter parliamentary interference in their affairs, and the power of dissolution has become simply a tactical weapon in the hands of the Prime Minister to enable him to choose as favourable a date as possible to fight an election."[30]

A major effect of a mass electorate desiring more and more "collectivist" policies has been the necessity for a high degree of co-ordination among the different parts of government. The attempt to ensure social justice through positive state action has disrupted the older pattern of governmental functioning. Using essentially the same kinds of institutions that in the past were employed for routine governmental tasks, governments today seek to perform tasks that are not only quantitatively, but also qualitatively, different. The maintenance of the highest possible level of employment, the control of wages and prices, the provision of social services – these and many other responsibilities (for the stress upon "collectivism" here should not obscure the vital influence also of modern war, defence policy, and foreign affairs on the functioning of government) involve immensely more co-ordination in government than in the past. And the performance of this vital function has been vested, logically, in the cabinet and its ancillary bodies. Thus it is argued that the obvious unsuitability of the House of Commons for the performance of a co-ordinating function, or for acting with the swiftness now deemed necessary

30 / Vile, *Constitutionalism*, p. 341.

for governments, has greatly strengthened the hierarchical principle in government organization and fostered the growing ascendancy of a single man or a few men. Above all, the instrument which is credited with bringing this state of affairs about has been the modern mass political party, for the party process contains within it today the electoral, the legislative, and the executive processes (and, to a degree, the judicial also). Political parties have not only been of crucial importance in transmitting the demand for social justice from the electorate to the government, but they have also been indispensable in providing for the co-ordination of the activities of the various branches of government by the party leadership, and pre-eminently by the prime minister.

III
We can now consider the applicability of this interpretation of British constitutional evolution to Canada. It is at once apparent that neither before nor after Confederation was there an equivalent to the classic phase. In fact, the era from 1867 until the turn of the century can be much better understood by reference to eighteenth-century British political practice. On the one hand, the party system was in a primitive condition and party loyalties were very ill defined; on the other hand, the government employed all the devices available to it, from control of elections (in the years immediately after 1867) to the pork-barrel, to ensure that it enjoyed the confidence of the House.[31] The late Senator Power praised the "independent" member of Parliament of that day,[32] but other evidence suggests that this independence was used not so much to check the government as to support whatever government held office in return for the appropriate favours. Derby's apt definition of independent MPs as members who could not be depended upon could have fitted many of these individuals. And Macdonald would surely have agreed with Wellington's complaint about the unreformed House of Commons: "Certain members

31 / See, e.g., E. M. Reid, "The Rise of National Parties in Canada," in H. G. Thorburn, ed., *Party Politics in Canada* (Toronto, 1963), and also Norman Ward, *The Public Purse* (Toronto, 1962).
32 / C. G. Power, "Career Politicians," *Queen's Quarterly*, vol. 63 (winter 1956–57), pp. 478–90.

claim a right to dispose of everything that falls vacant within the town or county which they represent, and this is so much a matter of right that they now claim the patronage whether they support upon every occasion, or now and then, or when not required, or actively oppose; and in fact the only question about local patronage is whether it shall be given to the disposal of one gentleman or another."[33]

Certainly, Bryce's conclusion (quoted earlier) does not suggest a House of Commons capable of checking and scrutinizing the conduct of a government prepared to make unscrupulous use of the public purse to maintain itself in office. Private members' business was predominant and a "mass of private bills ... flooded the House,"[34] but these in no way impinged upon government policies, rather the reverse. Birch's comment upon eighteenth-century Britain could easily be applied to post-Confederation Canada: "The great majority of legislative measures were private bills, introduced for some such purpose as the enclosure of land or the acquisition of rights to build a canal or reservoir. These bills were frequently opposed by rival interests, and they were certainly of national, rather than of purely local concern. However, they did not affect the policies of the administration and were not the subject of ministerial decisions."[35] Only the last sentence might require qualification.

There are additional explanations for the lack of adequate control over government policy by the Canadian House. Most obvious was the lack of such a tradition before Confederation. Fennings Taylor pointed out in 1879 that, "Until the passing of 'the British North America Act, 1867', no legislature within the colonial dominions of Great Britain had been established to compare with the Imperial Parliament,"[36] and he laid stress upon the

33 / Quoted in Woodward, *The Age of Reform*, p. 26. Another interesting example of this analogy with eighteenth-century British practice can be found in Norman Ward, "The Press and the Patronage," in J. H. Aitchison, ed., *The Political Process in Canada* (Toronto, 1963).

34 / W. F. Dawson, *Procedure in the Canadian House of Commons* (Toronto, 1962), p. 22.

35 / Birch, *Representative and Responsible Government*, p. 30.

36 / Fennings Taylor, *Are Legislatures Parliaments?* (Montreal, 1879), p. 32.

failure of the colonial legislatures to scrutinize executive actions.[37] The other side of this was that in a colonial setting the executive power had been highly significant, and once autonomy in internal affairs was achieved much of this passed on to the prime minister. Furthermore, as can be observed in contemporary cases, the first leaders of newly independent states are usually relatively untroubled by serious opposition for some years – witness Nkrumah, Smallwood, and Nehru. In Canada it was not until the accession of Laurier to the leadership that the Liberal party was able to present a sustained and relatively cohesive opposition to the government. Finally, the fact that positive state action, in the sense of a policy of economic development, was a major part of the government's program caused members to be anxious to stand well with the government so as to secure their due share of benefits.

Rather, then, than the primary functional differentiation in the classic system of "governing" and "control of government," the Canadian case corresponded much more to the older functional dichotomy of "executive" and "legislature". And while the same kinds of tendencies were at work as in Britain to change the system, there were also significant differences in the subsequent Canadian pattern of development. These, in the main, derive from the facts that Canada was a federal union in a North American setting and that its party system at the federal level evolved along different lines from the British.

The franchise, as in Britain, was steadily extended despite a chequered history. Parties became more organized and more disciplined. Yet by British standards they remained rather loose groupings of sectional units – federal "broker" parties *par excellence*. If party leaders were to hold their followers and maintain the necessary degree of legislative cohesion, they could not afford to impose too many demands upon back-benchers. Thus the achievement in this century of a high degree of legislative cohesion by the major parties has been made possible by the relatively limited demands, in terms of adherence to specific policies, made

37 / *Ibid.*, pp. 118–19. He also complained about the inadequacies of the press in reporting public affairs.

by party leaders upon their followers.[38] And the relative absence of significant ideological differences between these parties has given the electoral struggle the appearance of being primarily a battle between "ins" and "outs." Only in a limited sense, therefore, could such parties be described as "mass" parties.

Furthermore, after the First World War the two-party system in Canada broke down. While it continued to be possible in the main to conduct parliamentary business as though a two-party system persisted, since ordinarily one party was able to secure a clear majority of the seats, nevertheless the existence of minority governments in the 1920s, in 1957, and again from 1962 to 1968 has acted as a serious check to the aggrandizement of the government in the House of Commons (especially when the government has also happened to be deficient in parliamentary skills).

Two additional comments can be made here. First, the diversity of the country itself and the nature of the major parties combine to place those chosen as party leaders in a far more exalted position vis-à-vis their ministerial colleagues than has been the case in Britain.[39] This elevation of the leader has been further emphasized by the populist device of leadership conventions. To a large extent, then, the "cult of personality" replaces party leadership based upon more orthodox considerations, and the route to party leadership is less and less through a lengthy apprenticeship in federal party ranks. Conversely, the leader of a major party who is unable to win elections is probably more vulnerable than his British counterpart. Second, if a party can secure prolonged electoral success, as the Liberal party did from 1935 to 1957, when the prospect of defeat seemed extremely remote, then the kind of situation described by Mackintosh[40] is more closely approximated.

Another point of difference from the British case lies in the

38 / See Leon Epstein, "A Comparative Study of Canadian Parties," *American Political Science Review*, vol. 58 (March 1964), pp. 46–59.

39 / See R. R. Alford, *Party and Society* (Chicago, 1963), p. 282, and an item from the *Toronto News* in 1905 reprinted in Dawson, ed., *Constitutional Issues in Canada*, pp. 121–5. The latter is also an interesting anticipation of more modern claims of "cabinet dictatorship."

40 / See p. 226 above.

expansion of state activity. For a variety of reasons, the demand for social justice was later in appearing in Canada and has never achieved the same intensity as in Britain. Again, until the First World War foreign affairs and defence were of relatively little significance and even since then they have not assumed the same importance as in Britain. In addition, until that time also there was no problem of obstruction of government business in the House comparable to that of the Irish Nationalists. Finally, Canada was, in a governmental sense, a "smaller" country than Britain, for while its size and diversity required a relatively large government apparatus, this was more than compensated for by the small population, the prevailing social philosophy, and the existence of a federal system which divided governmental responsibilities.[41] Thus it was not until 1913 that procedural changes in the House of Commons took place which were at all comparable to those effected in Britain in the 1880s. Indeed, it is doubtful if these changes were as substantial as the British ones,[42] but still Professor W. F. Dawson describes 1913 as "the most important single year in the history of Canadian procedural reform, [when] the House put into the hands of the Government the power needed to control the business of the House."[43] Even so, Canadian governments have shown themselves more reluctant to use this power than their British counterparts.

Relatively, then, Canadian governments experienced less pressure than British, and the changes to meet new demands in Canada occurred a generation later and in a more muted form than in Britain. Since the First World War the role of government

41 / Of course, it is also true that there is a long tradition of "positive" state activity in Canada. See A. Brady, "The Economic Activity of the State in the Dominions," in R. MacG. Dawson, ed., *Problems of Modern Government* (Toronto, 1941), pp. 106–18.

42 / At least one Canadian authority suggests that they were not. Before 1964–65, "Canadian procedure was to some extent where that of Westminster had been prior to the reforms of the 1880s. ..." Philip Laundy, "Procedural Reform in the Canadian House of Commons," *The Table (The Journal of the Society of Clerks-at-the-Table in Commonwealth Parliaments)*, vol. 34 (1966), p. 20.

43 / *Procedure*, p. 23.

has continued to expand. The two wars themselves and the post-1945 situation were powerful influences. So also was the Depression and the growing demand for social justice. But while there was a very marked growth in state activity, at the same time and largely for the kinds of reasons mentioned previously the necessity for the government to order the business of the House minutely has been much less than in Britain. Thus it remains the case that the pressure on back-benchers is a great deal lighter, and complaints in Canada about an overworked House subjected to stringent party discipline should be treated sceptically.

One further comment can be made about these developments. In Canada also there has emerged in the twentieth century a large, expert, and non-partisan civil service. Given the inevitable deficiencies of the governing parties as innovators and the increasing demand for "collectivist" policies, especially after the experience of the Depression, it is not surprising that the senior ranks of the bureaucracy in Canada have come to play a highly significant role in policy formation, probably much greater than that of the Administrative Class in the British civil service.

In short, while a development corresponding to that in Britain has also taken place in Canada, it has probably not gone as far because of the character of society and politics in this country. Indeed, it is probable that in Canada it is the bureaucracy which has come into its own, rather than governments proper. The balance of the classic parliamentary system was lacking from the outset and the House was a most inadequate scrutineer of governmental policies and actions. Yet it is doubtful if Canadian governments have in the last century strengthened their position in the House of Commons to the same extent as British governments, and at the same time there are indications that the contemporary Canadian House is a more vital and effective body than it was in the immediate post-Confederation years. This is not to say that by the standards of the classical model it is satisfactory, but it is probably less unsatisfactory than it once was. In a curious fashion, therefore, Canadian parliamentary government, which in the years after Confederation bore strong resemblances to that of eighteenth-century Britain, has by the middle of the twentieth century come to resemble mid-nineteenth-century British parliamentary government to a greater extent than ever before. And for those who value limited, balanced government the paradoxical consequence of this time-lag is that Canadian government now gives some indication – albeit weakly – of being a more truly responsible government than at any time in the past.

IV

It is by no means true today that the House of Commons is powerless vis-à-vis the government, even in Britain. Morrison comments that "if Governments are often saved from parliamentary defeat by the back-benchers' fear of a dissolution, it is no less true that Governments must treat their supporters with respect and understanding, because ... it is essential to the success and survival of the Government and its political party."[44] After all, the primary requirement of a party leader is to have followers and these cannot be kept in line simply by compulsion or the promise of patronage. There is a profound truth in Carlyle's contemptuous remark: "I am their leader, therefore I must follow."

But of great importance also are the structure and constitutional powers of the House itself. For while it is quite true that it is civil servants and ministers who are chiefly responsible for initiating and drafting legislation, they are not the only participants in the legislative process. Legislation requires the approval of the Commons and there is not a coincidence of interest between ministers, civil servants, and members of Parliament. (Indeed it is a fallacy to assume that such a coincidence must exist between ministers and civil servants.) Certainly governments do not normally anticipate defeat over their legislative proposals if they enjoy majority support, but their expectations are based upon the fact that they have gone through a complex process beforehand to ensure that this does not happen. While part of this consists of consultation with various interests, much of the process is occasioned by the necessity to secure approval in the House. Even more than this, the description of the Commons as a

44 / H. Morrison, *Government and Parliament* (3rd ed., London, 1964), p. 108.

"rubber stamp" is rendered meaningless by the obligation imposed upon the government to defend its measures there, in the
presence of an opposition which seeks to present itself as an
alternative government. Thus the government has to try and
convince the electorate and, more immediately, its own supporters
in the House that it deserves support and eventual re-election,
that its policies are correct, and its personnel competent. To this
extent, the role of the House in the legislative process can hardly
be termed a formality.[45] It is surely true that the Commons
"remains the one institution whose demise would involve the
virtual disappearance of everything characteristically democratic
about our political way of life. ..."[46]

Nevertheless, there is little cause for complacency. Given a
belief in the desirability of constitutionalism in government above
all else – in the idea that government should at all times be limited
and balanced and that there should be effective responsibility on
the part of the governors to the elected representatives – then it
is clear that the House of Commons is at a severe disadvantage in
its relations with the government. Of course, it is possible to
accept this as "inevitable" and suggest alternative control devices:
the "ultimate weapon" of elections; the pseudo-science of public
opinion polling; the pressures of officially recognized interest
groups; the "countervailing power" of provincial governments as
manifested, for example, in federal-provincial conferences; or
even the attempts to provide a "non-solution" to the problem
through the creation of semi-autonomous agencies or appointing
royal commissions.[47] But while some of these possess a certain
value, they are also highly imperfect modes of control and should
properly complement and supplement, not replace, the House
of Commons.

As has been suggested, the present condition of the House,
relative to its past, is not nearly as deplorable as is often argued.

45 / Cf. Vile, *Constitutionalism*, pp. 321–3, and B. Crick, *The Reform of Parliament* (London, 1964), pp. 25–8.
46 / A. H. Hanson, "The Purpose of Parliament," *Parliamentary Affairs*, vol. 17 (summer 1964), p. 295.
47 / There are in addition political scientists whose major concern is not with the irresponsibility of "the government" but with the irresponsibility of "private government," primarily in the case of giant corporations.

While much time continues to be unwisely consumed and while a minority have persisted in negative, obstructionist tactics,[48] members in general have increasingly shown a willingness and a capacity to engage in "discovering the facts on which policy is based and commenting on the conduct of that policy."[49] And the specific set of political conditions existing in Canada at the present time would appear to be favourable to a further improvement of the House. Such an improvement would in no way be prejudicial to the maintenance of effective government, but rather would be conducive to more responsible government in Canada.

What steps can be taken to further this improvement? The difficulty is to try and distinguish the wood from the trees. Many proponents of parliamentary reform appear to believe that by changing the length of the question period or providing additional time for private members' business or introducing television cameras into the chamber minor miracles will occur. They are in error. The primary changes must be much more general. Politics must be treated as a professional business and a parliamentary career must be regarded by politicians as something rewarding in itself. The first of these will require some change in the climate of public opinion (and hence in the manner in which members of Parliament and their activities are all too frequently caricatured by the press, radio, and television), but there is reason to be optimistic on the basis of the calibre of many members who have entered the House in recent years.[50] The second will undoubtedly require reforms that will make a strictly parliamentary career

48 / Undoubtedly, the very lengthy session of 1964–65 generated considerable criticism of proceedings in the Commons. But at the same time much of this criticism was founded on misapprehensions about the functions of that body.

49 / Mackintosh regards these as the "central functions" of the House. See "The Reform of Parliament," in B. Whitaker, ed., *A Radical Future* (London, 1967), pp. 36–55.

50 / It is interesting to note that Bryce in *Modern Democracies* (chap. 67) listed "Professionalism in Politics" as a serious defect in some of the governments that he surveyed. He objected strenuously to politics being made "a business occupation, in which the motive of civic duty is superseded by the desire of private gain." But this judgment must be considered in the light of conditions prevalent in certain countries, especially the USA, at the time when Bryce was writing, and also in the light of his own class preferences.

sufficiently attractive for a considerable proportion of those who seek election. It is here that proposals for research and secretarial assistance, for certain kinds of procedural alterations, for budgetary provision for committees, and so forth become important. But even more important is the necessity to assert the independence of the Commons by changing the present balance between front-benchers and back-benchers. It is quite misleading to describe the problem of executive-legislative relations in terms of "government" and "opposition." Over fifty years ago Belloc and Chesterton described the front-benchers as "one close oligarchical corporation" and a contemporary Australian political scientist has acutely described the situation now, in Canada as well as in Britain: "A study of the reform of Commons procedure ... is better seen as a study of the 'ins' and 'outs' of power rather than a study of the 'ins' and 'outs' of Government. There is a conflict of procedural interest in the chamber, but it is not the conflict to be seen on social issues; it is a contest of the interested back-bencher versus the rest. ... In the procedural struggle of House of Commons versus the executive there is more in common between two front-benchers, one of whom is a member of the Government and one a member of the Opposition, than between a front-bencher and a back-bencher of the same party. The front-bench political élite groups in the House have a coincidence of interest in power; neither group is particularly anxious that the floor of the House should develop in efficiency as the national forum wherein their power – *vis-à-vis* the rank and file – may be challenged. Both élites are sympathetic to trends that remove uncertainty and unpredictable elements from parliamentary debate. That is, both are opposed to the development of a wider scope for open politics in the parliamentary process."[51]

Today it is an essential principle of the parliamentary form of government as practised in Canada that the ministry should be members of one or other house of Parliament, and in fact that all but one or two should sit in the Commons. However, it is also basic to the effective and responsible functioning of parliamentary

51 / Gordon Reid, *The Politics of Financial Control: The Role of the House of Commons* (London, 1966), p. 27.

government that the ministry should be only a small part of the Commons numerically. Yet at present the ministry can number well over twenty persons and with the addition of parliamentary secretaries and whips (who are not formally part of the ministry, but must realistically be considered an adjunct of it) this number will normally total over forty. This is in the region of one third to one quarter of the membership on the government side ordinarily. On the opposition side there is another sizable contingent on the front-benches. Clearly it is no longer possible to regard the front-benchers as an insignificant proportion of the membership, and in qualitative terms it is to be expected that this group will contain some of the ablest persons in the House. A ministerial and "shadow ministerial" group of this size must necessarily be detrimental to the proper functioning of the Commons and prejudicial to the acceptance of the value of Parliamentary careerism. As Bernard Crick observes: "A backbencher must be exceptionally clear-headed and candid if, with such short odds, he does not believe that fortune will smile his way one day. Such numbers, then, do not apply their discipline merely upon those directly concerned; great expectations are created in others. A modern Prime Minister has a patronage beyond the wildest dreams of avarice of a Walpole or a Newcastle."[52]

It is an essential step in the improvement of the position of beck-benchers that a limit should be placed upon the proportion of office holders (including parliamentary secretaries) in the House in relation to the total membership. This would in turn have an immediate effect on the size of the opposition front bench. It seems quite reasonable to propose that office holders should constitute no more than 10 per cent of the total membership and that of this 10 per cent one half should be ministers of cabinet rank and one half parliamentary secretaries. Assuming that the House remains at its present size – and there are good grounds for not increasing it – this would allow for thirteen individuals in each group. It might be argued that this would place impossible burdens upon the ministers, but in view of the virtuosity with which prime ministers have been wont to reshuffle departmental

52 / *The Reform of Parliament*, p. 30.

responsibilities there is no reason to believe that this would be so. Rather, it should clarify the lines of responsibility and would hopefully lead to a more logical structuring of the executive branch of government. Furthermore, such a limitation would be advantageous for a prime minister besieged by claimants for office. While it would not, and should not, eliminate regional representation in the cabinet, other criteria of selection would also loom large. In short, the benefits of such a restriction would not accrue to back-benchers alone.

Coincidentally there would have to be a recognition by the front benches that it is necessary to seek that middle path between too much and too little party discipline over back-benchers. It has already been argued that party discipline is more flexible in Canada than in Britain, and while more slackening of the reins might not appear to the front-benchers to be in their own interests, this would be a very dubious and short-run criterion to employ. Back-benchers have no inherent desire to destroy their own leaders in the House and they would almost all support Disraeli's claim that "you cannot choose between party government and Parliamentary government. I say, you can have no Parliamentary government if you have no party government."[53] But the consciousness of a more relaxed party discipline would liberate back-benchers to a degree in certain kinds of activity, such as committee work. If such a relaxation were accompanied by a greater frankness between front-benchers and other members and by less insistence on the prerogatives of rank, then to the question, "What happens to Parliament?", we should be able to reply, in rather tortuous but optimistic fashion, "Both of its elements live together reasonably happily ever after."

53 / From a speech in the House of Commons in 1848, quoted in Butt, *The Power of Parliament*, p. 73.

12

Toward the Democratic Class Struggle*

GAD HOROWITZ

THE TERM "DEMOCRACY" has, like many other honorific terms, fallen victim to twentieth-century doublespeak, which is a device used by the practical-minded for the purpose of "adjusting their ideals to reality," thereby obscuring the gap between the ideal and the real, and substituting the name for the thing. We no longer use the term "democracy" to refer to a situation in which masses of people participate, directly and meaningfully, in the making of the decisions which shape the basic conditions of their existence. We have discovered that this is an unattainable ideal – which means not that it is absolutely, inevitably, and eternally unattainable, but that all our efforts to attain it have failed: limited as we are by ignorance, or by original sin, or by what seem to be inexorable social and economic necessities, we do not know how to attain it. We have therefore decided to adjust the ideal to the reality; that is, we have given up the ideal. We now use the term "democracy" to refer to the reality of our way of life.

Of course, there are large differences of opinion about the nature of that reality. Perhaps the most common view is that

*An earlier version of this paper appeared in the *Journal of Canadian Studies*, November 1966.

which was first formulated by Joseph Schumpeter, who defined democracy as "the rule of the politician," or, in a more extended phrase, as "that institutional arrangement for arriving at political decisions in which individuals acquire the power to decide by means of a competitive struggle for the people's vote." Those who hold this view believe that we have the second best thing to real democracy. The people do not have the power; their elected leaders have the power; the people act through their leaders. This is, surely, in this world, a satisfactory approximation to the real thing.

Assuming for the sake of argument that the people do act through their elected leaders – something that is not at all certain – and granting that the rule of politicians is a satisfactory substitute for the real thing, the question remains: Is this really a description of the reality of our system? Is our system one in which elected leaders make the political decisions? Do we have even this second best approximation to democracy? That depends on how one defines "political." What are political decisions? If they are simply whatever decisions are made by politicians, the definition fits the reality. But tautology is never satisfying. What if the political decisions are less significant, less powerfully determining of the fate of the community, than non-political decisions? Can we then say that the community is governed by its political decision-makers?

The only way of avoiding this difficulty is to define "political" non-tautologically, as "pertaining to the polity." Political decisions are decisions which are of importance to the community, decisions on public matters. And it is a fact that the most important of these decisions are not made by our political elite but by other elites which are not accountable to the community. The common or Schumpeterian definition of democracy is therefore not an accurate description of the reality of our system. We have not even achieved second best. We have not even approximated democracy.

I want to suggest that, among the roles that the party system in our society can and should play, the most important is to move our society toward democracy – not the "utopian" democracy in which the people rule, but the "attainable" democracy in which an elite accountable to the people rules.

If the party system is to play the role of moving us closer to democracy, if, in other words, our political elite is to be strengthened to the point where it replaces the corporate and bureaucratic elites as the source of the most important social decisions, our party system must be polarized on a left-right basis, and the main issues raised for discussion in the political arena must be class issues. I will argue not only that this change in the party system ought to be brought about, but that it can be brought about, and with no evil side effects.

The Democratic Class Struggle

We are interested in strengthening our political elite in relation to other elites not because we want politicians to have more power for themselves, but because we want ordinary people to have more power. Power is what it takes to get what there is to get. Power is valuable because it is a means to other values; Lasswell classifies them as security, income, deference. To move closer to democracy is to redistribute power, and with it all other values, downwards in the social system. Some form of elite rule is probably inevitable in a modern industrial society; the political elite is the one which is most sensitive to the needs of the mass of the people; therefore the rule of the politician is the form of elite rule which comes closest to democracy.

To move closer to democracy requires (1) that the political elite include a powerful party of the "left," which I will define provisionally as a party which is more responsive to the needs of the underprivileged than to those of the overprivileged; (2) that this party succeed in mobilizing popular support for programs of social change, i.e., for policies which will reallocate social values in the interest of the underprivileged. This in turn requires attention to the latent, unexpressed, unarticulated needs of the masses as well as to their manifest needs, for the masses are seldom capable of expressing autonomously their need for power and the things that it can get. One of the techniques of oligarchy has always been to train the masses to be content with their lot, to minimize their demands, to want what they get. The task of a left party is to agitate – to train the masses to be discontented with their lot, to maximize their demands, to get what they want.

In a well ordered society, the privileged elites and the politicians responsive to them behave responsibly in the sense that they do not press their resistance to social change past the point where it would endanger the underlying consensus guaranteeing the stability of the society. The elite of the masses (the left) behaves responsibly in that it does not press the masses' demands for change past that same point, nor past the point of obvious impracticability. The political process is thus one of peaceful social change within a society which is fundamentally at one. The democratic class struggle is carried on within the framework of a broad integrating consensus; it is not a class war.

It should also be emphasized that change cannot proceed continuously at an intense rate without disrupting the society. Change in a well ordered society therefore comes in undulations or cycles. In the first stage of the cycle the left presses for change, the privileged elites resist. In the second stage the privileged elites absorb the change, while the left relaxes its pressure, whines that it has "run out of ideas," and one and all proclaim the "end of ideology" until the next undulation begins. The societal consensus is thus, as V. O. Key has pointed out, a moving consensus. It moves continuously from the stage of innovation, when social tension is great, to the stage of accommodation, when policy differences between left and right temporarily approach the vanishing point.

If popular support is to be mobilized for programs of social change, the main issues which are raised in the political arena must be left-right issues, that is, class issues: issues which have to do with the allocation of values among the different classes of society. Under these conditions the political system can be used to some extent by non-elites as an instrument with which to counter the power of elites. Power can continually be redistributed downwards in successive first stages of the moving consensus. Without the dynamism provided by a left-right cleavage, the political system cannot initiate significant changes in the social order; it cannot radically alter the structure of comparative advantages and disadvantages in the interest of the under-privileged. It can only reflect the existing structure of power and co-ordinate to some extent the activities of the disparate component elements of that structure. In other words, when politics is not a democratic class struggle, the political elite cannot innovate in the interest of the non-elite; it can only serve as a broker among established elite groups. It cannot articulate the latent desires of the non-elite; it can only arrange compromises among the desires that are strong enough to assert themselves without the articulation services of politicians.

The social progress we have had in this country has not been the result of a left-right cleavage. It has been a result of the important but marginal pressure of the CCF-NDP together with the "demonstration effect" of reforms in Britain and the United States. That is why we have not moved as quickly or as consistently in the direction of democratic goals as either the liberal Americans or the socialist Britons. Our political elites operate, more clearly than theirs, on the periphery rather than the centre of the structure of power. Our politicians are restricted, more clearly than theirs, to the tasks of adjustment and co-ordination. They make fewer new demands on behalf of the non-elite, because the leftists among them are a minor party which can never get close to the motor of the system.

I have argued that our party system should be polarized on a left-right basis. There are many who would agree in principle, but most of these would go on to take the line either that such a change is impracticable in this country or that if implemented it would have intolerable side effects. These people are operating with two erroneous theories which are epiphenomena of the conservative mood of the United States during the fifties. The first of these theories is the "end of ideology," which is the theory that the terms "left" and "right" have no relevance to the problems of the fifties and sixties. The second is the brokerage theory of party politics, the theory that North American parties are always and must always be nothing but coalitions of all the significant interests of society, and politicians nothing but brokers among these interests.

Both theories are false, or at the very best misleadingly half-true; both theories, while purporting to be value-free political science, are in fact conservative rationalizations; and both theories, while they reflected the mood of the fifties in the United States and Canada, are out of tune with the mood of the sixties. Since neither of these theories is stylish, both should be eschewed by our "new generation of urbane and intelligent people who live with a certain sense of style." Since neither of these theories is true, it is unfortunate that they have hobbled the political thought of left-of-centre academics in Canada and thereby damaged the cause of social progress in this country.

The End of Ideology?

There is always a certain amount of confusion about the meaning of the terms "left" and "right." They are used to refer to a great many differing historical, ideological, and political phenomena. There have been suggestions that these terms have lost all meaning and ought therefore to be dropped. In my opinion, it would be better to cut away their useless meanings and retain the useful ones. The terms "left" and "right" are most useless and most confusing when they are used to refer to the content of particular policy proposals. Here is an example. The term "left" is very often defined as advocacy of social welfare schemes, government intervention in the economy, and public ownership. Since all Canadian parties support these policies, it is very often observed that the terms "left" and "right" have little relevance to Canadian politics.

But – first of all – the fact that a party implements a "leftist" policy does not necessarily indicate that it is a left party. A policy is a means to an end. The same means can be used by people who have very different ends in mind, people who are operating with very different motives and responding to very different social stimuli. The German socialists pressed for welfare policies because they wanted the German people to have more of what there was to get. Bismarck implemented welfare policies because he wanted to steal the socialists' thunder and prevent revolution. Bismarck and the socialists favoured the same policy. Was Bismarck a leftist?

Second, there is often disagreement on the right about the relative merits of alternative means of achieving rightist goals, and there is always disagreement on the left about the means of achieving leftist goals. Socialists, for example, have always disagreed among themselves about the appropriateness of nationalization and centralization as means to the distinctively socialist goals of community and equality of condition. Some socialists have preferred more decentralized forms of public ownership, and some have opined that very little public ownership of any kind is required. But these latter groups are just as socialist, just as leftist in this particular way of being leftist, as the nationalizers and centralizers.

To take another example, the goal of the American left, which is not socialist but liberal, has always been to protect the "little man" – the individual pursuer of happiness in the great competitive society – against large concentrations of economic power, i.e., to preserve equality of opportunity. In the days of Andrew Jackson the means to this end were *laissez faire* and the destruction of monopolistic privileges. In the days of Franklin Roosevelt the means were government intervention and the regulation of concentrations of economic power. But Jackson and Roosevelt were both leftists, because they had the same broad ends in view. No one would call Jackson a right-winger even though he believed in *laissez faire*. In 1830 *laissez faire* was the policy of the American left: it was a weapon against the privileged. In 1930 *laissez faire* was the policy of the American right: it was a weapon for the privileged.

Finally, the policy differences between left and right, since they occur within a moving consensus, are nearly always matters of degree. It therefore will not do to say that since both parties favour the same policy there is no longer a left-right distinction between them. Both the Tories and the Labour party in Britain – during this second or relaxed phase of the moving consensus in that country – are in favour of the policies of the welfare state and the managed economy. But the Labour party is still the left, because it was the originator of those policies, because it wants to implement them more thoroughly and swiftly, and because it has leftist motives for implementing them. The Tories are still the right because they first resisted those policies and then made peace with them, because they move less thoroughly and swiftly in implementing them, and because they have rightist motives for implementing them.

Because the same policy can be grounded in differing motives, and because the same motive can lead to differing policies, and because policy differences in a well-ordered society are usually not very sharp, the terms "left" and "right" are least useful when they are applied to policy differences. They are most useful when they are applied to the broad, rather vague sets of attitudes – which we may call ideologies – which serve as one of the important grounds of policy (the other being expediency). Ideologies are in turn related, in a direct but complicated and ambiguous way, to the stratification system. We therefore define a left party as one which is more closely related to the lower strata and has an ideology oriented to redistributing social values to these strata; we define a right party as one which is more closely related to the higher strata and is ideologically oriented to resisting the redistribution of social values.

A leftist party believes that ordinary people should have more power in the society. To the degree that it is liberal it stresses equality of opportunity. To the degree that it is socialist it stresses equality of condition. A left party is the source of innovation, of social change on behalf of the non-elite. The parties of the right and centre eventually adopt leftist innovations for their own reasons, but they do not for that reason deserve to be called leftist.

Now the theory of the end of ideology is itself unmasked as ideology in the following manner. To say that the distinction between left and right is no longer relevant to our social problems is to say that the unequal distribution of social values is no longer a problem. But that is always the opinion of the privileged. It is unfortunate that a leftist should find himself repeating it. If he requests merciful treatment on the ground that what he really meant was that inequality is still a problem, but that no one is excited about it, he may or may not be correct, depending on the stage of the moving consensus. But if no one is excited about the problem, the task of the leftist is surely to rouse a bit of excitement. The distinction between left and right will always be relevant – until the dream of equality is realized. We know that in all likelihood it will never be realized. The roles of left and right are therefore never-ending.

It has been argued that the distinction between left and right is no guide to the solution of many troublesome Canadian problems – federal finance, regional development, bilingualism and biculturalism, American investment. In the first place, this is not so. An egalitarian ideology will have definite policy implications for these problems. In the second place, even if it were so, no one has ever maintained that leftism or rightism can be guides to the solution of every social problem; nor has anyone ever held that left and right must disagree about everything. They never do, in a well ordered society, which is the reason that blood is not flowing in the streets of London and Vancouver. In the third place, the very fact that bilingualism and biculturalism and federal-provincial finance are more salient in Canada than the issue of inequality is itself an indication of the weakness of the left in this country. The distinguishing mark of a leftist is his belief that, ultimately, inequality is the most noxious of social problems, that the issue of inequality should be most salient in the political consciousness of a society, and that the party system should therefore be polarized on a left-right basis. If other issues are more salient, the leftist will try to minimize them. If the party system is not polarized, the leftist will try to polarize it. The non-leftist will always take the opposite view on these matters. His feeling will be that the masses already have enough power, or too much power, that class issues should therefore be non-salient and the party system unpolarized. He will, in other words, profess the ideology of the end of ideology and the brokerage theory of party politics.

Brokerage for Ever?
The brokerage theory of party politics maintains that in North America both major political parties are nearly identical coalitions of all the significant ideologies and social forces of the

nation, that they must be coalitions of this type, and that all is for the best, in this best of all possible societies, when they are. We are told that the party system must have this character for these reasons: (1) North American societies are so heterogeneous, so diverse in their ethnic, religious, regional, and economic composition, that the introduction of the additional element of class conflict would be intolerably divisive. Because North Americans are so sharply fragmented, the role of political parties must be to unify rather than to divide, to act as agents of consensus (brokers) rather than agents of dissensus (agitators). The function of both parties must be to prevent new cleavages – to draw the divergent elements together into a majority by whatever means possible. (2) Again because North American society is so heterogeneous, electoral majorities are put together only with great difficulty. This impels each major party to appeal to all the elements of society for votes. In doing so, each party must either ignore or harmonize the differing views of various social forces. Both parties therefore end up with nearly identical social compositions, with nearly identical "lowest common denominator" approaches to the issues, unable to present the electorate with a sharp set of alternatives.

But all is for the best. The price that is paid for this kind of party system, the brokerage theorists tell us, is merely a low level of intellectuality in political discourse and the absence of a "real choice" in elections. I say "merely" because, for the brokerage theorist, the costs of such a system are far outweighed by the alleged gains: all significant elements of society are represented in each party – the demands of democracy are thus satisfied. Society is held together through moderation and compromise – the demands of social peace are thus satisfied.

The brokerage theory is unmasked as ideology in the following manner. (1) To say that a brokerage party is a "coalition" of all social forces, that it "represents" all social forces, is true only in the sense that its electoral support comes from all elements of the society. The language of "coalition" is a dangerously misleading language, because it obscures the differences which always exist between the leading or directing elements at the core of a political party and the heterogeneous elements in the electorate which support that core through their vote. The fact that a party is voted for by a heterogeneous grouping of voters does not make it the party of all those voters. For example, the fact that approximately 40 per cent of the British working class votes for the Tories does not make the Tory party a "coalition" of labour and business, because the directing core of the Tory party has a much closer relationship with the British business community than with the British working class. To return to North America, what the brokerage theorists like to think of as a "party of all the people" is actually a bourgeois party financed by businessmen and highly sensitive to corporate interests. The brokerage theory is in reality a class ideology, for it maintains that both our major parties must always be more closely related to the privileged elites than to the non-elites of our society.

(2) To say that the role of a party system is to serve as a non-ideological broker among existing constellations of power is first of all to conceal the fact that "non-ideological" is double-speak for "in accordance with the prevailing ideology," and second it is to deny that the role of the party system is to move us closer to democracy, i.e., to *alter* existing constellations of power in the interest of the non-elite. It means that the party system must reflect rather than alter the present state of affairs in which non-political elites are the primary source of decision-making and politicians are restricted to the task of mediating among elites. The brokerage theory is a rationalization of the interest of privileged elites in preserving their positions against the encroachments of politicians, i.e., against those who reflect the people's power.

(3) To say that politicians must eschew class issues in order to avoid disrupting the society is to say that non-class issues must be salient. The people's vote must never be an expression of their desire for more power and the things that it can get; it must always be an expression of their non-class interests – region, ethnic group, etc. – and of their opinion on non-class issues such as the personality of Trudeau, Gerda Munsinger, the flag, and so on. To say that non-elite votes which are captured in this way

make the party that gets them representative of the interests of the non-elite voter is the exact opposite of the truth, for these votes express all the interests of the non-elite voter except his interest as a non-elite voter. The brokerage theory is a rationalization of the privileged elites' interest in maintaining the non-saliency of class issues. Only the successful application of this strategy can keep a non-left party in power. The brokerage theory makes things very comfortable indeed for North American elites, for it insists that all major parties in North America must always follow this elite strategy.

The normative foundations of the brokerage theory are, I trust, exposed as bourgeois foundations and for that reason faulty. That the empirical foundations of the brokerage theory are also faulty will become evident through an examination of its false dichotomy of British-polarized and American-brokerage type party systems. According to the brokerage theory, a party system is *either* one in which the parties divide the electorate on a left-right basis, appeal to different classes, and present sharp policy alternatives to the voters, *or* a system in which the parties unite the electorate at the lowest common denominator, appeal to the same classes, and present nearly identical programs to the voters. A party system can perform *either* the function of building dissensus *or* the function of promoting consensus. It can *either* divide *or* integrate. It can be *either* British *or* American.

This is a false dichotomy because party systems that operate with any degree of efficiency – and this includes the British and the American, but not the Canadian – always perform both sets of functions: the consensus-building and the dissensus-promotion functions, though the relative emphasis given to these functions varies with the state of the moving consensus. The consensus model is not an accurate description of the American system and the dissensus model is not an accurate description of the British system. The party systems of both countries are really very similar in that both are polarized on a left-right basis (though the British is more polarized than the American) and in both all parties, left and right, perform both functions of consensus-building and dissensus-promotion.

The Labour and Democratic parties are both left parties; the Conservative and Republican parties are both right parties. The tendency of the left parties is to innovate in the interest of the lower strata; that of the right parties is to resist or retard innovation. The left parties receive much more electoral support from the lower than from the higher strata; the right parties receive proportionately much more from the higher than from the lower. The prerequisites for dissensus-promotion are thus satisfied. The electorate has a choice between a party which wants to move swiftly in redistributing social values, and which therefore tends to emphasize class issues, and a party which wants to move slowly or not at all and therefore emphasizes non-class issues.

At the same time, all these parties are coalitions of diverse interests, in these two senses: their directing cores are composed of factions representing differing interests which must be harmonized, and these directing cores, though they are broadly speaking either leftist or rightist, business-oriented or labour-oriented, are impelled by electoral exigencies to seek votes in every possible quarter. Thus, in Britain, the Tories do not call themselves "the party of the comfortable," but "the national party," and Labour does not call itself "the party of the downtrodden masses," but the party of "all who toil by hand and brain." In both countries, the right parties manage to get many votes from the lower strata, and the left parties get many votes from the upper strata. In both countries, the strength of the underlying consensus is such that left and right do not disagree on everything. In both countries non-class cleavages cut across rather than coincide with the class cleavage, thereby helping to integrate the society. In both countries most elections do not offer a very sharp set of alternatives to the voters except in the innovative stage – usually the briefest – of the moving consensus and in freak elections such as the Goldwater-Johnson confrontation. In both countries, left and right do not press their differences past the point at which social peace would be endangered. The British and American systems thus prove that left-right polarization is not incompatible with social integration. The democratic class struggle does not cause a society to fall apart in class war.

One is often told that British society can "afford" a democratic class struggle only because it is a very homogeneous society. But the fact that American politics are also polarized on a left-right basis proves that polarization can be afforded by a heterogeneous society consisting of many diverse regional, ethnic, and religious interests. The idea that Canada, because it is a heterogeneous society, must for ever be saddled with two major parties of the right or centre is beginning to be recognized as erroneous. The relationship between the consensus and dissensus functions is always complex, but the following simplification may be helpful. A nation which is in danger of falling apart on class lines may be held together by a politics which emphasizes non-class issues; that is, class cleavage can be mitigated by emphasizing the non-class cleavages which cut across it. But by the same token a nation like Canada, which is in danger of falling apart on ethnic-regional lines, may be held together by a politics which unites the people of various regions and ethnic groups around the two poles of left and right. The contention of the brokerage theorists that our heterogeneous society can be held together only if an "additional" class cleavage is avoided is the exact opposite of the truth. The promotion of dissensus on class issues is a way of mitigating dissensus on many non-class issues.

A class politics in Canada would take for granted that the nation exists and will not be dismembered. Political debate would focus on the question: Who gets what, when, how? The present non-class politics takes for granted that those who have the most of what there is to get will continue to get it, and political debate centres on the question of whether they will continue to get it in one nation or several, through the provincial governments or the federal. Class politics would translate popular discontent into demands for change in national social and economic policy. Non-class politics translates popular discontent into provincialism or separatism. Non-class politics perpetuates the power of established elites and endangers the existence of the nation.

The unity of this country will be assured only when a powerful party of the left operates at the centre rather than the periphery of our political power structure. Such a party will emerge only if the regionally and ethnically segregated victims of our society can be united by a set of common ideals and symbols based on class. To say that this will never happen because Canadians aren't class-conscious enough is to ignore the distinction between class consciousness *per se* and politicized class consciousness. Class consciousness exists in any stratified social system as a kind of natural resource which may or may not be mobilized by politicians. We are at least as class-conscious as the Americans. The difference between our system and theirs is that their system mobilizes class consciousness, makes it relevant to politics, harnesses it to the political system, while ours lets class consciousness lie unused, an untapped resource. No one can convince me that the ordinary Manitoban feels his antipathy toward the Quebecois more deeply than he feels economically and socially disadvantaged by his non-elite status. He is class-conscious, all right, and powerfully so; but he has to live with a political system which makes his ethnic identifications directly relevant to politics and his class identifications irrelevant to politics.

What people feel most strongly is not automatically perceived as politically relevant. It is the political elite of a society that decides which feelings will be harnessed to the political system and which will be allowed to remain politically irrelevant. In C. Wright Mills' terms, politics is the transformation of personal *troubles* into public *issues*. There is no major party of the left in Canada not because our people are too stupid to be conscious of the disadvantages of non-elite status, but because our business-oriented political elites have been reluctant to translate the personal trouble of non-elite status into the public issue of inequality.

When a major party of the left emerges in Canada, it will undoubtedly consist of leaders and voters who are now to be found in all four parties. I believe that the best way to develop a major party of the left is to strengthen the only left-wing party we already have – the New Democratic party. I respect the right of others to work for the same goal within the Liberal, Conservative, or Social Credit parties, but I believe that on this question, they, not I, are the utopians.

13

Public Power
and Ivory Power

J. E. HODGETTS

> Human knowledge and human power meet in one,
> for where the course is not known the effect cannot
> be produced.   FRANCIS BACON

TODAY, three hundred and fifty years after Francis Bacon penned
this aphorism, the task of finding ways of placing knowledge at
the service of power has perhaps become the supreme challenge
confronting mankind. In Bacon's day, power was concentrated in
the hands of absolute rulers, but the responsibilities of public
authorities were so limited that elementary skills in reading,
writing, and arithmetic were about all that was required of the
servants of the state. The clergy, as custodians of these rudimentary but necessary skills, tended to monopolize the bureaucracy –
a historical fact that has been ratified by the perpetuation of the
term "clerical" to describe the work they performed.

Even as late as the mid-nineteenth century this same low level
of knowledge met most of the requirements of public authorities
and, in large measure, also met the needs of private power centres.
Universities could afford to bask in the luxury of uncommitted
studies directed to the production of a handful of scholars who

were free to cultivate their humanist gardens in seclusion and leisure. Public and private power centres made few demands on their services; nor was there any mass tax-paying public to insist that they make themselves useful in the service of the community. Similarly the professions did not look to the universities for recruits, but, like the self-perpetuating guilds they were, found the knowledge they required by relying on experience gained from a prolonged apprenticeship whose conditions they themselves rigorously controlled. The scientific establishment was minuscule and still largely comprised the lone-wolf and gifted amateur who worked with primitive, hand-crafted equipment. It is true that, by the late eighteenth century, the scientific findings of these isolated minds were being placed at the disposal of economic power, but not until this century did the problem of bringing scientific knowledge to bear on the whole range of human power become, literally, a life-and-death matter.

The gathering momentum of the industrial revolution in the nineteenth century increased the demand from private power centres for technical, managerial, and economic knowledge. The ancient professions of accountancy and engineering, in all its branches, also made heavier drafts on knowledge, even as in this century the scientific establishment was called upon to place its increasingly sophisticated knowledge at the service of the community. The advent of political democracy and the rising tide of collectivist philosophy rapidly broadened the range of public power and progressively brought the private power of individuals and corporate interests under its domain. The range of knowledge and skills required to service the expanding needs of public power was, thereby, dramatically extended.

The altered and expanding demands for knowledge by private and public power centres, during the last half of the nineteenth and early part of this century, produced little change in the traditional reliance on the gifted amateur, the cultivated generalist, or the man trained in law. The informed layman – most frequently a lawyer – elected as our representative to Parliament was deemed sufficient for the knowledge needs of public power. Occasionally, he could be usefully supplemented by appointing *ad hoc* royal commissions of inquiry which were authorized to sound the public mind through public hearings and report their findings to governments for such action as they cared to take. In Canada, the almost invariable practice of drawing on the bench and the bar for the membership of such commissions simply confirmed the belief in the informed generalist skilled in the arts of probing the minds of other informed generalists.

Even the personnel of public bureaucracies reflected this preference, as they remained relatively unaffected by rising demands for more varied expert knowledge. In the 1850s, for example, the Macaulay-Trevelyan proposal to introduce an elite corps of administrators for the so-called "intellectual" work in British government departments was resisted on the grounds that the requirements were too mundane to warrant the deployment of such talents on quill-pushing operations. And, when the proposal was implemented, the basic philosophy remained unchanged: the cult of the cultivated amateur – the typical product of the Oxbridge curriculum of the day – was to persist for another century. As a consequence, universities experienced no immediate threat to their self-contained, autonomous pursuit of knowledge; not until well on in this century did the universities find themselves rather suddenly precipitated into the "public domain," partly as a result of the success attending their own pleas for state financing on grounds that they were the main suppliers of the knowledge and the knowledgeable required by all significant private and governmental power centres.

The situation confronting us today has been utterly transformed by a century that has witnessed unremitting extension of the long arm of Caesar into the lives and homes of every citizen, as it seeks to grapple with the social and economic problems created by unprecedented technological and ideological changes, secularization, urbanism, war, and a sequence of radical revolutions in communication, transportation, and new forms of energy.

The knowledge possessed by our lay representatives in Parliament has long since ceased to keep pace with the multiplicity and complexity of problems that burgeon on all sides. Their "intelligence" services are antiquated, still relying on the informal contact with constituents which were just barely adequate in a less complex age and at a time when the geographic basis for representation provided a method of tapping a more homogeneous set of interests, geared largely to an agrarian, local economy. Nor have political parties, as mobilizers of support and brokers for policies, compensated for the inadequacies of the representative: for example, they have not, as in the United Kingdom, developed a substantial research apparatus of their own. Within Parliament, the tale is much the same: mounting pleas for research assistance – at a minimum to be provided for committees – have so far had no effect; the prospect of providing, at state expense, researchers for each individual representative or a legislative reference service, as is done in the United States, is apparently even more of an idle dream of an unnecessary luxury. We increase the pay and the sitting hours of our members, but with little visible impact on either their quality or their performance. The outmoded machinery of legislatures creaks along, a source of mounting frustration for the eager neophyte MPS and a matter for endless bickering by the old hands who protest they "love this institution of Parliament" and yet will not give an inch when it comes to proposals for modernizing it.

In terms now made familiar by the systemic school of political scientists, parties have not equipped themselves to perform the basic task of aggregating interests and thereby bringing knowledge to focus on the public policies most appropriate to meet demands. They tend merely to respond to interests or seek the aid of the professional advertiser during campaigns in order to reduce policies to the low level of knowledge or understanding they are told to expect from the mass electorate. Parliament's task of defining and refining these demands and of validating choices in the public arena is not adequately performed because its machinery for appraising demands and developing a practical agenda of priorities still relies on outmoded "intelligence" links with the constituents it represents. And, as previously mentioned, Parliament still lacks any research resources of its own to provide support for its choice-making or, as David Easton puts it, "the authoritative allocation of values."

These harsh generalizations undoubtedly exaggerate the deficiencies of parties and parliaments as the instruments on which we have traditionally relied to bring knowledge to the service of public power. A measure of the validity of this diagnosis can be taken by examining at greater length the substitute instrumentalities to which we have increasingly had to resort in order to achieve this vital objective. Clearly, the more public power centres displace private power centres the greater is the need to bring knowledge of a more varied and sophisticated nature to the aid of governments. Yet, as has been argued, our conventional institutions for channelling and refining this knowledge for the multiple objectives of public power have proven increasingly inadequate for the task. In broad terms, the two agencies we have relied on most to fill the need are the public bureaucracy and what might be termed the new-model royal commission.

The Public Bureaucracy as a Repository of Knowledge
The recent tremendous expansion of the public services is a result of the attempt to harness knowledge to public power by the most direct means, namely, by recruiting into agencies of government those with the specialized skills and knowledge now deemed essential for the effective exercise of power. Data on public service employment in Canada are still surprisingly imprecise, particularly for provincial and municipal governments; nevertheless, even such rough approximations as are available are revealing. In the twenty years since the Second World War, the combined total of federal, provincial, and municipal departmental employees has increased from 221,000 to 636,000 – an increase of 187 per cent. Not only has government become the largest employer in the country (about one out of every seven salaried workers), but the rate of increase is greater than for other employers. The federal government still retains the largest share of this total, about 42 per cent as compared with 35 per cent and 23 per cent for the provinces and municipalities respectively. Nevertheless, it is important to realize that the rate of increase for provincial and municipal employment is much more rapid than for the federal government, a measure of the changing

balance of public power in our federal system. Twenty years ago there were nine federal civil servants for every 1000 citizens; today the ratio has crept up to eleven per 1000. For the provinces, the number of civil servants for every 1000 citizens has grown from four to ten; for the municipalities from five to ten for every 1000 persons.[1]

While these statistics substantiate the claim that we are in the era of big government, of greater significance is the qualitative change in the composition of governmental manpower, a qualitative change that is reflected in the general labour force as well. Historical data are not available, but current assessments of the public service reveal that the traditional emphasis on clerical workers and staff employed on routine servicing, maintenance, and operational tasks is changing. For the federal government these categories still account for about two-thirds of the total, but for the provinces they now stand at only half the total. The managerial, professional, and technical categories now comprise one-third to one-half of the total governmental manpower – strong evidence of governments' decision to "buy" the knowledge and skills required for their multi-faceted programs. Parenthetically, it should be added that much more refined analyses of American governmental manpower reveal the same patterns of growth and qualitative change.[2]

Impressive as these statistics are, they fail to reveal the full impact of the extending reach of Caesar: one should properly include the employees of vast state enterprises, such as the CNR, Air Canada, or Ontario Hydro, as well as the personnel employed in regulatory boards and commissions that have proliferated in all directions and display bewildering organizational variations that almost defy classification. This "second public service" numbers as many employees as the departments proper and tends to incorporate a larger proportion of scientific, professional, and

1 / These figures are based on an unpublished study prepared by O. P. Dwivedi, under the direction of the author.

2/ See, for example, US Civil Service Commission, *Federal Workforce Outlook, Fiscal Years 1966–69* (Washington, Nov. 1965); also Municipal Manpower Commission, *Governmental Manpower for Tomorrow's Cities* (New York, 1962).

technical skills. The growth of these non-departmental administrative entities, embracing major segments of the economy, demonstrates the enlargement of the grey area between public and private power centres. It also reflects the willingness of governments to adapt their administrative structures in order to improve their competitive position in a labour market in which the expertise or knowledge they wish to "buy" is in short supply.

It is clear that the effort of governments to supply their own power centres with the requisite knowledge by direct recruitment into departmental or non-departmental agencies has a number of interesting implications. The most obvious repercussion has already been noted – the dramatic expansion of public and quasi-public bureaucracies. Such rapid growth necessitates the allocation of more and more resources to the management and "care and feeding" of the bureaucratic machine. Such were the problems to which a team of over two hundred experts under the Royal Commission on Government Organization devoted nearly 80 man-years of research between 1960 and 1963. The five-volume report of this Commission has provided almost inexhaustible material for internal discussion, renewal of specific enquiries by outside firms of management consultants, and a continuous stream of organizational changes. It is obviously essential to pay unremitting attention to the techniques for improving the output procedures of the system, but this activity should not become an introverted absorption in techniques that distracts attention from the equally important task of considering the content of the output.

If it be argued that permanent servants of the state *should* concentrate their knowledge and expertise on means rather than ends, this is to blind oneself to the shift in the locus of power within the political system. Clearly, increasing attention must be devoted to means, as the organization and staffing of the public sector assume major significance; and it is equally clear we must look to civil servants, in the main, to assume responsibility for this task rather than anticipate helpful guidance from outside the public service. Nevertheless, the balance of power has also shifted to the permanent bureaucracy to such an extent that its senior members must also occupy themselves more than even before with the identification, refinement, and formulation of policy objectives.

The traditional functions assigned by our system to parties, legislatures, and the judiciary have, without any overt statutory changes in constitutional authority, gradually shifted to the bureaucracy. The parties' task of aggregating demands, the legislature's responsibility for sifting and arbitrating conflicting demands, and the judiciary's role of policing the implementation of policy have all tended, in varying measure, to be taken on by the public service. A good deal of the so-called brokerage function is now undertaken by direct negotiation between public agencies and the clientele interests they serve or regulate. The refinement of policy and arbitration of conflicting policy goals tend also to be handled by civil servants who have been vested with discretionary power to determine whether a health or safety measure is "adequate" or "safe," whether a person is "fit and proper" to receive a licence, and the thousand and one other variations on this theme thrown up by the collectivist state. Boards, commissions, and regulatory-cum-policy agencies of all kinds make similar inroads on the traditional functions of the judiciary by prosecuting cases involving the rights of corporate interests or by making determinations that affect the claims of individual citizens. That such agencies may also have legislated the terms in the first place simply compounds their power by making them legislators, prosecutors and judges (and perhaps even appellate courts) all in one. As definers and defenders of the public interest, they may often find it administratively convenient, in playing their brokerage role, to equate the interests of their clientele with a less clearly defined public interest: a *modus vivendi* mutually satisfactory to regulator and the regulated may produce a distorted version of the public interest.

These shifts in the locus of power have not failed to attract critical notice. Bar associations have inveighed against the preemption of the functions of the judiciary; legislators have desperately pleaded the cause of parliamentary supremacy; and now spokesmen appear to champion an ombudsman – a species of parliamentary auditor to report on the abuse of administrative powers. Whatever may come from these critics or from those who would add new controlling mechanisms, there is no sign that the locus of power will be shifted away from the public service. Some, who acknowledge that the clock cannot be put back, suggest that we must rely now on the sense of integrity of public servants: if responsibility cannot be imposed by traditional components of our political system then we must have faith, as we do for other professions like medicine and law, in self-imposed professional ethics to act as an internal constraint on the exercise of power that comes through the possession of special knowledge.[3]

Whether or not this line of thought is pursued, it is at least possible to observe two relatively recent developments within the public service that indicate a growing awareness on the part of the bureaucrat of the *de facto* power which he commands by virtue of his knowledge. First, there is the expansion of public information services within the government which has been viewed by some suspicious critics as an outright adoption of the public relations approach to the tax-paying public, akin to the Madison Avenue approach of many private business enterprises. It may be true in some instances that promotion of a favourable "image" lurks uncomfortably close to the surface of governmental publicity, but in most cases the growth of public information officers is a reflection of the increasing sensitivity of the bureaucrats to the power they command. Understandably, they wish to make their position clear by means of direct communication with the public rather than through intermediaries like legislators or parties.[4]

Closely related purposes are served by a second development – the association of formal advisory bodies with the formulation

3 / For a classical debate on this proposition see Carl J. Friedrich, "Public Policy and the Nature of Administrative Responsibility," in C. J. Friedrich and E. S. Mason, eds., *Public Policy* (Cambridge, Mass., 1940) and Herman Finer, "Administrative Responsibility in Democratic Government," *Public Administration Review* (1941), p. 335.

4 / For a description and critical analysis of the role of public information officers in Canadian government see the Royal Commission on Government Organization, *Public Information Services*, Report no. 13 in vol. III (Ottawa, 1963).

and administration of governmental programs. Again, this phenomenon is a response to the need to devise direct communication links between public power centres and the influential, affected, and possibly knowledgeable members of the community. That these advisory adjuncts are designed to supplement the inadequacies of our traditional communication links is demonstrated by their extensive application to recently developed regional schemes where representative institutions are lacking and where political parties do not have the appropriate organization. Indeed, as I have argued elsewhere, the concept of "region" is so far from being a natural by-product of a sense of community, deriving from spontaneously generated common interests, that public authorities have had to construct the regions themselves.[5] Thus, the program dictates the region, and administrators deliberately sponsor the formation of an advisory group to "represent" or discover the common regional interests. This development may be viewed as a Canadian substitute for the relatively unrestricted access enjoyed by organized interest groups – both functionally and regionally based – in the more open, fragmented American political system.

Whether the clientele for a government service has to be organized by the public authority involved or whether that authority makes use of already existing organized interest groups, the fact remains that communication links supplementary to or substituting for our traditional representative and political organs have had to be brought into play by the bureaucracy. Without these newer direct channels, knowledge and information vital to decisions taken by public power centres would be less effectively transmitted, and the agents working in such centres would lack the assurance that they were not developing programs in a vacuum.

The end result of this shift in the locus of power and of the new devices for bringing bureaucratic power centres into direct contact with their "publics" may be to thrust public servants much more

5 / "Regional Interests and Policy in a Federal State," *Canadian Journal of Economics and Political Science*, vol. XXXII, no. 1 (Feb. 1966), pp. 8–13.

into the open. The tradition of civil service anonymity has always had strong support, for if the servant of the state is openly identified with the policy or program output of the system he cannot preserve his capacity to serve political masters of various party hues. Thus, the permanency of the bureaucracy depends on anonymity, although the typically slow swing of the political pendulum in both provincial and federal jurisdictions has only rarely and sporadically tended to place this concept in jeopardy. It may be that, in their new search to fill communications gaps, public servants will be obliged to become more positively and publicly identified, not only through their direct advocacy of policies which are largely of their designing, but also through their direct association with the affected members of the public. If this is, indeed, to be the upshot of the developments noted above, then the permanency of senior civil servants may no longer be an acceptable pattern – or even a possible pattern, should political parties prove incapable in the long run of restoring the relatively stable pattern of governments with clear and long-term majorities.

Before one runs up the distress signals at the prospect envisaged in the foregoing analysis, it would be well to realize that in the United States there has never been a top administrative cadre comprising a permanent policy-making establishment. A quite different tradition was established in that country during the early days of patronage, reinforced by the Jacksonian egalitarian philosophy which made a point of Lord Acton's dictum that power corrupts, especially when it is conferred on permanent office holders. In more recent times, the antipathy to permanent careerists in the top policy ranks has been sustained by the peculiar "openness" of American society and the unusual mobility of its managerial and intellectual elite. As a result, there has been a remarkable two-way flow between the private centres of power and knowledge and the higher echelons of public agencies. Moreover, public authorities have been much more willing to "contract out" their needs for knowledge and skills, rather than staffing their own services with the experts who command the desired information and knowledge. No doubt a high price may be paid for this flexible interchange: for example, the recent revelations concerning the operations of the CIA imply a conspiratorial, somewhat underhand method of contracting out one's need for knowledge that is a threat to the spirit of free scholarly inquiry, just as the long-range dependance on government funds for many programs of scientific research in American universities may distort or unbalance the nation's priorities throughout the broad spectrum of science.

In contrast, Canada has tended to follow the British pattern of "buying" its knowledge by direct recruitment, thereby developing a relatively closed establishment of senior officers, highly trained and, on the whole, unusually well educated.[6] The egalitarian sentiments that influenced the openness of the American bureaucracy were never as strongly held in Canada and, more important, the supply of qualified persons has been so limited that governments have been inclined to employ such persons directly as the best means of ensuring full access to the knowledge they possess. In short, there has never been in Canada the same mobility of talent that has characterized the American scene; in particular, apart from the exceptional war years, there has been little evidence of a flexible exchange of experience and knowledge between public and private power centres.

The attitude of self-sufficiency engendered within the bureaucratic establishment by this pattern of development tends to impose a double-edged constraint on the exchange of knowledge. The bureaucracy may be overly complacent in assuming it has a monopoly on this commodity, and the outsiders with a contribution to make are reluctant to volunteer their services until they are asked – which all too seldom happens. There is an additional constraint that has operated particularly within the university community: the notion of preserving academic freedom and objectivity by refraining from engaging publicly in dialogues on policy issues. Such interventions as have occurred are at arm's length (witness the economists' blunt attack on Mr. Coyne prior to his departure from the Bank of Canada), have been viewed

6 / See John Porter, *The Vertical Mosaic* (Toronto, 1965), chap. XIV.

askance by some members of the academic community, and perhaps have tended to confirm the bureaucrats' suspicion of the unrealistic stance of the outsider when he elects to intervene. The fact that our politics, in C. P. Snow's term, are "closed," particularly at their heart and centre in the cabinet, and that the means of public access are restricted to the "letter to the editor" columns of the press and to relatively ineffectual legislative committees, diminishes both the opportunity and the inclination to make such interventions.[7]

One way in which this exchange can be effected is through the development of a working partnership between public and private power centres. Perhaps the most outstanding illustration of this arrangement is to be found in the peaceful uses of atomic energy. Spurred by peculiar wartime conditions, the Canadian government at first mounted the entire atomic energy program – from raw materials through pure research to final development – as a state monopoly. Successive relaxations in policy encouraged private participation in the provision of raw materials and ultimately in scientific research and development. As a result, the generation of electric power from atomic plants is now a combined operation, involving federal agencies, a large provincial utility, and a consortium of private firms.[8]

While this example, drawn from the field of scientific development of a unique and hazardous energy source, stands almost by itself as a demonstration of the merits of the partnership concept, it may be argued that a less direct form of partnership has also characterized much of the development in transportation and communication in this country. Part of the price of preserving the Canadian union is attributable to the necessity of constructing costly capital facilities to service the needs of a thinly populated continental domain, constantly threatened by potential inroads

7 / A recent improvement over this "arm's length" relationship was the selection of a personal "taskforce" of academic economists to advise Mr. Walter Gordon on the question of foreign ownership of our capital resources.

8 / See my *Administering the Atom for Peace* (New York, 1964).

from a wealthier and more vigorous country to the south. What has transpired as a result of this costly necessity of nation building is a mixed economy of "in-parallel" institutions, such as the CNR and CPR, Air Canada and CPA, CBC and the private stations, or the Bank of Canada and the private chartered banks. However, the public components in each of these segments of the economy have been vested with broader social responsibilities that extend beyond the mere management of an entrepreneurial activity. The notion of "chosen instrument" applies to these public agencies, and for this reason they should be viewed as more than senior partners combining forces with private entities in the provision of goods or service. Thus, there is actually little interchange of personnel or knowledge between the private and public segments of this mixed economy.

The communication gap between the knowledgeable activists in government and the various uncommitted centres of expertise outside government is especially serious when one considers the trend to extend the "brokerage" functions of permanent official-dom to which reference has been made above. If, indeed, public servants are increasingly obliged to substitute for the failure of parties to define issues and enlist support, and of legislatures to seek compromises on policy issues, then these barriers to communication and exchange between the bureaucracy and external centres of knowledge and expertise will have to be lowered.

There are obvious dangers in lowering the communication barriers. For the knowledgeable outsider, there is the implied threat to his independence, the fear that his own research interests will be suborned to the dictates of the particular needs of public power centres which he may be asked to service; the possibility that prolonged association with such centres may unduly inhibit his capacity to speak as a private, uncommitted citizen. For the bureaucracy there is the awkard prospect of having to lose its firm grip on choice-making, as the dialogue moves outside the traditionally closed circle of official advisers. If we have a concern for establishing a viable democratic polity, it is clear that we shall have to face up to such problems and likely objections. One can appreciate the convenience and tidiness of a relatively closed system for the bureaucrat, and yet it is apparent that our contemporary need for knowledge cannot be adequately supplied by a system that relies essentially on buying all its own experts and incorporating them in a tightly knit, secretive bureaucratic hierarchy. Democracies require countervailing knowledge centres that will provide full and intelligent discussion, without detracting from the ultimate authority of our responsible governing organs to make the ultimate choices.[9]

This proposition implies that if public power is to secure access to the knowledge pooled in its community, it must be prepared to face the time-consuming, untidy dialogue that will inevitably ensue in the effort to sort out divergent opinions. But this procedure is surely more effective in the long run than the traditional technique – so well illustrated by the recent armed forces unification program – of presenting the country with a *fait accompli* and then haggling interminably with irate opponents, whose delaying tactics merely reflect their frustration with a procedure that prevents them from getting access to the hard facts on which a sensible counter-brief could be prepared. Unless dialogue precedes decision and unless sufficient facts are made available to keep the dialogue relevant, rampant emotionalism is bound to displace cool reason. Unfortunately, with significant policy decisions, it is all too often a case of having to enter the dialogue too late in the day and with too little to support the criticisms. Meanwhile, governmental postures become increasingly intransigent and resistant to any amendment.

It should be clear by now that public power centres are growing, that their needs for knowledge have undergone a dramatic expansion, and that the traditional policy of buying such knowledge will not meet these needs and, in a democratic society, the knowledge should not in any event be monopolized by the bureaucracy. It has been suggested that the new, positive role of permanent officialdom derives from the attempt to fill communication gaps which have not been adequately filled by legislatures,

9 / The Economic Council of Canada apparently agrees: see its *Third Annual Review* (Ottawa, 1966), pp. 79 and 190.

individual MPs, or parties. Accordingly, public servants, exercising the functions of brokers, advocates, and arbitrators, have had to seek more direct means of establishing communication linkages with the public they serve and with the actual or potential centres of knowledge existing outside public agencies. Despite the inhibitions of the activists in government and of the knowledgeable outside government, certain steps have been initiated to bring the two parties together. In a general sense, the advent of public information officers provides one such instrumentality, but the flow is largely in one direction – to the public. More specifically, the proliferation of advisory bodies, associated with most new programs of governments, reflects a more systematic attempt, on a piecemeal basis, to bring outside interests and knowledge to the service of government. Being advisory, the representatives of various publics are less likely to feel their independence is being compromised by such participation, while public servants have the assurance that the dialogue is suitably contained and reasonably confidential. Like the contacts that are built up between numerous regulatory agencies and their clientele, advisory committees can, however, develop into overly "cosy" clubs, restricted to an inner circle of establishment or near-establishment participants with common vested interests in refraining from any overt statement or action that would rock the boat.

Royal Commissions as Transmitters of Knowledge
Apart from these somewhat limited efforts to close the communication gap and the government's own efforts to "buy" the knowledge it requires by direct recruitment into the bureaucracy, probably the royal commission remains as the most outstanding instrumentality for bringing knowledge to the service of public power in Canada. Royal commissions are by no means a new invention, for their ancestry goes back into the antiquity of Britain from which they were inherited by her colonial off-shoots. Even before Confederation, the Canadian provinces made extensive use of royal commissions, and there are few historians who have not had occasion to bless them for the bequest of a wealth of information in their voluminous reports. In the hundred years

since Confederation Canada has established well over three hundred royal commissions, an average of better than three per year.[10]

Until the Rowell-Sirois Commission on Dominion-Provincial Relations, 1937–1940, royal commissions were modelled from a pattern that was entirely consistent with the restricted needs of government for knowledge. They were nearly always small in size, often relying on a single commissioner; they invariably drew on the bench and bar for commissioners and staff; they pursued their inquiries by means of public hearings, frequently travelling across Canada for that purpose; their reports were based on the "evidence" in the transcript; their findings were placed before the executive as formal reports addressed to His Excellency the Governor General. In composition, procedures, and reporting, the traditional royal commission was akin to an *ad hoc* circuit court with carefully delimited terms of reference. As such, it was admirably suited to investigate one large category of subjects: that is, the non-recurrent problem where the facts had to be ascertained, by the same methods, for example, that a traffic court would use, and making recommendations to the executive in lieu of handing down a binding decision. Thus, a scandal in government, a fire in the Parliament Buildings, a riot in Halifax, the plight of the musk ox in the Barren Lands, the sex life of the oyster, the fall of a bridge, or a disastrous landslide – all these and many other equally out-of-the-ordinary occurrences lent themselves to this judicialized form of inquiry. The ordinary law courts were not geared to take on these extra-curricular assignments, but heavy borrowing from the judiciary and from the legal fraternity to staff the commissions suggested that the two operations were approached in much the same ways.

There were other commissions, of course, that studied problems of an entirely different order from those just mentioned, although their *modus operandi* was essentially the same. Numerous problems assigned to royal commissions have emerged out of our

10 / More detailed treatment of royal commissions is to be found in my article "Should Canada Be De-Commissioned?" *Queen's Quarterly*, vol. LXX, no. 4 (winter 1964), pp. 475–90.

growing pains as a nation: they embrace all of the significant social, economic, and cultural issues that have beset us in the past and continually rise to plague us as hardy perennials, showing an unfortunate reluctance to yield to once-for-all solutions provided by a single *ad hoc* investigation. As a result we have had to launch, repeatedly, investigations into transportation, communication, banking, taxation, the economy, our resources, and our culture.

The current crop of royal commissions, beginning with the immediate pre-war years, shows signs of the strain placed on them by the changing demands for knowledge on the part of our growing centres of public power. It is no longer possible to acquire "the facts in the case" by the traditional, judicialized procedures of the conventional royal commission. The skills of the bench in sorting out fact from fancy and of the bar in grilling witnesses at a public hearing are no longer the main skills required for most of the major inquiries launched in recent years. Nor are the issues dealt with likely to receive much illumination through the examination of witnesses, however vigorously conducted by counsel for the commission. Different skills, different procedures, and a much less casual array of witnesses must be brought to bear on the complex range of problems now set before royal commissions.

The new-model royal commission reflects these changed requirements not so much in any alterations in the size or composition of the commission proper – although even here the bench has lost its virtual monopoly of seats on royal commissions – but in the size and make-up of the staffs of commissions. In effect, royal commissions have been converted from specialized *ad hoc* judicial tribunals into sizable, temporary departments staffed by social scientists representing every discipline. While they may still continue the old practice of holding public hearings (and, as in the case of the Royal Commission on Bilingualism and Biculturalism, even associate discussion seminars with them), the facts now are primarily garnered by trained researchers, using the latest methods approved by their respective disciplines. The "evidence" on which royal commissioners have to base their recommendations relies less on the transcripts from public hearings and more on a massive accumulation of data, as well as sophisticated analyses or elaborate theorizing on the basis of the data. In short, the hard facts susceptible to proof or disproof before a judicialized tribunal give way to social facts with varying ranges of ambiguity and precision, susceptible to varying interpretations and, hence, to substantial differences of opinion as to the recommendations which should logically flow from such data. The struggle to achieve a consensus thus begins in the commission, while research staff frankly speak of trying to "educate" their commissioners.

It follows that there is not only a greater possibility of the executive disagreeing with the conclusions which its commissioners have reached from the research findings, but also the likely prospect of commissioners disagreeing quite radically with the conclusions which each of its researchers may have reached in the course of his individual inquiries. The last possibility is all the more likely, not simply because experts have been known to disagree and each has his own biases, but because the commissioners are responsible for producing a total package of recommendations whose contents are reasonably consistent. The research team exploring only one area of the subject referred to the commission need not worry about the compromises which may be forced on the commissioners in order to harmonize all parts of the report; at the same time, each researcher is bound to feel cheated or consider that the integrity of his work has been violated should the commissioners' broader concerns induce them to discard or alter his findings. Possibly we have been overly concerned about achieving consensus, and perhaps we should welcome minority reports as the norm rather than the exception. On the other hand, commissioners are, no doubt, correct in assuming that the impact of their report tends to be diffused and weakened by open dissent expressed in minority reports.

This problem is only one of a number of significant new issues raised by the transformation of recent major royal commissions into *ad hoc*, research teams. The relation of royal commissioners to the executive that appoints them has sometimes been at issue, though by and large royal commissioners have tended to share in the same prestigious autonomy that has long been a feature of our judiciary's relations with the executive. Of greater concern and still far from unresolved, is the matter of the most appropriate relationship to be established between commissioners and their research staff – a question that seldom arose when the staff might consist of one or two secretaries and a lawyer who possessed a well understood and uncomplicated relationship to his commissioner – usually a judge.

The clarification of the relationship between commissioners and research staff has an important bearing on the central theme under discussion. The new-model royal commission is a sensible response to the growing need to bring knowledge to the service of public power. But this knowledge is being purchased on an *ad hoc* and temporary basis so that the researchers must somehow retain their intellectual integrity and their capacity to return to the community from which they were drawn with no lingering sense that they were sold, or sold themselves, for a mess of commissioners' potage. Nor can commissioners, after their report is out, be expected to accept with equanimity the possibility of some of their erstwhile employees renewing a campaign for adoption of alternative recommendations which they were unsuccessful in selling to their commissioners while on the staff. Perhaps the best way of achieving the necessary balance between conflicting interests is to generalize the practice that has been followed by several commissions of making first claim on the researcher's report but giving the author full disposition over his manuscript in the event the commissioners are unable to use it or to publish it intact in appendices.

No doubt this problem and others which cannot be examined here can be resolved, but there are other innate deficiencies of royal commissions that are not so readily overcome. Clearly, few social scientists today could object to the remarkable coming of age of their disciplines that has been reflected by the growing calls on their talents by royal commissions. Nor would most social scientists object to the opportunities thus afforded them to bring their knowledge and expertise to the service of public power. Indeed, it may fairly be said that royal commissions have done the work of non-existent foundations, in getting more social science research projects off the ground, and encouraging the development of the disciplines with more generous financial support than would otherwise have occurred without their help. However, that being said, it is also proper to add that royal commissions may not be the long-term answer to the support of social science research or to the basic problem of bringing knowledge from the policy sciences to bear on public power.

In the first place, royal commissions are mounted as crash programs of research, sometimes but not invariably (*vide* the Royal Commission on Bilingualism and Biculturalism) constrained by their terms of reference. Because they work on a limited time schedule, it is not uncommon for commissions to underestimate the time it takes to design from scratch a massive research plan or the time required to complete that research. Invariably, pressure for a report is brought to bear and commissioners, faced with an overwhelming mass of research data, half-formulated conclusions, and some still in gestation, will be unable to make adequate use of the findings. In short, there is wastage: first, at the build-up stage in trying to clarify objectives, create an *esprit de corps*, and educate untried researchers; second, when the push is on to bring out a report, much that has been done is seen to be irrelevant to the immediate objective and is scrapped, loosely cobbled together, or (under recent sensible regulations) interred in the Archives.

The obvious difficulties associated with the abrupt and unforeseen demands for the services of outside experts may be coupled with another defect: the discontinuous nature of the research operation. A royal commission dies as it gives birth to its reports; the research apparatus, assembled at such cost and brought to a productive working peak, is dismantled and scattered; the report is left to the tender mercies of the executive with no continuing pressure group remaining behind to urge decision and action. The next time the recurrent issue reaches crisis proportions and is considered ripe for another inquiry, the new team has to be found and the research starts afresh, seldom building on the findings of its predecessor. These elements of discontinuity and lack of follow-up have, in fact, induced governments to institutionalize, as it were, certain royal commissions by creating permanent agencies to carry out their functions on a regular, day-to-day basis. Three illustrations of this phenomenon are: the creation of permanent Labour Relations Boards to handle industrial disputes which some years ago were invariably assigned for piece-meal study to royal commissions; the creation of the Restrictive Trade Practices Commission, in lieu of repeated royal commission inquiries into combines; the recently formed Economic Council of Canada, which may be viewed as the permanent equivalent of the *ad hoc* Royal Commission on Canada's Economic Prospects. These examples show the inevitable tendency of governments to "buy" the necessary skills by recruiting staff for permanent public agencies; as such, they accentuate the trend toward governmental monopolization of knowledge for its own power centres.

Finally, it is common knowledge that the new-model royal commission – even taking into account the changing value of the dollar – has inflated the cost of conducting public inquiries. Prior to the First World War the most costly royal commission (on Industrial and Technical Education) spent $100,000, although the average commission cost less than half this amount. The Rowell-Sirois Commission, which typifies the first of the new-model royal commissions, exceeded the half-million dollar mark. This sum pales into insignificance when compared with the major royal commissions of recent date: $1.5 million for the Royal Commission on Canada's Economic Prospects; $2.8 million for the Royal Commission on Government Organization; $3.3 million for the Taxation Commission; and, surpassing all by far and still incomplete, the Royal Commission on Bilingualism and Biculturalism with latest cost set above $9 million. Twenty million dollars would be a fair estimate of the cost of seven major royal commissions appointed during the past ten years to deal with recurrent problems that will not disappear as a result of their findings and recommendations. Could some better way be found of allocating sums of this size to the task of bringing knowledge to the service of power?

What seems to be required is a somewhat more institutionalized *applied research* resource that would encourage continuous study of the prominent policy issues confronting the nation, a more careful and systematic planning of research, a less casual assembly of qualified researchers, and an accumulation of findings which can be built upon over the years. The stop-and-go, "crash" nature of the inquiries conducted by the new-model royal commissions are obviously better than nothing, but as long-term solutions to the problem of bringing knowledge to the service of power they are less than adequate. In at least two respects, however, the revision of the working methods of the current crop of royal commissions has come to grips with realities. First, they have recognized that applied policy research demands a team effort, drawing on skilled resources found in many allied disciplines. Second, they have shown the value (as well as the costliness) of overcoming the problem of the isolation of our scholarly community which is scattered in pockets across a continental domain.

Both these features of the new-model royal commission should be recognized in any permanent institutionalization of the applied research function. One possible method of achieving this objective would be for governments to "endow" a number of applied policy research institutes to be attached to universities across Canada, the endowment to consist of the equivalent funds which otherwise could have gone to the creation of further royal commissions. Using the figures quoted above, for example, twenty million dollars would provide most useful "seed money" of five million dollars to each of four such institutes. An alternative would be to endow a single, privately governed Foundation for Applied Policy Research which, like the Canada Council, would allocate funds to task forces prepared and equipped to undertake long-term research in such areas, for example, as resources, communications, transportation, taxation and finance, urban and intergovernmental problems.

The adoption of one or other of these arrangements would not in any way trespass on the invaluable contributions now being made by the Canada Council to developing both a strong cadre of trained researchers and allocating funds to research in the social sciences and humanities. The Canada Council, unlike its counterpart the National Research Council, has deliberately refrained from undertaking research within its own establishment. In this respect, it has broken from the traditional preference, which was described earlier, of "buying" knowledge by direct recruitment to the bureaucracy. Its role is facilitative; its concern is to help young scholars develop themselves and maturer scholars to pursue their own valid research interests – irrespective of the specific relevance of research to the problems of the day. Thus, the Canada Council successfully avoids trespassing on the freedom of the academic community and allocates its funds in such a way as to eliminate the notion that it is "contracting out" research or seeking to dictate the areas in which research should be undertaken. It would, therefore, be improper to vest the Council with the responsibilities envisaged above for an Applied Policy Research Centre or even to place it in charge of the allocation of funds specifically ear-marked for applied policy research.

If our objective is to facilitate the development of independent centres of countervailing knowledge on policy issues, the Canada Council, despite its quasi-independent relationship to the government, is still too closely allied to the government to be vested with responsibility for sponsoring probes into the most sensitive policy areas of the nation. Perhaps the situation is sufficiently different in the field of science to make the National Research Council a viable active researcher on its own; but in the domain of the policy sciences one would be less confident that objectivity could be ensured. In any event, the government is already fully equipped within its own establishments, in such agencies as the Economic Council of Canada, the Department of Finance, Trade and Commerce, Industry, Manpower and Immigration, and the Dominion Bureau of Statistics, to undertake the applied policy research functions. What is lacking, and what even the new-model royal commissions only partially and temporarily supply, is an equivalent set of independent centres of countervailing knowledge that could be expected to be both sounding boards and sources of critical appraisal for the policy programs initiated from within the bureaucracy.

Democracies, as we have argued earlier, rely on informed dialogue. In a system such as ours, where policy initiatives are either germinated by experts in the bureaucracy and ratified in the secrecy of cabinet enclaves or compromises worked out behind the closed doors of *ad hoc* dominion-provincial entities of all descriptions, there is great danger that public apathy will be assumed to be a fact of life. Counter-measures must be deliberately designed and promoted to the end that governments will not be viewed, or view themselves, as the ultimate repositories of all knowledge. If knowledge is to be brought to the service of public power, its custodians outside government must be related in more meaningful and institutional ways with public power centres, but in such ways as not to destroy their intellectual independence. Governments will have to accommodate themselves to the more open and less convenient situation envisaged here, just as knowledge centres outside must be prepared to run the risk of "contamination" which their contacts with public power may bring. The case for co-operative pluralism in the application of knowledge to the contemporary needs of public power is strong but, its implementation will continue to stretch our ingenuity in the years ahead.

14

Conclusion:
Government as Dialogue

TREVOR LLOYD

OUR SOCIETY IS within measurable distance of sliding out of
control. Loss of control is by no means inevitable; it is probably
not yet an even money risk. All the same, there is a possibility that
one day we shall find that the odds have changed, and that only
an uphill effort will save us.

These essays have been concerned with one aspect of this loss
of control – the questions of political economy. Anyone with a
clear imagination can see a whole lot of other ways in which
society can go wrong: this book started with an attempt to show
the way that society is losing its ability to match means and ends
because the old objectives and the old explanations no longer
satisfy us and are sometimes dangerous. It then looked at a few
of the institutions by which we try to organize our political and
economic affairs and tried to suggest ways in which these institutions can be improved.

This is a modest goal: Keynes once said that economists were
the trustees, not of civilization but of the possibilities of civilization, and this goes for politicians as well. And politicians have a
great many problems apart from those we look at – the population
explosion, the difficulties of living in cities, the problem of making

sure that we do not stray into a war. But these frightening possibilities for the future are only special examples of the general danger that society will drift out of control. What we are doing here is to look at the techniques that people will have to use in the course of looking after all of their problems, potentially catastrophic or not.

This book provides perspectives for the future, but does not give any great ideological answers. Under the surface the authors are committed to the normal everyday values of North Atlantic liberals: liberty, equality, fraternity, the pursuit of happiness, and a considerable (though not unrestrained) respect for the gross national product; but they do not go round discussing these values in public. The articles are discussions of the best way to reach generally accepted objectives, which are taken for granted without argument.

Because the editors invited people to write who are sympathetic to the principles of the University League for Social Reform, the articles are inclined in favour of greater equality in economic and other matters; and because the editors asked rather firmly for proposals for definite action, most of the articles are directed toward the future. But there is an interesting change since the thirties, when the League for Social Reconstruction published *Social Planning for Canada*. Thirty years ago the authors were arguing in favour of economic planning, and they were very concerned that it should be carried out in a way that Parliament could supervise. A great deal of the mechanism of economic planning that they wanted has now been established, though, of course, neither the nationalization nor the equalization of income that they wanted has taken place. But the planning mechanism, which has given the government so much more power than it had thirty years ago, is not brought under popular control in the way that seemed necessary a generation ago.

The authors are democrats in the normal North Atlantic sense of believing in free elections, universal suffrage, equal opportunities for all, and political parties, but they are not directly worried about this problem of finding constitutional machinery for popular control. For people writing in the sixties, efficiency is the standard to appeal to. Questions of efficiency have grown more interesting and look easier to solve than in the past, and questions of broad principle have become either much simpler or much harder. Equality for negroes in the United States can be expressed in straight-forward terms; linguistic equality in Canada looks uncomfortably like an impossibility – compulsory bilingualism is the only way to enable everybody to feel at home (as opposed to being able to buy postage stamps) everywhere in Canada, but imposed bilingualism is on the present evidence the policy least likely to succeed.

It is nothing new for reformers to be primarily concerned about efficiency. At the beginning of this century progressively minded men like Theodore Roosevelt and Lord Rosebery wanted change for the sake of efficiency rather than for any higher purpose, though the policies they supported in the name of efficiency could be adopted by other people for more idealistic reasons. "Honesty is the best policy" is not a moral attitude, but it may lead people to be honest; and reform for the sake of efficiency is none the less reform.

The editors are less efficiency-minded than the writers. We asked our authors to write on more speculative topics, and they declined to do so; we invited people who, we believed, were concerned with the broad issues of moral purpose, and they declined to write at all. Authors, at least among our acquaintances, are not eager to write about the whole wide world and its problems. And why should they be? There is something uncomfortable about the idea that universities are full of people who can lay down the way that mankind ought to develop. Poets may have lost their place as the unacknowledged legislators of mankind, but professors would have a little difficulty qualifying to succeed them. The only advantage the academic community can claim is that it has plenty of time to think, and the writers in this book have spent their time thinking about their own areas of special interest.

The result is that the articles here are concerned with the relationship between knowledge and power. There are two aspects of the problem with which they are particularly concerned: they are afraid that the government does things without knowing enough about the effects of its policy, and they are afraid that ordinary people cannot find out enough about the activities of government to know whether it is doing a good job or not. The link between the two problems is that the government appears to think that information is something rather dangerous, which should not be spread around too much.

Because these authors have a personal interest in research and earn their living by dealing in knowledge, they may overstate its importance. In academic circles it is a fair reply to a problem to say that more research is needed; a politician, who has to decide things in a hurry, does not always have time for research to find out whether he is making the right decisions. So perhaps the authors' conclusions should be looked at with care. Is there something about the modern state which makes all this emphasis on knowledge necessary, or is it just a conspiracy of the academic class? The Liberal party gets a lot more support from the university than the Conservatives do; when elected, it spends a lot more money on research. Does the Commission on Bilingualism and Biculturalism act as an elegant way of paying election debts?

Nobody can read the minds of the contributors, much less explain why the government behaves the way it does. But there seem to be genuine reasons why the modern state leads to greater dependence on research, and there are also reasons why its subjects want more information about what is going on. The power of the government has become much greater than it used to be. The authors argue that there is no particular advantage in imposing limits on what the government can do, and that the law courts have become less eager to impose limits than they were in the past. This readiness to accept strong government has often been associated with a desire to give more power to the federal government. In some papers the argument is that governments should do more, but that the provincial governments are the ones that should be most active, and the authors who feel that the government has grown too fast for the means of regulation to keep up are not saying that governments should get smaller; they are saying that the means of regulation should be improved.

If governments become more important, they have to do more

complicated things. In any case they are acting in a more complicated world than the simple, mainly rural setting of a century ago. A hundred years ago governments dealt with problems caused by people living too far apart: building railways, establishing a market by means of a system of tariffs, running a Post Office and a police force which got its man by chasing him across the trackless wilderness. At the present day governments face problems caused by people living too close together: building roads inside cities without expropriating too many houses, enabling French-speaking and English-speaking people to live inside the same country (separatism is an artificial way of making people live further apart), pollution, deciding who has the right to use the crowded radio and television wavelengths, and dealing with organized crime, which flourishes inside cities large enough to provide a market for some illegal service such as gambling. The problems of overcrowding may not be more difficult than the problems of distance – people were just as hard to please in the nineteenth century as they are now – but they are more complicated: more things have to be taken into account before any answer at all can be given.

The increase in complexity can be seen in the way the Budget is run. In the nineteenth century governments did not balance their Budgets as often as might have been expected, but at least they knew what they ought to be doing, and everybody could see whether it balanced or not. At the present day we expect a government to lower taxes if it foresees a recession, or to raise them if there is a risk of inflation. These movements are rather harder to measure; how much should taxes be lowered or raised? Once you have left the solid ground of balancing the Budget you have to face all the dangers of lowering taxes too much and over-stimulating the economy, or raising taxes too much and suffocating it. The decision to regard the Budget as a way of manipulating the economy is one that can only be taken by politicians, but once they have taken it somebody has to deal with all the extra technical problems that follow from it; and most of the technical problems can only be answered when a good deal is known about what is happening in the economy.

Again, in the nineteenth century labour exchanges helped

employees and employers to get in touch with each other. Today the area of manpower planning has expanded to cover the whole country, and it takes note of what people need some time in the future, and tries to provide training to meet these future needs. None of this need involve coercion or even legal compulsion. Private individuals could set up a manpower planning system – for some of the more highly paid jobs there are private agencies which will find posts for executives or executives for posts, but the size of their fees shows that this would not be an economic way of filling the average run of job. None of these agencies have yet gone into the business of predicting future demand. In this field the role of the government is unchallenged, but it holds this place not because it has coercive power in the nineteenth-century sense but because it possesses information.

If government is to go into this sort of work, more or less as a supplier and co-ordinator of information, it has to be sure that it has asked the right question and got the right answers. When the government set up the National Research Council it was providing a service for private industry, which might be expected to be the principal customer for the products of government-sponsored scientific research. Whether the taxpayer gets a fair return on the support he gives to private industry in this way is a complicated question. But as we move toward increased government support for social science research, we find that the government, at various levels, will be its own largest customer. Educational research is mainly used by governments, even though it is useful to private industries to make sure that government does not neglect educational research. Large firms are involved directly in the work of educating their employees at a rather higher level than simply teaching people what lever to pull on a machine, but they cannot do much unless they are provided with adequate human resources by the provincial governments. When the government's Social Science Research Council is set up, it will accumulate information that will be helpful for churches, trade unions, and business corporations, but most of the time it will be working directly for the government.

Finding out what the government does with all this information will not be easy. Readers will have found that, while the authors in this book do not want to limit the powers of the government, they are not particularly ready to trust the government to do the right thing all the time. But the safeguard suggested is that the electorate should have more information given to it.

Governments find it much easier to act unfairly behind closed doors. It is hard to be certain where the boundaries of unfairness are drawn. For instance, it has been suggested that when franchises for private television stations were distributed a few years ago, they were handed out on a basis of political favouritism: nobody would attempt to justify in public a policy of rewarding one's political friends in such a way, but obviously nobody would think it impossible. There are various ways of dealing with this sort of borderline activity; it can be limited by changing the rules under which the game is played or by making sure that everything is done more publicly. On the whole people are ready to let an active and efficient government – especially at the provincial or municipal level – get away with quite a lot, as long as its infringement of the law does not intrude itself on the public. The signs are that, at elections, nobody is at all interested if skilful detective work produces a well-concealed piece of scandal; this is not the sort of information that anyone really cares about. If a government is to be held in check it must be by an explicit decision that its actions must take place in the open.

At the same time as the public has grown less interested in scandals about the government – less interested in the sense that they do not change their votes as a result; they are quite willing to read about scandals – the actions of government have become harder to understand than they used to be. The public realizes that, because the government takes on so many new jobs, it is more important to find a competent government which can get things done than used to be the case, and as a result a little corruption does not matter so much. But this is only a shift of attention from one area that used to be important to the more pressing questions of the present day. Government affects people more directly than it used to, but its impact has not become easy to understand.

To some extent this is the result of changes in the method of communication. The media of communicating political argument have been invented in the wrong order for Canada. In the nineteenth century, when people were concerned with such problems as Confederation or building the CPR, television would have been ideal as a way of showing what lay at the other end of the country. A large number of modern issues cannot be dealt with in that manner. The problems of international liquidity are not suited to television: I have watched people trying to make a program on this subject, and giving it up. When the Carter Commission presented its report on taxation, this was something that could affect everybody in Canada, because everybody pays taxes or at least is affected by the way they are collected. Some newspapers devoted 20,000 words to the Report; it would take three or four hours to say as much on television. One picture can say as much as a thousand words, provided that the message is one that can be put into a picture. Information about the methods used by police in the southern states of the USA can be given by a picture; information about oil-depletion allowances cannot be given by a picture. To the extent that television can give pictures about a report, it will show the more trivial features – for example, it is quite easy to show that there are a lot of pages in the report and that it is rather heavy, but what does that do to help people understand what is being said? One of the problems for the Canadian public is that the sort of issues facing government at the present day are only comprehensible through the medium of print, and because print is no longer the dominant medium for the general public "the medium censors the message." The result is that just at the moment when the public needs access to more complicated information to work out what the government's policy will do to it, information becomes more simplified than before. There may be no way out of this problem; in that case the public will become less able to control the government than it has been for the last hundred years or so.

Parliament has been designed as an instrument for confronting government with the views of ordinary people; if ordinary people do not know what is going on, members of Parliament will lose their usefulness as a means of keeping the government on the rails. It will continue to be true that governments will not want to offend the public, but this does not solve the problem of deciding what will offend it. Opinion polls will tell a government what is popular at the moment, but the trouble is that when a policy is put into practice it has many more effects than the public foresees when it is asked its opinion. The theory has been that MPs will be able to assess these effects and work out what the electorate will think when it has to live with the results of a policy. The recommendations on foreign investment in the Watkins Report are very interesting but only after a great deal of study can any-body know what is involved. This is not an excuse for avoiding action; anybody can see that what is being proposed would involve a large change in the way the Canadian economy is organized, and it is not a change to be undertaken without thought. Is it (or any proposal of comparable dimensions) some-thing that can be understood by the general public?

Underestimating the intellectual capacity of the electorate is rather worse than overestimating it, and perhaps policy can be explained to the people in the future as it has been in the past. But the question is vital for Parliament; giving MPs more in-formation about the activities of the government will not make them any more useful if they lose touch with their constituents. Even if rules and constitutions change the government will be able to ignore MPs, unless they know what is going on. Elections in Canada sometimes produce MPs who are chosen more for the capacity to understand their constituents than for their capacity to understand the problems with which the government is faced. MPs should be able to understand both their constituents and the specialized problems of government, and they will not be able to do their job unless they know about both sets of problems. If they do not know enough to check and advise the government, the pressures that lead governments to expand and take on more powers will persist and will even grow in strength because there will be no opposition to them.

Governments have always been in two minds about MPs. On the one hand, what a minister really likes from an MP is applause and flattery, preferably with no tedious reservations or requests for assistance for his riding. On the other hand, ministers know that they have to find out what public opinion is doing – ministers, just like MPs, need to keep in touch both with expert opinion and public opinion. Ottawa has shown fairly clearly over the last dozen years what is involved: the Conservative government spent all its time worrying about public opinion, had rather a poor view of expert opinion and as a result never knew what could be done (and expert opinion need not have meant civil service opinion, if they were afraid civil servants had Liberal sympathies); the recent Pearson government was rather better at finding out what expert opinion was, but did not find in what direction public opinion wanted it to deploy its experts. Without public opinion behind it a government cannot develop much momentum, and there was less momentum behind the Pearson minority government than there was behind the 1945–59 Liberal minority government. In terms of the worries of the authors in this book, the Conservatives neglected the work of research and the Liberals neglected the work of information.

Information is a two-way business; the people want to know what the government is doing in order to prevent it from doing something unpleasant, but this sometimes makes governments frightened of giving information to the public when it would be useful as a way of guiding public opinion. At a pessimistic level, people can hardly rally round a government's policy until they know what it is; more realistically, getting something done is always hard because people who are going to suffer from a change are always quick to see that their interests may be endangered. Only when a government has built up public support for its policy or has been carried forward by a wave of opinion, can much get done.

This has been shown by the way in which governments have proceeded while they have been getting bigger and bigger. Sometimes they have had a popular mandate to be active and to get things done, sometimes they have been confronted by a large obstacle that can be cleared out of the way only if the people will support the government. Public opinion has stood behind extensions of government power for a lot of different reasons: to fight a war, to deal with a depression, to cure some abuse in society, to get expensive long-term development work carried out. It is practically impossible to find a case where public opinion has supported an extension of government authority simply because government authority is thought to be a good thing in itself. Some very intelligent people have thought that government authority is a good thing for its own sake, and on the strength of this belief have prepared schemes for new government activity which have been taken up by public opinion because they fitted the needs of the occasion and have been passed into law.

The advocates of big government can take some satisfaction from this, and can even argue that it shows the general principle of their approach to be correct. For the majority, the question will continue to be one of examining the problems of modern life one by one, and finding out enough about them to know whether the government can be useful in a particular case or not. It is still possible that, on a general examination of the causes of the characteristic problems of our time, there will turn out to be underlying connections between most of them. So far as there are attempts in this book to provide overall explanations of what is going on, they suggest that the complications of the modern world are going to require more government intervention in the future. This is not just a matter of laments about public squalor or the search for what is now called in politicians' slang "quality of life." Private affluence itself depends on a foundation of government activity, and there is no sign that this dependence will diminish. If society is going to do complicated things, it needs a co-ordinator to link its various activities together. Short of setting up a monstrous universal cartel, private industry cannot do this job: if information means competitive advantage, information cannot be shared freely. There is no reason why the government should have to insist on additional powers to enable it to act as a co-ordinator of information; its services will be valuable enough and important enough to grow of themselves.

But, still, what sort of life are we going to live in a government-co-ordinated world – that is to say, in a world so complicated that somebody had to co-ordinate it? Most of the authors in this book are more concerned with the problems of holding society together, and of examining the way that this has led to an increase in the power of government in the past and looks like leading to a further increase in the future. When they look a little way ahead, and ask what sort of world we are making for ourselves they are worried by the prospect, but not so worried that it distracts them from the immediate work in hand. It is a "subject for further research" to discover how we shall live with the inevitable growth of government.

The future development of government is not going to be a process of peaceful growth which is always acceptable to everybody in the community. But the chances of peaceful and universally accepted change, government or no government, are so slight that friction and opposition will come as no surprise. The growth of government as a general proposition can be accepted fairly easily, but in individual instances it will cause a great deal of trouble. Like all other processes of political change, it will appear at the time to be a matter of conflict and it will appear in the perspective of the historian to have been a natural and uninterrupted path of advance.